A DNA WAS A FEMALE VERSION OF A WRESTLER

A DNA WAS A FEMALE VERSION OF A WRESTLER

An Abbreviated Herstory of
World Wrestling Entertainment

Scarlett Harris

A Diva Was a Female Version of a Wrestler: An Abbreviated Herstory of World Wrestling Entertainment
© 2021 Scarlett Harris

Book designed by Scott Ryan
Author photo by Linzie Meagher
Cover, inside titles designed by Lauren Moran
Back cover designed by Lauren Moran and Jay Zeller
Edited by David Bushman

Published in the USA by Fayetteville Mafia Press
Columbus, Ohio

Contact Information
Email: fayettevillemafiapress@gmail.com
Website: fayettevillemafiapress.com

ISBN: 9781949024180
eBook ISBN: 9781949024197

CONTENTS

Prologue:
WOMEN'S WRESTLING FANS ARE SUCKERS FOR PUNISHMENT

#GiveDivasAChance was a fan-led social media movement that took hold in early 2015 in response to a thirty-second women's wrestling match on World Wrestling Entertainment's (WWE) flagship weekly television show, *Raw*.

The tag team match pitted the babyfaces (good guys, also shortened to 'face or face), the youngest Divas champion in history, Paige, and happy-go-lucky Australian Emma (from my hometown, Melbourne), against the twin magic heel (bad guys) team of Brie and Nikki Bella, the latter of whom was the Divas champion at the time. Anyone even a little bit familiar with professional wrestling might wonder if thirty seconds is enough time to make a tag. Seeing as neither Nikki nor Paige entered the revered space known in wrestling as the squared circle between the ring bells sounding to signal the beginning and end of the match, with Brie hitting one of her signature moves, the Bella Buster (a sit-down facebuster), on Emma for the pinfall victory, the answer would be no: thirty seconds is not enough time to make a tag.

Though this wasn't the first time women wrestlers received a dismal amount of time on WWE programming to "get their stuff in"—perform their signature moves—and it wasn't the last, for some reason the company's lack of faith in its women employees that night resonated with wrestling fans. We'd finally had enough.

To be a women's wrestling fan, particularly one who patronizes WWE, which this book focuses on, is to be constantly disappointed. Pop culture and wrestling analyst Allyssa Capri wrote in *Women Love Wrestling: An Anthology on Women & Professional Wrestling*, which I also contributed to, "Fans of professional wrestling often half-jokingly say that the people who hate wrestling the most are wrestling fans. . . . It's often exhausting and downright hard to be a wrestling fan. But, it is even harder for those of us with marginalized identities to choose to love wrestling in spite of the insidious oppression that plagues the industry."

For years we grasped at any straws thrown our way. That's what happens when a historically misogynist industry retroactively factors women into its marketing plan, instead of making them a priority from the beginning, I suppose.

The one-step-forward, several-steps-back vacillation of the women's division in recent years (in contrast to the sustained regression of the past) was documented by wrestling fan and graphic designer Kate Foray in her *Raw Breakdown Project*[1] infographics. From September 2015 to late 2018, Kate charted the weekly ebbs and flows of women's wrestling on *Raw* and occasionally *SmackDown* during this time, which featured women's wrestling matches in the main event of wrestling shows, such as Sasha Banks vs. Charlotte in October 2016, both the first time women had been given the final match on a pay-per-view and the first time they were allowed to wrestle in the steel structure known as Hell in a Cell. But this fluctuation also resulted in the haphazard allocation of time being given to the women's division on these shows. Kate told me in January 2017[2] that "since the *Raw Breakdown Project's* inception, women['s wrestling has] not gotten more than 16 percent of

---

1   Kate Foray, *The Raw Breakdown Project*, n.d.

2   Scarlett Harris, "Why WWE Needs Quotas," *Paste*, January 3, 2017.

airtime. . . . The longest streak [occurred between] July 7, 2016, [and] November 7, 2016, with an average airtime of 10 percent. Since then, [it] has been far from consistent."

We've given you your women's evolution; what more do you want? it would seem WWE executives were telling their fans. Yet somehow we still stick around as the company squanders its women talent.

The slow gains being made in women's wrestling in WWE in particular began in 2012 with its developmental brand's relaunch from Florida Championship Wrestling (FCW) to *NXT*. The creation of the *NXT* women's championship in 2013 in a match between Paige and Emma signaled a tectonic shift, positioning women's wrestling as more than just slapping, hair pulling, and ripping off each other's clothes.

Two years after Paige and Emma paved the way for the #DivasRevolution and the subsequent #WomensEvolution, both WWE-conceived hashtags that piggybacked on the organic #GiveDivasAChance from five months earlier, WWE seemed to finally be listening to its audience. On July 13, 2015, WWE's chief brand officer and heiress to the company throne, Stephanie McMahon, "set the table of opportunity" for women in WWE, she said, citing the success of tennis superstar Serena Williams; the U.S. Women's National Team in soccer, which had just won the World Cup; and Olympics bronze medalist and mixed martial arts champion Ronda Rousey, who enjoyed a rendezvous with wrestling herself, in sports more broadly at the time.

In actuality, McMahon granted opportunity to only three members of the *NXT*'s Four Horsewomen faction: Charlotte Flair, daughter of the legendary Ric Flair (who spearheaded the original Four Horsemen group in the 1980s), flame-haired Irishwoman Becky Lynch, and then-*NXT* women's champion and all-around star Sasha Banks, all of whom had been tearing the house down in *NXT* on a weekly basis with their fourth member, Bayley, while #GiveDivasAChance continued to trend on Twitter, to no avail in WWE proper.

Flair, Banks, and Lynch were sorted into groups with a handful of other women wrestlers based largely on race. The biracial Banks was paired with fellow women of color Naomi and Tamina because, McMahon said, "she thinks a lot like you do" *insert side eye here.* Flair and Lynch joined Paige, while the Bella Twins and Alicia Fox, also all women of color, remained in their already formed trio. They then wrestled in variations of those teams until the concept was exhausted, as is wont to happen in WWE.

McMahon's assertion that she and her husband, Paul "Triple H" Levesque, who runs *NXT* and was, indeed, chiefly responsible for the platform women received through that subsidiary, basically invented the women's wrestling evolution rubs many the wrong way. If McMahon and Levesque, high-ranking executives in WWE for at least a decade, were the arbiters of gender equality in wrestling, why did it take them so long to grant it?

I've been a wrestling fan for over half my life, since catching my first glimpse of the carnivalesque world at a friend's house after school. I was hooked by the aerial in-ring stunts of the Hardy Boyz, Chris Jericho, and Kurt Angle. Lita, the Hardy Boyz's valet at the time, also piqued my interest, for being able to hold her own with men. Though I'd seen the occasional Litacanara (Lita's version of the Hurricanrana, a headscissor takedown), I hadn't known women wrestlers could do the things male wrestlers could do, because WWE had never let them.

Actually, my initial introduction to WWE was probably six months before I really developed a passion for it. It was late one night at a different friend's sleepover. Her dad had WWE *Raw* on in the living room, where we were to sleep that night, specifically a late-2000 episode in which WWE patriarch Vince McMahon, father of Stephanie, made out with his much younger on-screen girlfriend, Trish Stratus, in front of his "comatose" real-life wife, Linda McMahon, who later headed up the Small Business Administration (because a multibillion dollar company such as WWE qualifies as a "small business") during the first two years of the Donald Trump—a frequent WWE personality and member of its Hall of Fame—presidency. It's no wonder I, and many other wrestling fans at that time, couldn't fathom that women wrestlers could be anything more than eye candy in bra and panties matches.

Bra and panties matches were a staple of the Attitude Era—the late 1990s to early 2000s—which traded in the hypersexualization and cartoonish violence that is front of mind when most people think of wrestling. The concept of the match is as follows: the first woman to strip her opponent down to her lingerie wins. But really, wasn't everyone a winner in a bra and panties match, amiright boys? There were variations, such as an evening gown match (first woman to rip off the evening gown wins); the lingerie pillow fight, which was decided like a regular match, by pinfall or submission, but the women wrestlers were already in their undergarments as they entered the ring; the festive Thanksgiving gravy bowl match and eggnog match; and general food fights and mud matches. There was the *Playboy* pillow fight, which didn't always transpire in the ring but invariably featured the WWE Diva who posed nude for the magazine that year, a partnership the two conglomerates flirted with in 1999 and 2000 with Sable and Chyna getting their kit off, respectively, but really solidified between 2003 and 2008, with six Divas posing for the magazine during this time.

You'll notice that I mentioned the word "Diva" in that last paragraph, and indeed, it's the first word (insomuch as a hashtag can be considered a word) of this book. A Diva is not just the female version of a hustler, as Beyoncé defined it, but, as this book's title implies, also was the WWE's female version of a wrestler for the better part of a decade and a half. It's unclear exactly when the word officially entered the company's vernacular. Sable and Sunny, controversial figures whom I write about throughout this book, both vied for first dibs in the late 1990s. By the mid-2000s, WWE had leaned into the term, branding its women's roster the Divas division, with a brand-new, butterfly-shaped championship belt being introduced in 2008, because how would we be able to tell it was a women's championship if it didn't have a sparkly pink visual metaphor for female genitalia on it?

In 2013, the E! reality show *Total Divas* premiered, following the lives of many of the WWE women employees who are featured in this book, from the Bella Twins (who have their own spinoff, *Total Bellas*) to Paige, an irregular cast member due to issues in her personal life. The mainstream success of the show, which has been running for nine seasons at the time of writing, cannot be overstated, crystalizing the marketing power in the mainstream of not only women's wrestling, but also the term "Diva."

Multiple past women wrestlers have said they don't identify with it, though. Trish Stratus eschews the word. "We get it: you're beautiful and you're a woman. Great, now let's get in the ring. Let's be athletes," she told famed wrestling announcer Jim Ross on his podcast in 2014.[3] Indicative of the one-of-the-boys attitude that has attracted many wrestling fans to her, Lita has said she feels "Diva" is another term for "window dressing," adding "not to be sexist," she was always "thinking like a guy" in the ring.[4]

So it was only fitting that Lita be the one to announce the dissolution of the term in 2016, with a brand, spankin' new women's championship to replace the Divas title to boot, giving ~~Divas~~ women wrestlers a chance to be more than hot babes slapping each other around for a few minutes once a week. Granted, just because they weren't reduced to a sexist epithet doesn't mean that WWE saw them as capable of anything else.

For months after abolition of the term, which coincided with the beginning of my career writing about women's wrestling, WWE declined to give its women wrestlers their versions of classic men's matches, such as the Royal Rumble and Money in the Bank (both of which they eventually would receive).

But no matter how badly WWE flubbed many of what should have been defining moments in the history of women's wrestling, somehow I still kept watching. I kept watching after a man, James Ellsworth, retrieved the briefcase with a championship contract inside for his female colleague, Carmella, in the first-ever women's Money in the

---

3   Jim Ross, *Grilling JR with Jim Ross*, Official, "Trish Stratus Shoot Interview," YouTube, July 26, 2017.

4   Chris Jericho, *Talk Is Jericho*, "WWE's Lita," Omny, March 20, 2014.

Bank match in 2017. I kept watching as WWE refused to acknowledge the contributions of Joanie "Chyna" Laurer by inducting her into its Hall of Fame, even after her untimely death in 2016, because of her past in sex work and her romantic involvement with Levesque. (She was eventually inducted, in 2019, not for her own achievements but as part of the politically incorrect group D-Generation X, which also consisted of her exes Levesque and Sean "X-Pac" Waltman.) And I kept watching as WWE biannually shipped its male wrestlers off to perform in the Kingdom of Saudi Arabia, where women were not permitted to attend sporting events unchaperoned by a male relative or guardian, let alone wrestle.[5] You'll read about many of these things and the issues I have with them in further detail throughout this book.

I actually took a break from watching wrestling, from about 2010 to 2013/2014, not for any specific reason but more so because it didn't fit my lifestyle. I had moved away from home for the first time, into my own apartment, which I could barely afford the rent on, let alone cable TV. It was during this time that I "discovered" feminism. This is not to say that I wasn't a feminist before I started reading literature on the topic, as I have always believed in independence and autonomy for women, but it was the first time I had the tools to be able to identify my belief system.

When, at my cousin's wedding, I bumped into a family friend and wrestling fan who invited me to be a part of a wrestling mockumentary he was filming, I was thrust back into sports entertainment,[6] pondering how to reconcile my renewed love of wrestling with my newfound feminism.

Total Divas in 2013, the renaissance of women's wrestling in *NXT* that aired on the company's streaming service, the WWE Network, in

---

5   Beginning in late 2019, WWE began hosting one women's match per show in the country.

6   Wrestling may appear to be a competitive contest, and the wrestlers involved are no doubt athletes, but their sole purpose is to entertain the audience, not to win a legitimate bout; hence the name sports entertainment, trademarked by WWE because capitalism.

2014, and #GiveDivasAChance in 2015 all coalesced, and the rest is fraught herstory.

Why do you even watch WWE if all you do is criticize it? default avatars with three followers bark at me on Twitter.

It hasn't always been easy. I've wanted to, and have, quit on several occasions, as you'll read throughout this book. But wrestling must have imprinted itself on my impressionable young brain, and much to the chagrin of my mother, who thought I was over wrestling the first time I stopped consuming it, at this point it's part of my DNA. Or, at least, a focal point of my career.

But as another maligned woman on the internet, Anita Sarkeesian of the *Feminist Frequency* YouTube gaming series and podcast, puts it, it is "both possible and even necessary to simultaneously enjoy media while being critical of its more problematic or pernicious aspects."[7] No piece of pop culture is perfect, least of all professional wrestling.

Wrestling may be derided as "fake," but it is no more unrealistic than *Game of Thrones* or superhero movies or video games, all of which have followers just as dedicated as wrestling fans and have been deemed worthy of cultural criticism by the media.

A Diva Was a Female Version of a Wrestler is loosely chronological, ranging from the 1950s to the "end of the women's evolution," as WWE dubbed it: the first women's main event of *WrestleMania 35* in 2019. I have also included a handful of notable happenings after that, such as the first women's match in Saudi Arabia and some developments with the Four Horsewomen. But it is not a history lesson chronicling every woman in WWE's wins and losses. For that you can check out some of the books I've listed in the "Women's Wrestling Syllabus." Rather, I group wrestlers and ideas together to look at what they mean to the industry and culture in general, with a reverence that often wasn't afforded to them at the time. Or even now.

---

7   Anita Sarkeesian, *Feminist Frequency*, "Damsel in Distress: Part 1—Tropes vs Women in Video Games," YouTube, March 7, 2013.

1.

The Fabulous Moolah &
How We Tell Women's Stories in Wrestling

Content warning: *This chapter contains mentions of sex trafficking, rape, murder, financial abuse, drug and alcohol abuse, ableism, racism, and unfair-labor practices.*

The Fabulous Moolah Memorial battle royal was set for *WrestleMania* 34 in 2018. With the women's wrestling evolution in full swing and WWE's women's roster growing immensely, it was only right that women get a partner match to the men's version, named in memoriam for Andre the Giant, which had been running since 2014 in an effort to get every wrestler under WWE contract on the *WrestleMania* card.

A battle royal consists of a bunch of wrestlers all in the ring at the same time, with elimination occurring when a wrestler is thrown over the top rope with both feet landing on the floor outside of the ring. Historically men were the main competitors in such a match, with women's eliminations allowed to occur when the wrestlers fell out of the ring through whichever rope. You know, because women lack the upper-body strength to propel another person that high. Women's battle royals have since been changed so that the rules are now the same as the men's version.

Andre the Giant was well known for his involvement in battle royals in his day and was one of the most recognizable figures in wrestling, so it seemed fitting for this *WrestleMania* tradition to be named in his honor.

The legend of The Fabulous Moolah, born Mary Lillian Ellison in 1923 and also known, in her early days, as Slave Girl Moolah, began in 1956 when she won a battle royal to become the National Wrestling Alliance (NWA) women's champion.

"Starting that night in 1956, I held the championship for twenty-eight years," she wrote in her 2002 memoir, *The Fabulous Moolah: First Goddess of the Squared Circle.* (I use the term "wrote" loosely, as most wrestling autobiographies are ghostwritten—by and about men, of course.) "You can look that up."

Moolah shouldn't have encouraged anyone to take her claims at more than face value, as researching her supposed twenty-eight-year reign exposes the controversy it was imbued with.

Firstly, due to the politicking of Billy Wolfe, owner of NWA at the time and Moolah's former manager, whom she bitterly parted ways with, Moolah's victory was not recognized until 1964, when the former title holder June Byers retired for good. (Byers had previously tried to retire the championship along with her, leading to the battle royal for the title that Moolah won, but Byers was coaxed back by the chance to best Moolah as one of her many rivals.)

Wolfe, in addition to controlling NWA, the governing body of what at that time was known as the territory system of regional wrestling companies that operated throughout North America, Japan, and Australasia, controlled the terms of employment of many women wrestlers, such as Moolah; his first wife, Barbara Ware; his second wife, Mildred Burke; and his daughter-in-law Byers.

Burke, born Mildred Bliss in 1915, was the foremother of women's wrestling in the US and helped to popularize it in Japan but rarely gets the recognition she deserves. Burke approached Wolfe for training in the 1930s, but she was initially rebuffed with the renouncement that women can't wrestle, like many of the women wrestlers discussed here. However she proved her worth by wrestling hundreds of men, as an early pioneer of intergender wrestling.

"I didn't know girls could do this! I didn't know they did this!"

Moolah exclaimed[8] when she saw Burke—who later became her trainer—as a young girl.

Burke divorced Wolfe in 1952, sick of his philandering ways, and was quickly muscled out of the industry by Wolfe and the women he groomed to take her place, Moolah and Byers.

Moolah said that during her time working for Wolfe he would trade bookings for sex, both with him and promotors from other territories. It seems Moolah learned a lot from Wolfe, which I'll get to.

In actual fact, Moolah's first reign did last an impressive ten years, and she went on to hold the championship four more times, each for a period of several years. But in order for Moolah to credibly claim she held the women's championship uninterrupted for nearly three decades, she sold the title and her exclusivity to Vince McMahon, Jr.[9] As part of that deal, the lore of the title that would become known as the WWE women's championship was rewritten, so that no title changes since Moolah's victory in 1956 were recognized by the company.

This gospel according to WWE is exemplary of its propensity for revisionist history. *Contingent Magazine* defines revisionist history as "conscious, intentional misstatements about things in the past, whether distant or recent."[10] It is firmly rooted in nostalgia, which *New York Times* culture critic Wesley Morris calls a "romancing of reality."[11]

LaToya Ferguson, author of the book *An Encyclopedia of Women's Wrestling: 100 Profiles of the Strongest in the Sport*, notes that because professional wrestling is built on kayfabe—the scripted world wrestling exists in and the penchant for wrestlers to stay true to their characters

---

8   Lillian Ellison and Larry Platt, *The Fabulous Moolah: First Goddess of the Squared Circle*, 2002.

9   McMahon, Jr., whom I will refer to as McMahon throughout the course of this chapter and book, had just taken over World Wrestling Federation (WWF)—what has since become World Wrestling Entertainment (WWE), which is how I refer to it throughout this book, for cohesion—from his father, Vince McMahon, Sr.

10   Erin Bartram, "What Is Revisionist History?" *Contingent Magazine*, August 8, 2019.

11   Wesley Morris and Jenna Wortham, *Still Processing*, "Delicious Vinyl," *The New York Times*, April 2, 2020.

in their real lives—it's hard to parse what is truth and what is fiction.

"I would read and watch a lot of interviews . . . where wrestlers would say one thing, then in another . . . say another," Ferguson told women's wrestling site *Bell to Belles*.[12] "And it would be just so slightly different it would take me down wormholes trying to confirm. A lot of cross-referencing and a lot of removing things from the book that could be true but there were too many conflicting stories about."

Moolah's contentious title history is a distant example of revisionist history, while the WWE's women's wrestling evolution is a more recent one.

As discussed in the prologue, what is now known as the women's evolution began in 2015 as a fan-led social media movement with the hashtag #GiveDivasAChance, Divas being what WWE called its women wrestlers at the time.

Once WWE realized the hunger for better women's representation wasn't going away, it finally parlayed that into the Divas revolution and, when the Divas brand was dropped the following year, simply the women's evolution.

This marketing strategy smacks of WWE's party line, which positions itself as being at the forefront of cultural change, when WWE was the one halting progress and endangering its performers in the process.

In 2020, when the COVID-19 pandemic forced us indoors and put a halt to all events and attractions, WWE pushed forward on its fifty-two-weeks-per-year wrestling schedule and had its wrestlers reclassified as "essential media personnel" by the state of Florida[13] in order to keep working (and let dozens of them, along with crew members, go from their contracts days later), even though at least one of their performers

---

12   Lauren Founds, "Exclusive: Author Details *Encyclopedia of Women's Wrestling* As Labor of Love," *Bell to Belles*, May 14, 2019.

13   WWE moved its traveling circus to its training facilities in Orlando in March 2020. After the state's stay-at-home order was issued in early April, a super PAC for the reelection of Donald Trump run by Linda McMahon, Vince McMahon's wife and former head of the Trump cabinet's Small Business Administration, agreed to spend $18.5 million on advertising in Florida. Shortly thereafter, "employees at professional sports and media production with a national audience" were deemed to be providing "essential services," per Florida Governor Ron DeSantis.

was diagnosed with the virus. "We're putting smiles on peoples faces," WWE justified it as,[14] a refrain that was likely also heard when *SmackDown* was the first live event after 9/11, and when WWE decided to continue a pay-per-view after a wrestler died in the ring.[15]

Another example of this is the company's foray into the Middle East. WWE touted that it put on the first-ever women's wrestling match in Abu Dhabi in 2017 between Sasha Banks and Alexa Bliss, when there had been women's wrestling in the United Arab Emirates since at least 2010.[16] The much-repeated talking point about that match is that the entire arena was chanting "This is hope"; only some attendees close enough to the ring for the recording equipment to pick the chant up were calling it out.

The furor from fans—myself included, in one of those aforementioned moments that made my question my patronization of this company—when WWE expanded its Middle Eastern presence into the conservative Muslim country Saudi Arabia in 2018 was loud. Prior to Saudi Arabia's involvement with WWE, as part of its Vision 2030 campaign to portray a more progressive country to the rest of the world, women were not permitted to play sports there. The tandem promotion of WWE's Saudi Arabian shows and its women's evolution—the *Evolution* pay-per-view was held the same week, which some proponents of gender equality saw as a consolation prize[17]—hinted that WWE's end goal, aside from the money, was the good press that would come with being the first company to host a women's sporting contest there. In late 2019 that goal was reached with Natalya and Lacey Evans wrestling in the country, seemingly in place of a second installment of *Evolution*, which would have occurred around that time. Apparently gender equality was only

---

14   Corey Erdman, "*WrestleMania* Will Go on Despite the Coronavirus Pandemic. It Shouldn't," *Vice*, April 2, 2020.

15   Owen Hart fell to his death from inadequate rigging equipment as he made his entrance from the rafters of the arena that held the unfortunately named 1999 show *Over the Edge*.

16   David Bixenspan, "Stephanie McMahon: WWE's First Saudi Women's Match to Feature 'Different' Costuming," *Forbes*, October 30, 2019.

17   This is not to mention the assassination that same month of journalist Jamal Khashoggi, which, the CIA concluded in 2018, was ordered by Saudi Crown Prince Mohammed bin Salman.

achievable for two White, blonde women.

Like Saudi Arabia, WWE has historically erased women from its history. Recent wrestling documentaries, such as the Viceland series *Dark Side of the Ring* or HBO's Andre the Giant doco, seldom cast women among the copious talking heads. WWE put out a docuseries, *Ruthless Aggression*, on its streaming platform, the WWE Network, about the early-to-mid-2000s period of the same name. Granted, women were still portrayed as eye candy capable only of putting on— or taking off, as it were—a bra and panties match, a holdover from the previous, sex-drugs-and-rock-'n'-roll-heavy Attitude era. But they were present, not that many of them were included in the *Ruthless Aggression* doco, with only current women wrestlers Becky Lynch and Natalya asked to provide insight. Lita, who was jumping off ladders and performing in "live sex celebrations," received what amounted to less than a minute of talking-head time in one episode for her efforts. You'd think the second-season episode about the Diva Search, a reality competition to find WWE's next woman wrestler, would rectify this, but alas, the men who controlled the industry at the time—and still do today—were entrusted to tell this story too. On the odd occasion that women are called upon in these documentaries to give their opinion, they are the wife or romantic partner of the man being chronicled— rarely the subject. Case in point: Beth Phoenix was credited as Edge's wife in the *WWE 24* documentary about his return to the ring, not as the four-time women's champion and youngest Hall of Famer who wrestled while bleeding profusely from her head the very same night.

Or, more often than not, women are portrayed in these documentaries as victims, murdered by their partners or left to die by the industry. If we've learned anything from the clearer lens stemming from the #MeToo movement, it's that we should be creating space now for those who were overlooked then.

But revisionist history is not all bad. Sometimes we have to engage in it in order to tell the stories of those who weren't enshrined in it the first time around. Revisionist herstory, if you will . . . .

WWE probably didn't think that its christening of The Fabulous Moolah Memorial battle royal in Moolah's honor would result in attention being drawn to her shady past.

Within days, the company abruptly changed tack and the name to just the generic *WrestleMania* Women's Battle Royal™, but remained resolute on designating it the "first ever" match of its kind at *WrestleMania*, as was customary during the women's wrestling evolution, not realizing that this actually amplified the fact that WWE itself had prevented women from achieving each of these firsts years before. There had been plenty of battle royals consisting of women at *WrestleMania*; it's just that they were called Divas at the time and also one of those matches was won by a man. Shockingly, this was not the last time that would happen. If you'll recall: the first women's Money in the Bank ladder match in 2017, in which a male manager retrieved the championship contract from atop a ladder and threw it down to his female charge and the actual competitor in the match, Carmella, to claim the victory.

But I'm getting ahead of myself.

Moolah made the move to WWE at just the right time. Vince McMahon, Jr., was expanding the company from its roots in the tristate area to cable syndication across the United States, thus largely putting the territory system out of business.

A major factor in this was WWE's partnership with MTV in the mid-1980s, called the Rock 'n' Wrestling Connection. Wrestlers such as Captain Lou Albano, who starred in multiple Cyndi Lauper videos as her father, Wendi Richter, and Hulk Hogan were all over Saturday-morning TV screens in an attempt to infiltrate mainstream pop culture and create a wider audience for wrestling, just as *Total Divas* would do thirty years later.

"A lot of new fans were coming to wrestling because of Cyndi," Moolah wrote in her book. "I remember looking out at the crowd . . .

and seeing groups of young teenage girls, dressed just like Cyndi and with that crazy bright red hair, holding 'Girls Just Want to Have Fun' signs."

It all came to a head at *The Brawl to End It All*, which was telecast live on MTV in 1984. A feud had been set up between Lauper and Albano, with each selecting a woman wrestler to represent them in the ring. Lauper chose Richter, who appears as the waitress in Lauper's video for "She Bop," while Albano was in the corner of champion Moolah, who put her title on the line.

WWE, capitalizing on Richter's growing popularity, which skyrocketed after this match, scripted the ingenue to win the title, much to chagrin of Moolah, who dropkicked the referee after the match.

"Wendi was over as big as Hogan, and maybe that was the problem," Princess Victoria (real name Vickie Otis), a former student of Moolah's, said on Viceland's *Dark Side of the Ring*.

To reiterate: wrestling is predetermined. Except on rare instances, as I'm about to discuss, everyone has agreed upon the outcome of the match and who comes away with the title beforehand. But Moolah wrote in *The Fabulous Moolah: First Goddess of the Squared Circle* as if these matches were real and Richter actually got the better of her that night in a legitimate sporting contest, instead of acknowledging that WWE's hitching of the title to Richter's star power was what was best for business. Perhaps this is testament to the importance of kayfabe during the time when Moolah was coming up, and her blind adherence to it, or maybe Moolah's ego was so large she really couldn't fathom someone else holding the title. With Moolah working so hard to uphold her reign as the only one worth recognizing, having a young upstart deemed worthy enough to end twenty-eight years of revisionism must have really dented her pride.

Judging from what transpired in the following year or so, this is a fair assumption. Moolah took Leilani Kai under her wing and helped her defeat Richter for the title in early 1985 at *The War to Settle the Score*, but Richter reclaimed it at the inaugural *WrestleMania* a couple of months later.

Kai began training to wrestle with Moolah right out of high school in the mid-1970s. Though Kai was ethnically White, Moolah allegedly thought she looked "a bit Hawaiian"; hence the name, an illustration of the unfortunate trend of racism and cultural appropriation that appears throughout wrestling history. Later, Kai became a two-time women's tag team champion with Judy Martin as the Glamour Girls, who were the last women to hold the titles before they were deactivated in 1989. (The titles were brought back in 2019 after a thirty-year hiatus, which WWE once again inaccurately lauded a "first.")

Richter began speaking out about her mistreatment at the hands of WWE. Given that her popularity was akin to that of Hulk Hogan's at the time, she should have been paid to reflect this.

According to wrestling journalists Pat Laprade and Dan Murphy's reporting in the 2017 book *Sisterhood of the Squared Circle: The History and Rise of Women's Wrestling*, Hulk Hogan received up to a $100,000 payday for *WrestleMania*, while Richter was paid just $5,000.

"I found out early in my career that the men were getting paid more than the women," she said on *Dark Side of the Ring*. "But if I'm the only one saying that, one person can be replaced."

And replaced she was.

Later in 1985, Richter defended her title against Moolah, who was wrestling under both a mask and the moniker The Spider Lady, who up until that point had been a wrestler named Penny Mitchell, in what would become known as "the original screwjob."[18] It was alleged that Richter did not know that Moolah was The Spider Lady and that Vince McMahon orchestrated the screwjob because he was pissed that Richter was asking for more money. "I had wrestled The Spider Lady before and I didn't recall her being that size. . . . I couldn't tell who it was," Richter claimed on *Dark Side of the Ring*; however, others have disputed this. Either way, it was clear that something was afoot. Moolah walked away from the match again a champion—which she remained on and off for the next two years—after the referee fast-counted the pin, which Richter visibly kicked out of. Richter, at the height of her

---

18   The other is known as The Montreal Screwjob, or just the Screwjob, a 1997 match between WWE champion Bret Hart and Shawn Michaels. Hart was under the impression that he would be leaving WWE to go to competitor World Championship Wrestling (WCW) while still holding the title. Vince McMahon allegedly felt that this would diminish the value of the title, and instead colluded with Michaels, the referee, and other personnel to fix the finish and put the title on Michaels.

popularity, left WWE and never returned.

Moolah continued to use her reign to monopolize WWE's women's division, which had been thriving since 1983 and the addition of the women's tag team championships. In 1989, the singular women's championship was deactivated as well, with only three others—Sensational Sherri, Rockin' Robin, and Velvet McIntyre, whose title run in Australia lasted six days before Moolah won it back again, because what happens in Vegas etc.—having held it since the screwjob.

Setting reign records rarely does anything for anyone except the person holding the title.

"Moolah held wrestling back probably for forty years," Richter said in *Dark Side of the Ring* of the woman who was best known for wrestling of the hair-pulling, cat-fighting variety—both markers of the Divas era—rather than any real technical savvy.

Moolah climbed the ladder from "Slave Girl" to arbiter of much of women's wrestling for a time.

"Before I came along, the girls had no power," she wrote.

Instead of lifting other women up with her, she sought to keep them subjugated.

Moolah had been operating a women's wrestling school in some form since the 1940s and fifties. Women who went through her doors include Judy Martin, Joyce Grable, Ida Mae Martinez, Sensational Sherri Martel, and Richter herself, who claims that Moolah purposely trained her students inadequately or not at all, with Moolah's third husband, Buddy Lee, Leilani Kai, and other students such as Donna Christanello providing most of the training.[19] Moolah's own daughter, Mary, wrestling under the name Darlin' Pat Sherry, and a stable (wrestling speak for a group of wrestlers) of dwarf wrestlers rounded out the troupe. In her book, Moolah troublingly calls Katie Glass, a dwarf wrestler known as Diamond Lil (Lil being short for Lillian, Moolah's

---

19   Pat Laprade and Dan Murphy, *Sisterhood of the Squared Circle: The History and Rise of Women's Wrestling*, 2017.

real name, in an example of the paternalism and ownership Moolah exerted over "my girls"), "my damned midget."

"She calls me Ma, and I guess I have been a sort of mother figure to her," wrote Moolah, which is exemplary of the exploitation she treated her mentees with.

Moolah verbally berated the women who entrusted their wrestling training to her, as well as enforcing strict dress, hair, and makeup codes, a curfew, and no dating.

"I was pretty hard on the girls who came through," Moolah continues. "I made a lot of demands outside of the ring. . . . I didn't want them hanging around bars and dating guys in bars, because most of the guys in those bars back then were married and they had wives at home."

Perhaps she wanted to make sure the wrestling promoters she foisted onto her trainees in exchange for bookings were the only men they were spending time with. For as vocal as Moolah was about the treatment she and other women wrestlers had received under the tutelage of Billy Wolfe, she exhibited many of the same behaviors.

"She was trained by him, so I guess you know she got it from him," Judy Grable said in the 2004 documentary *Lipstick & Dynamite, Piss & Vinegar: The First Ladies of Wrestling*. "What goes around comes around. She got it done to her, and she was doing it to everyone else."

It has been alleged by several women wrestlers that Moolah was a sex trafficker—despite her protestations in her book that she "ain't no damn madam" when her trainees wanted to fraternize with the opposite sex—and exchanged their nonconsensual sexual services for wrestling bookings.

Sweet Georgia Brown, born Susie Mae McCoy in 1938, was the first African American woman wrestler at Moolah's school. When wrestling in the South during segregation, Brown often had to be surreptitiously ferried into venues to avoid the ire of the racist crowd and townsfolk, and she was not permitted to wrestle White women. She was treated as a second-class citizen not only by wrestling fans but by her trainers as well. Brown's daughter Barbara Harsey said her mother was plied with drugs and alcohol and forced to sleep with men on the road[20,21] and that most of her siblings were conceived during these encounters. They suffered discrimination and abuse within their family and community for being mixed raced,[22,23] and when their mother died, they were forced to watch as her wrestling gear, in a box marked "whore stuff," was burned by Brown's brothers.[24] Brown's son Michael McCoy believes his father is Buddy Lee, Moolah's husband at the time.[25]

Ella Waldek (born Elsie Schevchenko in 1929), another wrestler whom Moolah trained, alleged in *Lipstick & Dynamite* that she was raped by Moolah's previous husband, boxer and wrestling trainer Johnny Long, but Moolah didn't believe her. Moolah admits as much, telling the filmmakers that "I took her ass out to the woods and taught her what cheating was and put her on the bus home."

Luna Vachon, of the infamous Vachon wrestling family, began training under her aunt Vivian and Moolah in her teens in the late seventies. According to an interview in 2002, Luna claims that Moolah sent her to a creepy—albeit fully clothed—photoshoot when she was still a teenager.[26]

Moolah also financially abused her trainees, forcing them to live on her property—where they were charged rent as well as tuition—while she deducted travel, food, and booking fees. In some cases the women received only half of their rate, as Moolah would take the rest for herself.[27] "Can you imagine: four girls in one little house; she's getting $1,200 a month—in the eighties?!" said Princess Victoria, who claims that after she broke her neck and couldn't wrestle, Moolah tried to

---

20   Murfee Faulk, "Baby of Sweet Georgia Brown," *Free Times*, December 20, 2006.

21   "The Fabulous Moolah," *Dark Side of the Ring*, Viceland, May 15, 2019.

22   Faulk.

23   "The Fabulous Moolah," *Dark Side of the Ring*, Viceland, May 15, 2019.

24   Faulk.

25   "The Fabulous Moolah," *Dark Side of the Ring*, Viceland, May 15, 2019.

26   Brandon Truitt, "Gangrel and Luna Vachon Shoot Interview," *TheSmartMarks.com*, November 3, 2003.

27   "The Fabulous Moolah," Wikipedia, last updated May 1, 2020.

pimp her out in order to make some money for rent (when Victoria wouldn't do it, Moolah kicked her out. "I never wrestled again," she said.).[28] "And on top of that she's taking 25 percent off of what she's telling us we're paid. Bull pucky."

Suddenly the name Moolah makes a lot more sense . . . .

Though society's fledgling willingness to believe survivors of abuse in the wake of the #MeToo movement has shone a light on these allegations, they were made long before Moolah's death in 2007, and in some cases she herself boasted about or foretold them.

"She was smart enough to see through that old trick," Moolah recalled fondly of her friend Mae Young when Moolah offered to handle her money for her.

Johnnie Mae Young, after whom WWE named a women's wrestling tournament that began in 2017, was Moolah's best friend and was seldom seen without her during their later years.

Young was born in 1923 and grew up wrestling on her high school amateur team, breaking gender barriers at the tender age of fifteen. She continued to do so throughout the course of her career, which began professionally in the late 1930s and early 1940s (the exact year is contested) when, as a fan, she challenged the champion Mildred Burke,[29] a figure we know loomed large in both Moolah's and Young's herstories.

The three Ms trained and wrestled together, and Young made history by being among the first women, along with Burke, to wrestle in post-World War II Japan. If we are to believe that her first match was in the thirties, Young was the first person whose career spanned nine decades, with her last match being in 2010 at the age of eighty-seven.

When Moolah and Young started appearing in WWE—Young effectively made her debut for the company; she had previously

---

28   "The Fabulous Moolah," *Dark Side of the Ring*, Viceland, May 15, 2019.

29   The promoter wasn't having that, so he allowed Young to challenge Burke's scheduled opponent that night—Gladys Gillem—instead. Laprade and Murphy.

wrestled for its early incarnation, under Vince McMahon, Sr.[30]—in the late nineties Attitude and early 2000s Ruthless Aggression eras, they were in their seventies and able to roll with wrestlers forty and fifty years their junior, getting thrown through tables by the Dudley Boyz and attacked by 3-Minute Warning.

Conversely, the women who spoke out or went against Moolah, like Burke, saw themselves iced out of the industry.

Penny Banner, one of Moolah's contemporaries, fell victim to Wolfe and Moolah's revisionist history. Recognized in some territories as the NWA world champion while Moolah claimed to have held the title, Banner doesn't appear in official records as an official recipient.[31]

"Due to politics, the places she could work narrowed," wrestling journalist Dave Meltzer wrote of Banner. "Moolah was booked by most NWA promoters as world champion, and since Banner didn't play ball with her, a lot of her booking opportunities dried up."[32]

Mad Maxine, a fellow figure of the Rock 'n' Wrestling Connection era and one of Moolahs' trainees, verified stories of sexual and financial exploitation by Moolah on numerous occasions.[33,34] In an attempt to rebel against Moolah's rigid beauty guidelines and be rid of her shady dealings, Maxine (born Jeannine Mjoseth in 1959) shaved her hair into a bright green mohawk, catching the eye of Vince McMahon and the creative powers behind *Hulk Hogan's Rock 'n' Wrestling* cartoon show, who wanted to feature her as a character.[35] Maxine, who was being managed by Moolah on WWE TV, claims she had no knowledge of

---

30 Laprade and Murphy.

31 "NWA World Women's Championship," Wikipedia, last updated April 11, 2020.

32 Laprade and Murphy.

33 Bill Fernow, "Mad Maxine Has Quite the Story to Tell," *Slam Wrestling*, October 6, 2014.

34 Ryan Satin, "Fabulous Moolah Trainee Speaks Out Against WWE Tribute, Claims Hall of Famer 'Pimped Women,'" *Pro Wrestling Sheet*, March 13, 2018.

35 Concept Art of "Mad Maxine Ryder" is still available on WWE's website as of this writing. WWE. com, n.d.

this until after she had left WWE due to Moolah's treatment of her and Moolah's likeness appeared on the cartoon instead.

Moolah and WWE also tried to lay claim to lifting the ban on women's wrestling in New York State in the early 1970s and cited Moolah's match against Vicki Williams at Madison Square Garden in 1972 as the first women's match in the state.[36] However, Moolah and WWE appear nowhere in the New York State Athletic Commission records regarding licensing of women's wrestling, with women wrestlers[37] such as Betty Niccoli and Titi Paris doing a lot of the activism in order to get the ban lifted. *The New York Times* credits the commission with making the change.[38]

For their efforts, Niccoli said, Vince McMahon, Sr., prevented her from achieving her dream of being the first woman to wrestle in the iconic Manhattan arena, and Moolah froze Niccoli and Paris out of working any venues in which WWE promoted shows.[39]

Leilani Kai, who was managed to WWE women's championship victory by Moolah, was also fired from the company because of her. When Kai and Judy Martin tag teamed as the Glamour Girls, they suggested WWE bring in some women from Japan to freshen up the division.

"Moolah was having none of that idea," wrote Pat Laprade and Dan Murphy in *Sisterhood of the Squared Circle: The History and Rise of Women's Wrestling*. "[She] had no interest in bringing in women who weren't under contract to her, especially the ultra-athletic Japanese women with whom she could no longer compete."

During an event in Japan between WWE and All Japan Women, the

---

36   There is some consternation over whether this is the first women's match in New York State, which *The New York Times* states as fact. Pat Laprade, in *Sisterhood of the Squared Circle*, writes that Titi Paris and Cora Combs wrestled at a boxing gym four months earlier; however, there are no other records of this available.

37   According to available documents held by the New York State archives provided to me by archivist Kristin Lagerquist, based on her own research.

38   Arthur Pincus, "19,512 Quiet Fans See Women Wrestle for First Time in State," *The New York Times*, July 7, 1972.

39   Laprade and Murphy.

Glamour Girls challenged the Jumping Bomb Angels to the tag titles. Although the Angels were all set to retain the titles, Moolah apparently made a call to WWE officials in Japan,[40] claiming that the head office had asked her to communicate to them that the Glamour Girls would actually be winning the championship that night, and so, that's what happened.

"Upon returning to the U.S., Judy and I found out that we were no longer employed in the WW[E]," Kai said.[41] The company was furious that they would go into business for themselves, with Moolah feigning ignorance.

And of course we can't forget the fate of Wendi Richter.

After Moolah had been gone from WWE for a few years in the late 1980s and early nineties, the women's title was brought back, with Alundra Blayze, the late Bertha Faye, and Bull Nakano, the at-once-hulking-and-iconic Japanese woman wrestler who wore her hair in a mohawk and had blue markings resembling fault lines painted on one side of her face, challenging for and holding it. They tried to gain back some of what women's wrestling had lost during the heavily policed era of Moolah, though this momentum was prematurely halted again in 1995 when Blayze, whom the division was built around, was informed that WWE was going in a different direction (ie. once again deactivating the title) and she was no longer needed.

That's when she took the title to World Championship Wrestling (WCW) and threw it in a trash can, arguably igniting the Monday Night Wars that would burn between the two entities for the rest of the 1990s and signaling the devaluation of women's wrestling for the better part of the next two decades.

The institutionalized sexism that Moolah leveraged to get what she wanted was clearly still at play. Instead of existing as a rigid division

---

40   Laprade and Murphy.

41   Ibid.

at the mercy of one or two power players, women's wrestling was practically disregarded, and most of the serious women wrestlers were let go from their contracts, making way for the debuts of Sunny, Sable, Debra, and Marlena (later known as Terri Runnels) in the late nineties: blonde, highly sexualized bombshells whose skills were as managers rather than wrestlers. Though most of them[42] made forays into the ring, with Sable winning the reactivated women's championship from the first Black title holder, Jacqueline, in 1998 despite having less wrestling ability than those half-trained by Moolah, athleticism was not the main objective, and it became even less important as the Attitude and Divas eras were ushered in.

All told, Moolah wrestled in seven decades of her life. For the many wrestling fans who were not privy to all of this information thanks to the revisionist history of WWE, it seemed like a no-brainer that Moolah be the patron saint of the *WrestleMania* women's battle royal in 2018.

But WWE didn't take into account the power of social media and online organizing, which kicked into gear pretty much as soon as the announcement of the match was made.

Just like with #GiveDivasAChance three years earlier, the increasingly diverse and fed up wrestling fandom immediately started tweeting the aforementioned allegations against Moolah and petitioned *WrestleMania* sponsor Snickers to pull out if the match continued as a memorial to her.

The resulting change was swift. Two days later, the match was blandly renamed the *WrestleMania* Women's Battle Royal, some "first evers" thrown in there for effect.

Snickers's parent company, Mars Wrigley Confectionery, released the following statement:

---

42 Sunny didn't wrestle during her time in WWE, though she did sporadically for other companies later in her career.

"We were recently made aware of the World Wrestling Entertainment Inc's (WWE) decision to honor a former wrestler during the upcoming *WrestleMania 34* event. As a principle-based business that has long championed creating inclusive environments that encourage and empower everyone to reach their full potential, this is unacceptable. We are engaging with the WWE to express our disappointment."

Followed by WWE's version:

"After further consideration, we believe it's best to proceed with the name '*WrestleMania* Women's Battle Royal.' What remains most important is that this historic match is part of WWE's unwavering commitment to the Women's Division."[43]

If Mars Wrigley hadn't stepped in, it's likely that The Fabulous Moolah Memorial Battle Royal would have continued on in perpetuity, as would Moolah's standing as the bastion of women's wrestling. She is a woman after WWE's own heart. What WWE does today—classifying wrestlers as independent contractors who can't work for anyone else, but you can be damn sure they have to pay for their own travel expenses and health insurance as they're forced to work brutal schedules—finds its roots in Moolah's practices.

Despite this, naming a battle royal after someone whose commitment was first and foremost to herself, not to the women she had subjugated throughout her seven decades in the business, is antithetical to the very concept of such a collaborative match. Now that the company realizes audiences have soured to Moolah as the foremother of women's wrestling, WWE has engaged in a new kind of revisionist history. She is conspicuously absent from recent marketing around the women's evolution, such as the 2020 book *Kicking Down Doors*.[44] I just wish there

---

43   John Pollock, "WWE Changes Name of The Fabulous Moolah Battle Royal," *Post Wrestling*, May 15, 2018.

44   Moolah does appear in this book; however, it's as a part of Wendi Richter's story and those of the other women she did dirty thirty-five years ago.

could be a measured conversation about Moolah's prominence in the industry as well as the women she climbed over to reach that position. I hope I've done that discussion justice. Although Moolah is inextricably linked to the women I've written about, I've tried to illuminate their herstories instead of focusing on the gospel according to WWE and Moolah, which largely casts a shadow over their contributions to the industry.

2. THE TRAGIC JOURNEY OF THE WOMEN'S WRESTLING TRAINWRECK

Content warning: *This chapter contains mentions of rape, drug abuse, alcoholism, mental illness, intimate partner violence (IPV), racism, and murder.*

Society loves a bad boy made good. Professional wrestling is no different; it's a wasteland of bad men who've committed intimate partner violence (IPV), sexual assault, and, in some cases, even murder. Let me count the ways . . . .

Scott Hall, better known as Razor Ramon, killed a man in a bar fight in 1983,[45] he revealed on an ESPN special about his life, and was charged with IPV, though the charges were later dropped.[46]

Purveyor of the Superfly splash off the top rope, Jimmy "Superfly" Snuka was in 2015 charged with the 1983 third-degree murder and involuntary manslaughter of his girlfriend at the time, Nancy Argentino. Charges were dismissed in early 2017 due to Snuka's mental incompetence to stand trial,[47] and he died twelve days later from stomach cancer. He was memorialized with a video package on WWE

---

45   John Cobbcorn, "ESPN *E:60* and Scott Hall: The Most Shocking Revelations," *Bleacher Report*, October 20, 2011.

46   "Scott Hall off the Hook in GF-Choking Case," *TMZ.com*, May 4, 2012.

47   David Bixenspan, "The Dismissed Murder Case Against Jimmy 'Superfly' Snuka," *Paste*, January 5, 2017.

TV,[48] which shockingly *insert sarcasm here* didn't acknowledge his alleged crime.

Chris Benoit murdered his family in their home over the course of a weekend in 2007 before killing himself, yet debates still rage about whether WWE was right to scrub him from its revisionist history, a rare occurrence when it comes to bad men. In early 2020, he was the subject of the first movie-length episode of the second season of Viceland's *Dark Side of the Ring* docuseries.

Jerry "The King" Lawler was the vocal bane of the Attitude era, punctuating the debauchery and degradation therein as a color commentator whose biggest contribution to the craft was screaming "puppies!" at women's breasts. Before that he was a celebrated Memphis wrestler and also an alleged child rapist.[49] In addition, he was arrested for IPV in 2016.[50]

His metaphorical cellmate on the latter charge is Stone Cold Steve Austin, who, in addition to being one of the most famous wrestlers of all time, is a multitime IPV perpetrator.[51,52]

Hulk Hogan is not only wrestling's first crossover star into pop culture—both imploring us to take our vitamins on 1980s Saturday-morning cartoons and taking down Gawker Media, changing the media landscape and freedom of press as we knew it—he's also a huge racist. WWE used Hogan as an example by removing him from its Hall of Fame in 2015 when stolen footage in which he used the N-word and admitted he was racist was published by Gawker, resulting in the aforementioned lawsuit. Apparently three years was the arbitrary period of atonement, as Hogan began appearing on WWE TV again as part of its equally problematic Saudi Arabian shows in 2018 and was reinstated

---

48   Bixenspan, "WWE's Shameful Tribute to Jimmy 'Superfly' Snuka," *Paste*, January 18, 2017.

49   Bixenspan, "Jerry Lawler Wrote a Really Dumb Letter to Prosecutors in his 1993 Rape Case," *Deadspin*, February 13, 2018.

50   "Jerry 'The King' Lawler, Fiancée Arrested after Dispute," *WMCActionNews5.com*, June 17, 2016.

51   Lloyd Vries, "Pro Wrestler Accused of Wife-Beating," *CBS News*, June 17, 2002.

52   "Stone Cold Steve Austin Roughs Up Girlfriend," *The Smoking Gun*, March 29, 2004.

to the Hall of Fame the same year.[53]

These are just some of the bad men in the annals of professional wrestling, accumulating accolades while leaving fallen women in their wake.

Historically, women in wrestling have not been beneficiaries of the redemption story, or at least of being the subjects of the separating-the-art-from-the-artist—in this case, the wrestler-from-the-wrestling—debates that rage around bad men and the cool things they created.

This is no doubt thanks to the patriarchy that puts down women who don't adhere to the rigid guidelines set for them. Be fierce and pretty, but once cellulite appears on your exposed thighs or your cosmetic surgery becomes too obvious, you're outta here. For most of the women I will discuss in this chapter, the average amount of time spent contracted to WWE was four years.[54,55]

Often this is due to the physical and mental tolls of pregnancy and motherhood, but opportunities for older women to continue working in nonwrestling roles such as on-screen managers or authority figures and behind-the-scenes creative and producing positions have traditionally been few and far between. In recent years this has changed, with multitime women's champion and Hall of Famer Beth Phoenix commentating for *NXT* and pay-per-view events; the annual women's Royal Rumble match providing opportunities for departed stars to return; and former WWE wrestlers Lita, Gail Kim, and Christy Hemme starting their own wrestling show, called *Kayfabe*, a biting reference to the scripted reality of wrestling that should never be revealed, especially by women. Becky Lynch notably announced her pregnancy while she

---

53   Matt Bonestee, "Hulk Hogan Reinstated to WWE Hall of Fame After Suspension over Racist Tirade," *The Washington Post*, July 16, 2018.

54   In the case of Paige, who actually signed with WWE's training program Florida Championship Wrestling, which then became *NXT*, I've included only her time spent wrestling on the main roster of WWE, which was between 2014 and 2017, but not including her year-plus hiatus due to the injuries and personal issues discussed in this chapter. All told, Paige has been continuously employed by WWE in some capacity since 2011.

55   Alicia Fox and Rosa Mendes both spent over a decade working for WWE.

was the longest-reigning champion of the modern era[56] and the face of WWE, appearing on mainstream magazine and video game covers and fielding offers from Hollywood. This made her one of only a few to actively choose motherhood while on top of the industry[57] rather than as the socially acceptable next step in a woman's gradual retreat from the public eye.

More frequently than any of us would hope, though, women wrestlers just disappear from view and, thus, the collective consciousness of fans. Wrestling is notorious for punishing the body with death-defying stunts, rampant drug use, and relentless travel, so many women without the support of family, friends, and the industry fall through the cracks, reemerging only when their lives have become tragic enough to be considered trainwrecks.

Jude Ellison Sady Doyle wrote in their 2016 book about famous trainwrecks, which greatly inspired this chapter and my pondering of the bad girls of wrestling, that female trainwrecks are "the villains of the story; they're our monsters and demons, images of what we fear, and who we fear becoming."

Published just prior to the election of alleged-rapist-in-chief Donald Trump and a year before sexual assault and harassment survivors started sharing their stories under the hashtag #MeToo, a movement originated in 2006 by activist Tarana Burke, *Trainwreck: The Women We Love to Hate, Mock, and Fear . . . and Why* was ahead of its time in granting troubled women of pop culture's past the opportunity to have their stories reexamined through a more sympathetic lens.

Since then, women who were written off as crazy bitches and footnotes to men's history, such as Lorena Gallo (nee Bobbitt) and Monica Lewinsky, have been reconsidered with empathy and the all-too-clear benefit of hindsight.

It's only right that the trainwrecks of women's wrestling are afforded the same reexamination.

---

56   Post-WWE women's championship, which was retired in 2010 in favor of the Divas championship.

57   Other women, such as Brie Bella and Ronda Rousey, have retired from wrestling specifically to *try* to get pregnant.

Like other national sweethearts, such as Princess Diana and Marilyn Monroe, Miss Elizabeth, known as the First Lady of Wrestling, met a tragic end. Born Elizabeth Hulette in 1960, she was designated as such due to her beloved status as manager of her real-life husband, the late "Macho Man" Randy Savage. Elizabeth was perhaps the first woman in the industry to be portrayed in a nonwrestling role, and paved the way for many of the women I discuss throughout this book.

Though their relationship was the cause célèbre of the wrestling world, with their kayfabe wedding becoming pay-per-view main event programming in 1991, behind the curtain it was less than ideal. Savage was jealous of the attention Elizabeth received and exhibited controlling behavior toward her. Jerry Lawler, who would know that type of behavior when he saw it due to his aforementioned arrests, said that Savage "would literally lock her in his room"[58] when he couldn't be around to monitor her whereabouts.

Jimmy "Mouth of the South" Hart, who also managed Savage for a time, as part of the Mega Powers tag team with Hulk Hogan, agreed:[59] "They were doing an angle one time where Liz was not on the road with him. He got her twenty-one TV dinners: one for breakfast, lunch and supper [for each of the days that he was away]. She was not allowed to go out of the house. And that's a true story 'cause she told me that." When Savage turned heel, he mistreated Elizabeth on-screen. Given the things people have said about their relationship, one has to wonder whether art imitated life.

The two eventually divorced, in 1992, and she went on to valet for, and become romantically involved with, Lex Luger, a wrestler in WWE's rival promotion WCW, who was married to someone else.

In the *Dark Side of the Ring* episode about Savage and Elizabeth, Hogan's ex-wife, Linda Bollea, expressed concern over the control and

---

58   Macho Man: *The Randy Savage Story*, 2014, WWE.

59   Ibid.

forced isolation Luger exerted over Elizabeth, similar to what she had experienced in her marriage to Savage.

"'Where are you living? Do you have an apartment?'" Bollea said she asked Elizabeth at the time. "She's like, 'No, he's got another place he's keeping me in. But the weird thing is, it's in the same complex as where he and his wife live.'"

In April 2003, law enforcement responded to an IPV incident involving Luger and Elizabeth. Luger was charged with misdemeanor battery and released on bail. (He was arrested again two days later for DUI with Elizabeth in the car.) Two weeks later, paramedics responded to another emergency call at the apartment, after Luger reported Elizabeth unresponsive and not breathing. She was pronounced dead at the hospital of acute toxicity. She was forty-two.[60]

In a rare show of empathy for the toll wrestling takes, Vince McMahon, owner of WWE, said in an episode of the now-defunct show *WWE Confidential*[61] that "the irony of the innocence of Miss Elizabeth juxtaposed [with] the way that she died, there's a message there somewhere . . . of falling from grace and not dealing with it . . . . Not having a purpose in life beyond our business. . . . It's something that performers in our business have to learn from so that they do not repeat the same mistakes that were repeated by others before them."

Randy Savage was not the only thing that bound Miss Elizabeth and Sensational Sherri Martel together. It was also their tragic demise.

Born Sherri Russell in 1958, Martel rose up the ranks as both a wrestler, being trained by the dreaded Fabulous Moolah, and a manager. Whereas Elizabeth managed just two men, Martel left her mark on many of the biggest acts in wrestling, accompanying Savage, "The Million Dollar Man" Ted DiBiase, Shawn Michaels, Ric Flair, and the tag team Harlem Heat to the ring throughout her career.

---

60   "Miss Elizabeth," Wikipedia, last updated April 24, 2020.

61   Aired May 10, 2003.

Martel was the rare valet who was just as talented in the ring as she was outside of it, holding the women's championship for over a year and being one of the standard-bearers for the dark ages of women's wrestling in the late 1980s and 1990s. Her feud with Luna Vachon was also a high point.

Moolah, who gave Sherri her stage surname, wrote of her hard-partying ways: "She turned out to be one of those girls who had a problem living by my rules. She liked nightclubbing and going out, and that just didn't go with me."[62]

Martel and Miss Elizabeth were polar opposites as wrestling managers: one was a demure damsel in distress and the other was a brash vector of action. In the end, they both fell victim to the curse of the trainwreck, with Martel dying of a drug overdose in 2007 at the age of forty-nine.

Luna Vachon, born into the fabled Canadian wrestling family as Gertrude Vachon in 1962, the goddaughter of the late Andre the Giant was another casualty of the wrestling industry, never receiving her due within kayfabe and suffering an early death outside of it.

Coincidentally, Nancy Benoit, the wife of wrestler Chris Benoit, who murdered her and their son, Daniel, in 2007, christened Vachon with the first name Luna. "At the beginning they wanted to call me Moaning Mona," Vachon said, due to her deep voice, "but Nancy . . . said that I didn't look like the moaning type. So she proposed Luna, short for lunatic. It was actually Nancy who shaved my hair. She was one of the rare female friends I've ever had."[63]

"Luna Vachon was never the WWF Women's Champion. And it was something that, unfortunately, ate at her," wrote LaToya Ferguson in *An Encyclopedia of Women's Wrestling*. " . . . Luna had arguably done everything she was supposed to in order to at least get one run with the championship." Vachon appeared in WWE for two stints across the

---

62   Lillian Ellison and Larry Platt, *The Fabulous Moolah: First Goddess of the Squared Circle, 2002.*

63   Pat Laprade and Dan Murphy, *Sisterhood of the Squared Circle: The History and Rise of Women's Wrestling,* 2017.

1990s. During the first, she primarily valeted for male wrestlers and thus was a side character in their feuds, although she unsuccessfully challenged longtime rival Alundra Blayze for the women's title shortly before both women's departures from the company. Upon Vachon's return, she was again paired with men, and she fell prey to the burgeoning focus on women's looks rather than their wrestling skills as the Attitude era arrived in the late nineties. Vachon said she was set to win the women's title three times, but on two of those occasions the champion, the notoriously spiteful Sable, "forgot" to bring the title to work with her. On the third occasion she was suspended for a backstage fight with Sable. Vachon left WWE for a second time in 2000 amid growing dissatisfaction with the sexualization of the women's division.

"My aunt Vivian was a wrestler, so [she] knew the kind of toll that wrestling could take on a woman's body," Vachon told *WWE.com*.[64] Perhaps a call for help, as Vachon was found dead of a drug overdose at the age of forty-eight in 2010.

Feasibly wrestling's best-known female trainwreck is Chyna. Her impact on the sport is evident from the amount of times she's referenced throughout this book. Though Chyna passed away too soon of an accidental alcohol and drug overdose in 2016 at the age of forty-six, her fingerprints are all over many of the topics discussed herein.

Born Joanie Laurer in 1969, Chyna entered the wrestling industry in 1995, and despite her fearsome expression and the muscles to match, by all accounts—most notably her 2001 memoir, *If They Only Knew*—she was a smiley, happy-go-lucky ingenue.

Chyna was not only a pioneer in the ring, proving that women could go toe-to-toe with men, but was also regarded as the first woman to publish a wrestling memoir.

Chyna used this platform to talk about things considered taboo not just in wrestling, but in society in general. She wrote of her abusive

---

64   "Catching up with Luna Vachon," *WWE.com*, March 5, 2007.

mother and the "abandonment issues that a crate of Paxil and ten years' worth of psychotherapy couldn't put a dent in," wrought by her scheming, alcoholic father, both of whom she was estranged from at the time. She also revealed that she was preyed upon by a teacher, gang-raped at a party during college, and physically assaulted by a boyfriend.

Her formidable record wrestling against men could be seen as a reclamation of the power she had lost. During her time in WWE, she was the first woman to enter the Royal Rumble match, the first female challenger in the King of the Ring tournament and for the WWE world championship, and the first woman to hold a men's title, the Intercontinental championship. After accumulating all these accolades, Chyna moved to the women's division, where she won that title too, which could be seen as a demotion of sorts, especially considering she was pitted against men due to the lack of viable women's competition during her tenure.

Chyna left WWE shortly after winning the women's championship under messy circumstances that we would now dub workplace sexual misconduct, involving her former lover Paul "Triple H" Levesque and his now-wife Stephanie McMahon, daughter of the WWE chairman. Levesque defended[65] his family's longtime gatekeeping of Chyna from being acknowledged by WWE's Hall of Fame in 2015 due to her past in sex work thusly:

> "I've got an eight-year-old kid and my eight-year-old kid sees the Hall of Fame and my eight-year-old kid goes on the internet to look at, you know, 'There's Chyna; I've never heard of her. I'm eight years old, I've never heard of her,' so I go, 'Put that in,' and I punch it up, and what comes up? And I'm not criticizing anybody, I'm not criticizing lifestyle choices. Everybody has their reasons and I don't know what they were and I don't care to know. It's not a morality thing or anything else. It's just the fact of what it is. And that's a difficult choice. The Hall of Fame is a funny

---

65   "Stone Cold" Steve Austin, *Stone Cold Podcast*, "Triple H," WWE Network, February 2, 2015.

thing in that it is not as simple as 'This guy had a really good career, a legendary career, he should go in the Hall of Fame.' 'Yeah . . . but we can't because of this reason. We can't because of this legal instance.'"

Yet how many of the aforementioned bad men are in the Hall of Fame? But I digress . . . .

Chyna wrestled for a short period of time in New Japan before making headlines for an IPV arrest, working in the adult industry, and starring on *Celebrity Rehab with Dr. Drew.*

The mother whom Chyna was estranged from reconciled with her daughter prior to her death, and is producing a documentary about the woman who described herself as a "very sensitive, fragile little music box." Is it any wonder she became broken? Or, more to the point, that we broke her?

Sunny, born Tamara Lynn Sytch in 1972, was widely considered "the original Diva," a designation shared with her archnemesis, Sable. Sunny grew up in the suburbs of New Jersey as an adored youngest daughter who was studying premed at college when she was thrust into the wrestling world as a valet for her first love, wrestler Chris Candido, and instantly revolutionized the role of the female manager.

Despite Sunny's stratospheric success, which could be sustained for only a short period of time, her life has been marred with tragedy. During her early wrestling career, both her father and her niece died suddenly, followed by Candido in 2005. These profound losses caused Sunny to spiral further into alcohol and drug abuse during her brief affair with Shawn Michaels, who has since become a born-again Christian and is heavily involved in mentoring the next generation of WWE wrestlers, but at the time was wrestling's biggest bad boy.

"I can't remember when I took my first pill, but it was shortly after I took my first drink with Shawn" at age twenty-three, Sunny wrote in her memoir, *A Star Shattered,* about developing pancreatitis from drinking, a side effect of which is weight gain.

"I grew greatly depressed and self-conscious. My self-esteem was gone," she wrote of her illness.

A Star Shattered chronicles but a few of Sunny's numerous stints in rehab as well as multiple arrests for IPV and violating a restraining order over the course of several weeks in late 2012 and early 2013, which landed her in prison. In fact, *A Star Shattered* could be considered a prison memoir, as it was written during her incarceration. She has been in and out of prison since, mostly for driving under the influence.

Like Chyna, Sunny parlayed her wrestling career into a starring role in an adult film, in 2016.

A notoriously unreliable narrator, as many trainwrecks are, Sunny avoids responsibility for her actions and readily claims the descriptor of the "female Hulk Hogan"—Wendi Richter might have something to say about that!—which holds even more weight in light of her racist tweets.[66,67,68]

"I have been abused, ridiculed, harassed, imprisoned and blasted in the media for making the same mistakes that everyone in this world makes," she maintained.

However, Sunny does make a valid criticism of how women are exploited by the prison industrial complex. "Too many women in prison are victims," she wrote. "They are victims of abuse, rape and manipulation, and they are suffering consequences that they shouldn't have to [be] experiencing."

In this way, Sunny is exemplary of how wrestling has historically turned smart, vibrant, and talented women into husks of their former selves, descending into addiction, crime, mental illness, and poverty.

"And when she did," wrote Doyle in *Trainwreck*, "we would be there. Ready and waiting to take her down."

---

66   @WWEHOFerSunny, Twitter, January 18, 2016.

67   David Dennis, Jr., "Sunny Used the N-Word on Twitter and It Only Got Worse from There," *Uproxx*, January 19, 2016.

68   Brad Hunter, "WWE Diva Turned Porn Queen Sunny Denies She's Racist," *Toronto Sun*, October 25, 2017.

If Sunny was the original Diva, then certainly she was the patron saint of the Diva Search.

The Diva Search was a competition that was rooted in the pages of *WWE Magazine* in 2003, with winner Jamie Koeppe receiving a spread, but by the next year it was a segment on WWE TV consisting of ten finalists undertaking weekly challenges that had little to do with wrestling until a single woman was left standing, a WWE contract firmly in her grasp. Winners of the Diva Search included Christy Hemme, Layla El, and Eve Torres, while other entrants, such as Maria Kanellis, Candice Michelle, Michelle McCool, Maryse, and the Bella Twins all ended up in the company as well. Many of these women became multitime champions and accomplished wrestlers in their own right, but the Diva Search will be best remembered as a harbinger of the much-maligned Divas era, in which wrestling was of less concern than looking hot. It's no coincidence that many of the Diva Search winners and finalists went on to pose nude for *Playboy*, which garnered them a title shot and a marquee match at *WrestleMania*.

One such recipient of all of these accolades was Ashley Massaro, the 2005 winner.

Massaro grew up in an amateur wrestling family, with both her father and brother having competed. She tried out for many hosting and modeling gigs before hitting the big time with WWE, where she competed until 2008, when she allegedly requested to be released from her contract to care for her young daughter, Alexa. Perhaps not uncoincidentally, in May of that year she had been named in a *Rolling Stone* exposé as working for the Bella Models escort company.[69]

During her time with the company, Massaro could never be confused with being a skilled wrestler. Instead, she had the honor of competing in such first-ever clashes as a two-on-three bra and panties match, a gauntlet bra and panties match, and a Diva Invitational, which was not a match at all but a "talent" show that ended in Massaro revealing her breasts, covered in *Playboy* Bunny-head pasties as promotion for her

---

69   Vanessa Grigoriadis, "The Sex Queen of L.A.," *Rolling Stone*, May 15, 2008.

pictorial.

This focus on Massaro's physical attributes rather than physicality in the ring proved detrimental to her health. In a harrowing affidavit for a CTE (chronic traumatic encephalopathy) class-action lawsuit against WWE that she was a part of, Massaro said that she was entered into matches for which she lacked sufficient wrestling training, in addition to alleging rape on a US military base in Kuwait during a tour there, after which WWE urged her not to pursue charges:

" . . . [S]hortly after I started performing for WWE, on or around September 5, 2005, I had a match with Torrie Wilson, and while rehearsing for our match, she performed a move on me known as the neck-breaker. Again, I did not know how to safely be on the receiving end of this move, and as a result, I was knocked unconscious for five minutes. I received no treatment for the concussion. . . . "[70]

Massaro also sustained a broken knuckle—from which, she alleged in the affidavit, she was "ordered" to return early, forcibly having her cast removed backstage before a match—and a fractured fibula and tibia over the course of her career. According to an *AskMen* article,[71] these last two injuries "resulted in a spiral fracture, a severed nerve and several broken bones in her foot that required the insertion of a five-inch metal plate and eight screws" as well as several follow-up surgeries. Massaro wrote she was "forced" to perform in a storyline while she was healing, which resulted in her being in a position "where I was likely to get hit or have someone fall on me (which happened—Trish [Stratus] fell on top of me accidentally during the match)."

Massaro stated that she became addicted to pain medication as a result of these injuries and "suffer[ed] from depression, for which I take medication; migraine headaches; and severe short-term memory loss," likely stemming from "routine repetitive blows to the head."

---

70   "Ashley Massaro, Laurinaitis et al. v. WWE et al," *WWE Concussion Lawsuit News*, May 5, 2019.

71   "Ashley Massaro," *AskMen*, n.d.

She made reference in the affidavit to Chris Benoit, the aforementioned wrestler who killed his wife, son, and then himself in 2007, sending the wrestling world into a tailspin and compelling WWE to drastically overhaul its response to prescription drug use, though some are critical that its policy essentially does nothing and that substance abuse is still rampant within the organization. Benoit's brain was later examined and it revealed that he suffered from CTE, a neurodegenerative disease caused by repeated blows to the head like those Massaro described. Headaches, memory loss, depression, and suicidal ideation are all symptoms of CTE.

Because of all this, after departing WWE Massaro was by and large a footnote in wrestling history until her death by suicide in 2019. It was then that the industry paid the slightest amount of attention, granting her an in-memoriam credit at the beginning of that week's WWE programming. In life, Massaro felt used during her time with the company; in death, her story was appropriated as instructive about mental health and suicide prevention, becoming the ultimate cautionary tale of the trainwreck.

In contrast, the aforementioned male trainwrecks who've met an untimely death—and, in wrestling, that is not uncommon, with male professional wrestlers 2.9 times more likely to die earlier than American men of the general population, according to a 2014 study by researchers at the University of Eastern Michigan[72]—such as Jimmy Snuka and Chris Benoit, received glowing tribute videos and, in the case of the latter, an entire show dedicated to his memory (that was before WWE learned of Benoit's role as a family annihilator, the term given to men who kill their entire family). Those who've managed to stay alive despite their debauchery are met with redemption stories in the form of WWE documentaries. Wrestlers such as Scott Hall, Jake "The Snake" Roberts, and The Ultimate Warrior have had their tumultuous lives immortalized

---

72   Christopher W. Herman, Anna S. C. Conlon, Melvyn Rubenfire, Andrew R. Burghardt, Stephen J. McGregor, "The Very High Premature Mortality Rate among Active Professional Wrestlers Is Primarily Due to Cardiovascular Disease," *Plos One*, November 5, 2014.

in hour-plus-long telecasts. WWE docuseries *Untold* has had no episodes about women wrestlers as of this writing. The Viceland series *Dark Side of the Ring* dedicated only one episode to a woman's story alone, that of the controversial Fabulous Moolah, over the course of its first two seasons, and seldom featured women as talking heads. Other episodes that featured women, such as Miss Elizabeth, Nancy Benoit, Nancy Argentino, and Martha Hart,[73] focused on their victimhood, giving priority to the men in their lives, who, all too often, were the men who victimized them.

We know the patriarchy of wrestling and that those—again, usually men—who document it often neglect women's stories, so women wrestlers have taken it into their own hands, as we see with Sunny's memoir, the Chyna-estate-produced documentary about her life, and even the E! reality show *Total Divas*, which has some of its stars as producers. And while men dominate the podcasting world too, several women have carved out a niche by amplifying female voices in a business that usually silences them.

Former WWE ring announcer Lilian Garcia has cornered this market with her podcast *Chasing Glory*, previously *Making Their Way to the Ring*. On it, she talks to wrestlers about things that are not often openly discussed in the vocation, like mental health, abusive relationships, and eating disorders. But the focus on trauma and tragedy over all else can be off-putting. Garcia has commodified trainwrecks, if you will.

For example, after Alexa Bliss[74] had gone into great detail about her debilitating eating disorder, which almost killed her as a teen, Garcia fished for more, asking her what other struggles Bliss had endured during her youth. Um, I think mental illness and a near-death experience just about does it for one adolescence and, indeed, one episode.

And when guests haven't had enough tragedy in their lives for Garcia's liking, she pathologizes (which I could find no evidence that she has the

---

73   Martha is the widow of Owen Hart. She was awarded $18 million from WWE in a wrongful death lawsuit in 2000 for the 1999 fatal in-ring stunt that WWE is alleged to have forced Owen to do without the proper safety precautions. By all accounts, Hart was a stand-up guy and a victim of the industry himself.

74   Lilian Garcia, *Chasing Glory*, "Alexa Bliss," Apple Podcasts, September 4, 2017.

credentials to do) their childhoods and personal struggles, as if the vast majority of us don't have issues of some kind. Garcia's calling card is trauma porn, and if you've agreed to guest on *Chasing Glory*, you better be ready to bare yours.

Her lines of questioning, or the deductions she makes from them, at least, are conservative in nature. In a 2018 episode[75] with the first open lesbian, Sonya Deville, in WWE, Garcia asked whether the fact that both Deville and her sister are gay had something to do with the way they were raised and said that "you have to give people time" to accept that queer people are worthy of being treated like humans too. Similarly, when Paige[76] made her much-anticipated appearance on *Chasing Glory*, Garcia admonished her for taking sexual photos and videos in the first place, not the hackers who stole them and published them online without Paige's consent.

You'd think that despite her prominence in the aforementioned Bella Models sting and her involvement in the CTE lawsuit, Massaro would have been a prime candidate for Garcia's armchair confessional. (It's rumored that WWE will continue to allow its contractors to appear on non-WWE podcasts only as long as the presenters of said podcasts toe the company line. Former WWE talent Vickie Guerrero claims WWE denied her requests to interview its wrestlers on her podcast, *Excuse Me*, after she did a guest spot on rival promotion All Elite Wrestling,[77] so that tracks.) But again, Massaro was held up as the moral of the story, not the story itself, when her former colleagues spoke to Garcia about how her passing had brought them closer together.

"Women who've succeeded too well at becoming visible have always been penalized vigilantly and forcefully, and turned into spectacles," Doyle wrote in *Trainwreck*. We want them to bare their souls, repent for stepping out of the bounds society has set for them, and accept their penance. Once they've done so, women trainwrecks are offered redemption by the industry that shunned them, but too late, as with

---

75   Lilian Garcia, *Chasing Glory*, "Sonya Deville," Apple Podcasts, March 12, 2018.

76   Lilian Garcia, *Chasing Glory*, "Paige," Apple Podcasts, December 11, 2017.

77   Alistair McGeorge, "Vickie Guerrero Claims WWE Blocked Podcast Interviews after AEW Appearance," *Metro*, February 20, 2020.

Chyna's posthumous induction into the WWE Hall of Fame in 2019, though notably as part of the group D-Generation X, not on her own merits. In wrestling, as in wider culture, we've deemed women's stories worthy only when they've sacrificed themselves on the altar of public approval. That is, when we bother to listen to them at all.

If there's one paragraph in Doyle's *Trainwreck* that sums up the fate of women wrestlers, it's the following:

> "Women disappear because they've been wrecked—because we've hated them for long enough to get bored of them. But they also disappear due to being misunderstood, or condescended to, or ignored. They vanish into irrelevance, but they also disappear into poverty, or addiction, or domesticity, or day jobs. The natural tendency is to see these disappearing girls as titillating unsolved mysteries. But they weren't spirited away to never-never land; they were talented professionals whose careers were put on hold for decades, or for the rest of their lives."

An exercise in the aforementioned revisionist history that WWE is wont to engage in was the erasure of Rita Chatterton, the company's first female referee. Instead, current referee Jessika Carr is promoted by WWE as having that distinction. Why has Chatterton been lost to history? Because in 1992 she alleged on an episode of Geraldo Rivera's *Now It Can Be Told* that in 1986 Vince McMahon pressured her to give him a blowjob, and when she refused, he raped her.[78] McMahon denied the allegations and filed a lawsuit against Chatterton and Rivera, later dropped.[79] (McMahon has also been accused of sexually assaulting a

---

78   Shaun Assael and Mike Mooneyham, *Sex, Lies, and Headlocks: The Real Story of Vince McMahon and the World Wrestling Federation*, 2002.

79   Ibid.

tanning salon employee, in Florida in 2006.[80]) Little can be found about where Chatterton is now.

Women wrestlers sometimes disappear quite literally, as in the unsolved case of Samantha Fiddler, a Canadian mother of three who also wrestled under the names Lucy Morningstar and Samantha Steele. Fiddler apparently dated wrestler Teddy Hart (real name Edward Annis), of the famed Hart wrestling dynasty, who in 2014 was wanted for sexual assault,[81] though the charges were later dropped,[82] and faced multiple arrests in early 2020 alone, one of which was for allegedly strangling his girlfriend, wrestler Maria Manic.[83] Fiddler trained under Hart as well as convicted statutory rapist Chasyn Rance,[84] who has also been accused of threatening to kill a sex worker.[85] Neither Hart nor Rance is a person of interest in Fiddler's disappearance.

Fiddler is also of Cree First Nations descent, which is a risk factor given that Indigenous Canadian women are more than six times more likely to be murdered than non-Indigenous women.[86] She has been missing since 2016, when she was released from jail, following her second arrest that year for trespassing.

And we already know the story of Sunny, who has moved in and out of prison and the public eye since 2013.

What is more common is women wrestlers' metaphoric disappearance,

---

80   Ben Feuerherd, "She Said Vince McMahon Sexually Assaulted Her in a Tanning Booth. Police Found 'Probable Cause.' Prosecutors Shrugged," *The Daily Beast*, January 26, 2018.

81   Clara Ho, "Wrestler Teddy Hart Wanted on Charges, Including Sexual Assault,", *Calgary Herald*, December 5, 2014.

82   Chris Purdy, "Crown Drops Alberta Assault Charges Against Daredevil Wrestler Teddy Hart," *Global News*, June 9, 2016.

83   Marc Middleton, "Teddy Hart Charged with Strangulation Resulting in Wounding/Bodily Harm, More On Thursday's Arrest," *Wrestling Inc.*, March 27, 2020.

84   Brian Damage, "A Wrestling with Sin Mystery: The Disappearance of Samantha Fiddler," *Ring the Damn Bell*, December 13, 2019.

85   Jake Drury, "Registered Sex Offender, Wrestler and Vision Dojo Operator Chasyn Rance Threatened to Kill Sex Worker after Being Turned Down," *BodySlam.net*, November 11, 2019.

86   "Missing and Murdered Indigenous Women," Wikipedia, last updated September 7, 2020.

into domesticity or whatever else comes after wrestling.

Rosa Mendes, who broke into WWE as part of the Diva Search in 2006 and was a *Total Divas* cast member between 2014 and 2017, did just this when she became pregnant in 2016. Prior to that, though, she gave good reality TV when she returned from a stint in rehab for substance abuse (which road agent and former wrestler Michael Hayes—still a WWE employee—allegedly exacerbated when he went drinking with Mendes[87]) and frequently bared her new breast implants (censored, of course) on the show. She was also depicted possibly relapsing, struggling with her mental health, and playing into the trope of the sex-crazed bisexual who just can't make up her mind when she forcibly kissed several cast members without their consent. A baby mellowed her out and redeemed her, and Mendes quietly retired in 2017.

I wrote for *Sports Retriever*[88] in 2018 that "in many industries, it's fathers who keep working while their female partners take maternity leave and opt-out of the workforce to look after their children. Wrestling is no different, with a majority of WWE's male performers going home to families with children at the end of the week. Though many since-retired women wrestlers have gone on to have children, rarely do they parent and wrestle in WWE at the same time."

Alicia Fox, a member of the self-proclaimed "Three Amigas" on *Total Divas*, alongside Mendes and Paige, is no stranger to the trainwreck. Hell, her whole persona, which consisted mostly of her being various degrees of unhinged, revolved around the catchphrase "crazy like a fox."

Fox grew up with alcoholic and unpredictable parents, and battled feelings of low self-worth, as she revealed on a hard-to-listen-to episode of *Chasing Glory* in 2017.[89] Fox appeared to have succumbed to her genetic predisposition throughout 2018 and 2019 by exhibiting erratic behavior, such as getting into an altercation with a fellow wrestler's

87   Keith Harris, "WWE Suspends Michael Hayes for Getting Rosa Mendes Back on the Booze," *Cageside Seats*, October 9, 2013.

88   Scarlett Harris, "Wrestling While Mothering, It's Becoming More Mainstream," *Sports Retriever*, March 16, 2018.

89   Lilian Garcia, *Chasing Glory*, "Alicia Fox," Apple Podcasts, October 2, 2017.

husband[90] and allegedly wrestling while under the influence (like with Mendes, her road agent, former wrestler Arn Anderson, purportedly allowed her to do so).[91] Fox seemingly retired from WWE in late 2019, when her profile was moved to the alumni section of WWE's website and she appeared alongside other past stars as part of a reunion episode of *Raw*. She announced on Instagram around the same time that she was several months sober after undergoing treatment.[92]

The fabled herstory of the trainwreck is "vastly overpopulated with young, pretty, blonde white women," according to Doyle. Indeed, wrestling trainwrecks often tick off all of these boxes, but that's because not only are women who exist outside of these confines rarely allowed to mess up in the ways of their White comrades, they're also rarely given the fame and notoriety to do so in the first place. Hence the perhaps-puzzling-to-some inclusion of Fiddler, Mendes, and Fox here (of the three, only Fox appeared in LaToya Ferguson's *An Encyclopedia of Women's Wrestling: 100 Profiles of the Strongest in the Sport*.)

Paige rounds out the Three Amigas' "forcible exposure and public shaming," as per Doyle, having fallen from grace spectacularly over the course of her short but impactful career.

Born Saraya-Jade Bevis in 1992, Paige burst onto the scene in 2013 as the first *NXT* women's champion, the winner of a match with Emma, which I wrote about in the prologue, and which arguably started the women's wrestling evolution in WWE. She was the first and only dual *NXT* women's champion and Divas champion when she debuted on the main roster the night after *WrestleMania XXX* in 2014, and she was also the youngest Divas champion. Paige was cast on *Total Divas* in 2014 and was a cornerstone of the Divas Revolution—as WWE initially branded its investment in women wrestlers. She was a member of Team PCB along with Charlotte Flair and Becky Lynch as they fought against

---

90   Jake Lambourne, "*WrestleMania 34*: Alicia Fox in Fierce Argument with Travis Browne Ahead of Ronda Rousey's WWE Debut," *The Sun*, April 9, 2018.

91   Andrew Thompson and Sean Ross Sapp, "Report: Arn Anderson Was Let Go from WWE Because He Allowed Alicia Fox to Wrestle While Intoxicated," *Fightful*, March 4, 2019.

92   @thefoxxyone, Instagram, November 21, 2019.

Team B.A.D., consisting of Naomi, Sasha Banks, and Tamina Snuka (yes, the daughter of Jimmy "Superfly" Snuka), and the Bella Twins and Fox's Team Bella.

From there, Paige's personal life seemed to crumble. She was suspended twice for violations of WWE's wellness policy in 2016 involving drugs, and began a doomed, whirlwind relationship with former WWE wrestler Alberto Del Rio (also known as Alberto El Patrón). Paige proposed to him in the ring at a World Wrestling Council event in Puerto Rico later that year.[93] Several days later, she underwent neck surgery.[94]

In early 2017, nude photos and videos of Paige were stolen and posted online without her consent, for which she faced a barrage of online harassment.

"Unfortunately people don't see [that we are human and make mistakes] when they are behind a keyboard," she tweeted[95] at the time. "They don't think that we have feelings or that we don't suffer. Not only was I a victim of viral humiliation but a victim of cyberbullying. I had days were [sic] I wanted to physically harm myself."

In July of that year she was involved in an IPV incident with Del Rio, who was arrested on sexual assault and kidnapping charges (since dropped)[96] in an unrelated incident, at the Orlando International Airport, which police responded to, but no arrests were made.[97]

Appearing to have finally gotten her life back on track, Paige returned to the ring in late 2017 after more than a year out of action. Six weeks later, however, she sustained another neck injury, which forced her to officially retire from in-ring action in April 2018. She was twenty-five years old.

---

93 Joseph Zucker, "Paige Proposes to Alberto Del Rio at WWC Event: Details, Comments and Reaction," *Bleacher Report*, October 16, 2016.

94 Adam Martin, "Update on Paige Undergoing Neck Surgery on Wednesday, Posts Video about Three Screws Now in Her Neck," *Wrestle View*, October 19, 2016.

95 @RealPaigeWWE, Twitter, March 28, 2017.

96 Robert DeFelice, "Report: Sexual Assault Charges Against Alberto Del Rio Dropped, Accuser Issues Apology On Instagram," *Fightful*, November 29, 2020.

97 "WWE'S Paige off the Hook in Dom. Violence Case," *TMZ.com*, August 22, 2017.

At the start of this chapter I wrote about the male trainwrecks who have traditionally thrived in wrestling. Granted, the tracks are littered with women who've been wrecked, but society's newfound understanding of its own role in contributing to this and its empathy for the victim have resulted in some redemption stories for women in wrestling.

Paige is absolutely a warning of what wrestling can do to a talented young woman with the world at her feet; however, she's also perhaps the first woman wrestler to get her own redemption arc.

As if Paige didn't have enough to deal with before, her untimely retirement could have easily sent her spiraling into the afflictions of trainwrecks past and, indeed, her own past. However, Paige jockeyed her inactive status into becoming a well-loved general manager of *SmackDown* through most of 2018 and managed the Kabuki Warriors, consisting of Asuka and Kairi Sane, to women's tag team championship victory in 2019. She also briefly returned to the cast of *Total Divas*, laying further groundwork for her atonement, and started her own clothing and makeup line, The Saraya Store. Perhaps most notably, she is the only female WWE wrestler to have a Hollywood movie made about her life, *Fighting with My Family*, which starred Oscar nominee Florence Pugh and was produced by Dwayne "The Rock" Johnson in 2019.[98]

Australian wrestler Toni Storm, who was signed to WWE's *NXT UK* brand in 2018, was met with a much different response when her private images were leaked online in similar fashion in early 2019. Fans and colleagues took to Twitter with #WeSupportToniStorm, which went viral in the days following the breach of her privacy.

"#WeSupportToniStorm from someone that has experienced the same thing I strongly support you girl. It's gonna be hard and people

---

98   At the time of writing, Paige was dating musician Ronnie Radke, who has spent time in prison for violating his probation in relation to a 2006 fight he was involved in that resulted in the death of a man. He has also been charged with disturbance of the peace for striking his girlfriend in 2012 which was later dismissed, and has been accused of sexual assault.

are gonna be mean because they don't understand. But you're a strong, talented woman. You'll get through this. Your future is too bright to be dimmed," Paige tweeted.[99]

"I look at what she went through [which was] a lot more than I [went through], and I'm like, 'Thank God for her,'" Storm said of Paige on *Chasing Glory*.[100] "I don't think if she had gone through that and survived that and come out the other end, I don't know where I would be. She was a huge motivation to keep getting up each day. . . . She's living, walking, talking proof that you can get through it. And you really can. I never thought I'd be able to say that."

Storm reclaimed social media, which had been used in an attempt to undo her and, thus, her power and autonomy, Instagramming (a platform on which she has turned off comments in an attempt to protect herself from further online harassment) a picture of herself holding the *NXT UK* women's championship with the caption "reborn,"[101] her first venture back online.

Rebuffing Lilian Garcia's predictable attempt to get her to caution other young women, Storm—who also spoke about her experience with depression, anxiety, and self-harm—frankly said, "Everyone has sex. Everyone takes photos. . . . No one should ever be made to feel that they're a disgusting person [because of something like this]."

Storm appears to have also used her experience to help change the culture at fan conventions. When I attended *WrestleMania 35* in New York in 2019 and the accompanying Fan Axxess event, I noticed Storm had a sign up that stated that male fans were not permitted to touch her during her photo opportunity. The internet is peppered with photos and stories of fans getting too close to women wrestlers, from Becky Lynch being awkwardly enveloped in a hug by an overzealous male fan to Sasha Banks admonishing fans who accost her at airports at all hours of the night and early morning with a bagful of swag for her to sign,

---

99 @RealPaigeWWE, Twitter, January 3, 2019.

100 Lilian Garcia, *Chasing Glory*, "Toni Storm–Dealing with Betrayal, Anxiety and Depression," Apple Podcasts, December 9, 2019.

101 @tonistorm_, Instagram, January 15, 2019.

which she suspects later ends up on eBay.[102]

In the case of Japanese wrestler and reality star Hana Kimura, social media directly contributed to death by suicide in 2020 at the age of twenty-two. She was bullied and sent death threats for her behavior on the reality show *Terrace House*, on which she admonished a fellow contestant for ruining her wrestling gear. Her tragic death has forced Japanese authorities to overhaul cyberbullying laws and has prompted reexamination of the country's attitudes toward mental health, racial differences (Kimura was biracial), and obsessive fandom.

It's no coincidence that Paige's and Storm's experiences and the responses to them straddled both sides of the #MeToo movement. BC and AD, if you will. The ousting of film producer Harvey Weinstein and the copious men like him who exploit their power to harass, abuse, and efface women in their industries served as a tipping point. We are now realizing that people of marginalized genders have either accepted harassment and abuse to protect their livelihoods or come forward and been pushed into the background. Their silence allowed them a modicum of success and fulfillment, as opposed to "vanishing into irrelevance," as Doyle called it.

Paige's ordeal helped lay the tracks on the way to redemption, with her pulling up to the station just in time to not be completely undone by what happened to her. Storm was able to see the light at the end of the tunnel thanks to Paige and the graveyard of trainwrecks that came before her, as will the other women who will inevitably be targeted in the same way, because we still live in a patriarchal society that wants to keep women in their place by humiliating us.

What a difference a #MeToo movement makes.

These women didn't kill anyone, and in rare instances did they inflict pain on others that wasn't sanctioned within the squared circle. They mostly hurt themselves, yet we often treat them worse than the alleged rapists and affirmed murderers I mentioned at the outset of this chapter,

---

102 Sam Roberts, *Not Sam Wrestling*, "Sasha Banks," September 1, 2017.

whom the industry protects.

Wrestling hasn't provided these women the redemption stories most of them so richly deserve. It's seeing prominent women in culture forcing a reckoning in the wake of #MeToo that has helped us to reconsider the way we've treated the troubled women of wrestling. Podcasts, memoirs, reality TV, and, I hope, this book, are finally telling the long-silenced story of the women's wrestling trainwreck.

3. THE INTERNALIZED MISOGYNY OF NOT BEING LIKE MOST GIRLS

Content warning: *This chapter contains mentions of family violence, slut-shaming, mental illness, homophobia, transphobia, fatphobia, sexual assault, and internalized misogyny.*

Lauren Moran, the cover artist for this book, designed a T-shirt in 2018 sold through 123Pins that was emblazoned with the visages of women wrestlers Chyna, Nia Jax, Bull Nakano, Luna Vachon, and Awesome Kong/Kharma/*GLOW* star Kia Stevens, along with the tagline "Not Like Most Girls."

Moran used the phrase in this instance to celebrate the body diversity of these strong, bigger women in an industry that has mostly valued thin, ample-breasted ones, but its usual deployment in both wrestling and society at large is to jostle women up the patriarchal hierarchy so that they more closely align with male preoccupations, rather than traditionally feminine ones, such as makeup and clothes.

"I'm not like those other girls, who like makeup, fashion, and gossiping about boys. Ew!" goes the common refrain, which is usually accompanied by something about being a tomboy, liking and playing sports, and eating pizza and burgers with abandon.

Author Gillian Flynn christened another version of the Not Like

Most Girls trope—the "Cool Girl"—in her 2012 novel *Gone Girl*. Flynn describes the Cool Girl thusly:

"Being the Cool Girl means I am a hot, brilliant, funny woman who adores football, poker, dirty jokes, and burping, who plays video games, drinks cheap beer, loves threesomes and anal sex, and jams hot dogs and hamburgers into her mouth like she's hosting the world's biggest culinary gang bang while somehow maintaining a size 2, because Cool Girls are above all hot. Hot and understanding. Cool Girls never get angry; they only smile in a chagrined, loving manner and let their men do whatever they want. Go ahead, shit on me, I don't mind, I'm the Cool Girl."

If there has been one woman who personified being the Cool Girl who is Not Like Most both in and out of the ring, it was AJ Lee, who reigned supreme over the WWE women's division from 2011 to 2015.

April Jeanette Mendez Brooks was born in 1987 in New Jersey. She wrote in her 2017 memoir, *Crazy Is My Superpower: How I Triumphed By Breaking Bones, Breaking Hearts, Breaking the Rules*, of her unstable upbringing by teen parents. Her mom went most of Lee's life with undiagnosed bipolar disorder, a disease that Lee herself was later diagnosed with. Her father was an addict, and she witnessed him physically abusing her mother, who in turn foisted that violence on Lee as she spiraled deeper into her mental illness.

"I knew Dad's violence wasn't representative of who he really was," she wrote, after detailing graphic descriptions of his abuse toward her mother and older siblings.

On the other hand, Lee received the brunt of her mother's verbal abuse, precipitated by her suspicion that a preteen Lee was having sex (she would in fact remain a virgin into her twenties) and her ignorance of Lee's own mental illness, which emerged in the form of panic attacks, obsessive compulsive tendencies, and insomnia.

As someone who grew up in a similar environment, I do have empathy for Lee; however, her internalized—and externalized, in many cases—misogyny stemming from her mother's abuse rather than her acknowledgement of her father's is troublesome. She paired assertions like "It might be hard to reconcile the fact that I wore denim booty shorts for a living with the fact that I don't have daddy issues" with tirades against women who take selfies, demonstrating a rudimentary, Taylor Swiftian understanding of the dichotomy between the stiletto-wearing cheerleader and the girl watching from the bleachers in her Chuck Taylors.[103,104] "We get it, ladies; Daddy didn't hug you enough and with each 'let me cum on dem titties' tweet a forty-year-old living in his mother's basement sends you, that hole in your heart is slowly filled," Lee wrote. Never mind the fact that many people of marginalized genders and body types have adopted the selfie as a form of empowerment;[105,106,107,108] Not Like Most Girls doesn't make room for them.

This attitude was at the forefront of Lee's wrestling character—"a girl that every single guy would want to hang out with"—who was often positioned as the lone woman in the sea of men that made up the WWE roster at that point. Lee "enjoy[s] being one of the guys. I've always been more comfortable in the company of like-minded dudes who don't make me worry what my hair looks like." Her role was often that of the love interest, being coupled with copious men throughout her career. And even when she was permitted to stand on her own, fans would chant her husband's name, CM Punk, at her when she wrestled. This is an indication both of the sexist environment WWE hath wrought (other women wrestlers with famous significant others also received

---

103 The lyrics to Swift's "You Belong with Me" (2008) go "She wears high heels, I wear sneakers/She's cheer captain and I'm on the bleachers."

104 In Lee's infamous "Pipe Bombshell" promo she accused the rest of the women's roster of not being able to lace up her Chuck Taylors.

105 Melissa Blake, "I Was Told I Was 'Too Ugly' to Post Photos of Myself—So I Did It Anyway and Went Viral," *Health*, October 4, 2019.

106 Victoria Sanusi, "This Woman Made a Movement Online to Empower Plus Size Women," *iNews*, April 12, 2018.

107 Carta Monir, "I'm a Disabled Trans Woman Who Loves Taking Selfies," *Them*, May 18, 2018.

108 @carlyfindlay, Twitter, May 20, 2020.

intonations of their names) and of Lee's fundamental alignment with men rather than her fellow women wrestlers.

"When given a microphone, I let my freak flag fly," she wrote in her own version of the Cool Girl screed. "I talked about robot handshakes, playing Xbox, and eating pizza and displayed a vast knowledge of pro-wrestling history."

As more women arrive on the scene, both as wrestlers and as fans, with the advent of things like *Total Divas* and social media providing entry points that had previously been gatekept by men and girls who aren't like most, the idea of who a woman who likes wrestling is expanded.

Granted, Lee did a lot of that work, bucking the trend at the time of tall, blonde models. Lee was a short, scrawny (before she started training to wrestle and cultivated an enviable six-pack), and non-White self-described tomboy who "wasn't into designer dresses and high heels."

"I watched pro wrestling because I was a tomboy [who wasn't into] fashion magazine[s] or teenybopper show[s] about high school relationship drama," she wrote, not realizing that they aren't mutually exclusive. Take it from someone who was—and still is—into all of those things.

There's a video from the early 2000s that went viral of a young AJ Lee crying as she met her idol, Lita.

Born Amy Dumas in 1975, Lita was a breath of fresh air when she debuted in WWE in 2000. She was originally paired with the short-lived *luchador* Essa Ríos, her fiery red hair blazing as she sneak-attacked his opponents with a hurricanrana off the top turnbuckle, a move women were not doing at that time in WWE. Shortly thereafter, she made the jump to become part of "Team Extreme" with Matt and Jeff Hardy, the Hardy Boyz, frequently inserting herself into their matches, proving she could hang with the big boys.

Lita was a four-time women's champion, and she competed in the first three women's main-event segments of *Raw*: with The Rock against her real-life bestie but wrestling nemesis, Trish Stratus, and Triple H in 2000; three weeks later against Stephanie McMahon to win the women's championship; and in 2004 once more against Stratus to win her second women's championship. Lita also wrestled in the first women's cage match in WWE, and is a Hall of Fame member.

Lita was not only one of the first wrestlers to prove that women could be just as skillful as men in the ring, she also showed young girls and women that we didn't have to look like all the other girls to get a foot in the door. Current wrestlers such as Becky Lynch, Bayley,[109] and Sonya Deville,[110] all of whom break the mold in ways I will discuss throughout this book, have said that Lita influenced them to become wrestlers. Seeing an alt-tomboy feuding with a literal model in the form of Stratus showed these girls that there was a place for them in wrestling too (and perhaps provided fuel for the proverbial Divas-vs.-women-wrestlers fire that I will return to shortly).

It's clear that WWE and its fans saw Lita differently from her peers, one of whom was Chyna, who faced Lita for the women's championship in 2001 in what would be Chyna's last WWE match. At the time Lita was the rare women's wrestler who captivated both women and girls with her alternative look and men and boys with her big breasts and thin frame.

"Fans tell me that they think of Lita as a big sister or one of their best friends. There's a real personal connection that they feel," she wrote in her 2003 book, *Lita: A Less Traveled R.O.A.D.—The Reality of Amy Dumas*, as opposed to the "cartoon characters" and "Barbie doll types" who made up the rest of the roster.

The pitfall of performing the part of Not Like Most Girls is that the sisterhood isn't there to offer support when the pandered-to patriarchy inevitably tries to turn them into the cautionary tales of the wrestling trainwreck.

Lita's personal life became storyline fodder in 2005 when she cheated on her real-life partner, Matt Hardy, with their good friend and colleague Edge (real name Adam Copeland). The woman whom many young girls, Lee included, had projected themselves onto was

109 "Women's Evolution," *WWE 24*, WWE Network, August 16, 2016.

110 LaToya Ferguson, "Fire and Desire's Sonya Deville 'Ain't Got Time for Hate,'" RondaRousey.com, February 14, 2020.

now conforming to the hypersexualized ideal on screen, performing in "live sex celebrations" as Edge's evil paramour, and being slut-shamed for it both behind and in front of the scenes.

"For the most part, every woman in that locker room judged me. [All] of the other wrestlers' wives [judged me]. The boys judged me," Lita said of that time on Lilian Garcia's podcast, *Making Their Way to the Ring*, in 2017.[111]

Lita went out with little fanfare shortly thereafter, having her underwear auctioned off in a "Ho Sale" the night after her retirement match, which she lost, the following year.

"All that work, all the right moves," wrestling critic Mira Adama lamented.[112] "Punk rock chic and sexpot, both the things required of women. I watched my patron saint be shamed, her underwear and sex toys pawned off to the crowd. Men who had once offered her protection were now shaking dollars and laughing cruelly as she left the ring forever."

Lita has since returned on good terms to WWE, being inducted into its Hall of Fame in 2014 and wrestling in the first women's Royal Rumble match (wearing "#TimesUp" on her costume and the names of women wrestlers gone too soon on her wrist tape, no less) and the first all-women's pay-per-view, *Evolution*, in 2018. Her biggest non-WWE wrestling venture, though, is the forthcoming TV show *Kayfabe*, a play on what is kept secret in wrestling. Created with former WWE women wrestlers Gail Kim and Christy Hemme, the show will explore women's experiences in and out of the ring.

Contrary to profiting from the Not Like Most Girls hallmark of eschewing girlfriends in favor of stroking the egos—and other things—of men, Lita has clearly seen the benefit of befriending other women and perhaps protecting herself from what befell the women whose names Lita wore on her wrist tape.

As with the women's evolution more broadly, women's wrestling is

---

111 Lilian Garcia, *AfterBuzz TV*, "Lita Interview | *AfterBuzz TV's* Lilian Garcia's *Making Their Way to the Ring*," YouTube, April 10, 2017.

112 Mira Adama, "WWE: The Bella Twins Claimed a Space for Women in Wrestling," *Daily DDT*, February 25, 2020.

about collaboration and camaraderie, not cool girls and superiority.

Though wrestling might have fancied these women peerless during their tenures, as Moran's design attests, there have been those throughout wrestling history who've had the concept of Not Like Most Girls thrust upon them based not necessarily on their interests, but on their looks.

Chyna's impressive and exceptional physique immediately separated her from the other women in WWE when she arrived in 1997 as a bodyguard for male faction D-Generation X. What also differentiated her was that she primarily wrestled men in intergender contests, racking up accolades few or no women have since, such as being the first woman to enter the Royal Rumble, the first female Intercontinental title holder, and the first female challenger to the WWE world championship.

"I wanted to be perceived as someone who could handle all of it, not this high-maintenance, hormonal, sniffly problem," Chyna wrote in her memoir, *If They Only Knew*. "I guess if I had any real designs on competing with the guys, I had to act like one."

Downplaying her naturally bubbly and naive personality in order to make it fit perceptions of her did Chyna no favors when she was moved from the men's division after having achieved almost everything a woman feasibly could—and not just any woman, but one whose theme song began with the line "Don't treat me like a woman" and who was advertised as exceptional. WWE had spent so much collateral on making Chyna Not Like Most Girls that her character didn't mesh with the rest of the women's division. This, combined with Chyna's 2000 *Playboy* spread, which showed that women who have different body types can be sexy and desirable, would signify that she actually was like the other women who appeared in the magazine in the years after Chyna left WWE[113] and who were coded as fame hungry and male-gazey. It illustrated the false binary between being Not Like Most Girls and exactly like them: both appeal to the patriarchy, but in different

---

113 Beginning with Sable the year before, WWE women wrestlers posed for *Playboy* in an annual spread until 2008.

ways.

Luna Vachon, another unfortunate victim of the business, returned to WWE the same year as Chyna debuted, after having previously wrestled there in the early nineties. Vachon "didn't look like Sable or the other Divas [and that] was part of her appeal, part of what made her stand out," wrote LaToya Ferguson in *An Encyclopedia of Women's Wrestling: 100 Profiles of the Strongest in the Sport.*

Chyna wrote in her book that Vachon once told her, "We're shit out of luck. We're not strippers. We're not bimbos, we're not empty-headed females. We like the sport. We love to entertain. We didn't want to be in this sport to be close to men—we got in this sport because we love wrestling. . . . You know what the men have done to us? Besides paying us tons less than the men, objectifying us into eye candy, T&A, the little wet dream for the little weenies? They turned us on each other. . . made us back-stab each other, turned us into being nasty to each other instead of lifting each other up. And the real bitch is you try and get tough? You try to get beyond the girlie thing, you show 'em you're into the moves and countermoves and that you can take a dive off the top rope as good as any of them, they start calling you a man, a dyke, a 'roid-junkie, a muffin diver, all that crap."

Another woman who had these kinds of slurs hurled at her was Nicole Bass, born 1964. Made in Chyna's image and debuting as Sable's bodyguard in 1999, Bass was with WWE for a short-lived but fraught period. Bass's fearsome physique from her decade-plus award-winning career as a bodybuilder set her apart from all but Chyna in WWE, which played this up by pairing her first with the lithe Sable and then with Ivory and pitting her against them in bikini contests. This encouraged the tiresome transphobia (Bass was a cisgender woman) Bass was subjected to by the fans and the press (Bass filed a sexual-harassment lawsuit against WWE in 2000, which she lost, alleging she was sexually assaulted by another wrestler, "The Brooklyn Brawler" Steve Lombardi) and on-screen when Shawn Michaels called her "mister" in a promo.[114] In the Not Like Most Girls construct, Bass's body betrayed her: it extended

---

114 David Bixenpspan, "How Nicole Bass Was Slut-Shamed by WWE During Her Sexual Harassment Lawsuit," *Deadspin*, December 14, 2017.

too far outside of those restrictions, yet its vulnerability pulled her back in when she was allegedly assaulted. In 2017, Bass died from a stroke.

Not Like Most Girls is couched in the transphobia Bass faced. I don't think it's a coincidence that the women I've just listed have either masculine features, a dress size more in line with the average American woman[115] than that which pop culture would have you believe is standard, or oftentimes both. Though these women are cisgender to the best of my knowledge, wrestling's othering of them based on their appearance feeds into society's tendency to do so as well. Trans people face high levels of discrimination and violence and transgender women of color have an appalling life expectancy of thirty-five years[116] and are at a disproportionate risk of being murdered.[117] The portrayal of trans people in the media, which is getting better with shows such as *Pose*, still predominantly positions them as freaks or playing dress up, with cisgender actors such as Matt Bomer, Jared Leto, and Felicity Huffman cast in those roles. Trans actress, writer, and activist Jen Richards said that when cisgender actors play transgender characters, it reinforces society's perception of trans as "a performance. Trans actors rather perform THE STORY, not our gender," she tweeted in 2016.[118]

"If they cast a cis woman, they're ultimately saying a trans woman is a type of woman," Richards said during a trans-actor roundtable for *Variety*.[119] "They cast a cis man, they're saying that at the end of the day, a trans woman is a kind of man."

There are women, and then there are transgender women. Women,

---

115 According to a 2016 study published by The International Journal of Fashion Design, Technology and Education, the average American woman's dress size is between 16 and 18.

116 "Trans women," Wikipedia, last updated May 5, 2020.

117 Rick Rojas and Vanessa Swales, "18 Transgender Killings This Year Raise Fears of an 'Epidemic,'" *The New York Times*, September 27, 2019.

118 @SmartAssJen, Twitter, August 29, 2016.

119 "What It Says When Cis Actors Are Cast in Trans Roles," *Variety*, n.d.

and people who identify as women. Girls, and Not Like Most Girls.

A similar dichotomy can be seen in the Divas-versus-*real*-women-wrestlers argument. I write at length about WWE's Divas era and what the hell that word actually means in the next chapter, but it was basically the WWE-created period that began in the 2000s[120] when women wrestlers were valued more for their looks than their in-ring abilities, segregating them from male—read: "proper"—wrestlers and creating further division among the women who remained.

Since the word "Diva" and its accompanying championship were abolished in 2016 in favor of calling women wrestlers Superstars (what WWE trademarks its performers as), a debate as to which category they fall into has raged. Previously, real women wrestlers had been few and far between—another version of Not Like Most Girls, if you will. After the rebrand, Divas were holdovers from that era, while real women wrestlers were those such as the Four Horsewomen (Sasha Banks, Charlotte Flair, Becky Lynch, and Bayley): easily identifiable as not being traditionally beautiful in the way the women who came before them were, or having worked on the independent wrestling scene, or some combination of the two.

Those who seemed to subscribe to a more Divas-era look—i.e., those with backgrounds as models or nonwrestling athletes—such as blonde bombshells Alexa Bliss, Carmella, and Mandy Rose—were dismissed as Divas, despite debuting in WWE well and truly after the Divas prohibition. And let's be real, to be a woman in WWE has historically meant being beholden to traditional standards of beauty and trappings of femininity, such as hair extensions, cosmetic surgery, and breast augmentation.

Such adornments are prescribed to trans women who want to "pass" (appear as if they were assigned the gender they identify and live as at birth) as cis women. This medicalization, in addition to hormone therapy and top and/or bottom surgery, insists that that is the only way to be a woman, and any other choice is invalid.

---

120   There is some consternation over whether the Divas era began at the end of the Attitude era in 2002 or when the Divas championship, which was introduced in 2008, became the primary women's title in WWE, in 2010.

But when a trans woman does undergo such treatments, she's catering to the male gaze, as Black feminist scholar bell hooks accused trans activist and actress Laverne Cox of doing in 2014.[121] Conversely, cis women who receive cosmetic surgery are "fake" and therefore Not Like Most Girls. Even makeup is laden with meaning: how many times do straight men say they prefer women to be barefaced, not realizing what they really mean is that they prefer a time-, effort-, and money-intensive natural makeup look to hide things like wrinkles, blemishes, and bags that society deems unsightly. Attempting to satiate patriarchal notions of femininity is a zero-sum game.

Some of the more modern Not Like Most Girls exemplars straddle the binary of appearing to be outside of the norm physically and possessing personalities and pastimes that are more in line with the dreaded masses.

Nia Jax, who appears in the foreground of Moran's Not Like Most Girls shirt and who debuted in WWE's developmental brand *NXT* in 2015, seemed designed to exploit this contradiction. Heavily promoted with vignettes dubbing her as exceptional, Jax made her debut to the theme song "Force of Greatness," the lyrics of which scoff at "plastic little princess[es]" who are handed the world on a silver platter, and position Jax as "not like most girls."

Though she cuts an intimidating figure at six feet and 272 pounds (which is often announced as she enters the ring, a custom for male wrestlers but an anomaly for women, because God forbid people know our weight), Jax is like those other girls in a lot of ways: she previously worked as a model and, contrary to the lyrics of her theme song, she comes from the famous Anoa'i wrestling family that includes The Rock, which one could argue means she was "handed" her position in WWE. She has also appeared on the most recent seasons of *Total Divas* and is a fan of the affirming selfie, which contradicts the edicts of her theme song and the Not Like Most Girls notion more broadly.

121   bell hooks and Laverne Cox, The New School, "bell hooks and Laverne Cox in a Public Dialogue at The New School," YouTube, October 13, 2014.

Paige's pale complexion and gothic affectation differentiated her from the blonde, tanned ideal of women wrestlers in WWE when she was signed to a developmental contract smack dab in the middle of the Divas era in 2011 at the age of nineteen. She was depicted as clashing with such women in *Total Divas,* the cast of which she joined in 2014, and the biopic about her life, *Fighting with My Family,* in which she is played by Florence Pugh.

During her time in *NXT,* Paige formed a tag team with Ivelisse (known in *NXT* as Sofia Cortez) called the Anti-Divas, an ethos she would carry with her throughout her time as an active wrestler.[122] Her character, especially in the early days of her transfer to the main roster, seemed to be modeled in the image of Lee, whom she won the Divas title from in her first match on the main roster—making her the first and only woman to hold both the Divas and *NXT* titles simultaneously— and whom she would continue to feud and team with on and off until Lee left WWE in 2015. However, her true personality—or at least the one that was shown on *Total Divas*—seemed to buy into stereotypes about women, such as being immature (she was twenty-one at the time, whereas most of the other cast members were in their thirties, after all), petty, and flighty. Her postwrestling endeavors include fashion and beauty lines, which indicate that the Anti-Diva was merely performative, or that she values women as consumers and little else.

Although Paige's facade made her stand out and signaled to other women and girls that they are welcome in wrestling, her sexualized and unhinged character actually fit in well with what little character development there was in WWE at the time, which is to say, alternating between those two traits.

Being a female wrestling fan has often meant being Not Like Most

---

122 Paige was forced to retire in 2018 due to a neck injury.

Girls. I've certainly been told that a few times throughout the course of my twenty-year fandom, though I've never identified as one myself, what with my other interests, such as fashion and not caring what men think, precluding me from being a true member of that group.

Women in wrestling, especially throughout the two-decade period that overlaps with my own investment in the industry, have often been high femme and marketed specifically to appeal to that coveted eighteen-to-thirty-five male demographic. To be Not Like Most Girls is to be in defiance of the Divas aesthetic, an identity to cling to when WWE seems to be experiencing a second wave of homogenization, with many women wrestlers possessing fillers of both the facial and mammary kinds. Even those whose characters aren't expressly marketed as unlike the majority have engaged in its rhetoric: Sasha Banks told *Busted Open Radio* that "there's always gonna be, so to say, 'Divas.' And I'm in a category of 'wrestlers.'"[123]

So I can understand how women and girls who feel like they don't fit within those markers might seek to rebel against them by emphasizing the things they do have in common with the group that has historically been the largest consumers of wrestling[124]—men—and latching onto the few women wrestlers whom they feel a connection to based on this.

In the popularity of these women we see a reclamation of sorts of the girl who is not like most. But we have to be careful not to internalize the misogyny—and, indeed, the transphobia, racism, ableism, and fatphobia—that shades it.

It is still important to note that the women I have written about here who either claimed to be or were marketed as exceptional to other members of their gender are very similar to them: able-bodied, cisgender, and White or White-passing. They just had darker hair, wore thick eye makeup, and eschewed high heels. That doesn't make them Not Like Most Girls. It just makes them pretentious.

Trumpeting how sports and junk food and video games make one

---

123 Doug Mortman and Dave LaGreca, *Busted Open Radio*, "Sasha Banks on Changing Women's Wrestling, Bayley, Will She Be on *Total Divas* and More," YouTube, April 18, 2016.

124 According to WWE's corporate statement, 40 percent of its audience are women.

Not Like Most Girls contends that these things are inherently male interests, which is not true, and that stereotypically feminine pastimes and the people who enjoy them are less than.

4. A DIVA WAS A FEMALE VERSION OF A WRESTLER

Content warning: *This chapter contains mentions of sexual harassment, slut-shaming, and internalized misogyny.*

On October 28, 2018, WWE held *Evolution*, the first-ever all-women's pay-per-view in the company's sixty-six-year history (different from women's wrestling tournaments like the *Mae Young Classic*, which was classed as a WWE Network special, not an event that was also available in the increasingly outdated pay-per-view format).

The event took its name from the evolution of women wrestlers from being called Divas and wrestling thirty-second matches in their underwear to serious athletes who warranted a stand-alone show.

Evolution was a long time coming. The event inspired hearty debates about who is to thank for this change in the perception of women's wrestling.

Some would say that Paige and Emma's twenty-minute match on WWE's developmental show *NXT* in 2014 was the catalyst. Others credit the Four Horsewomen of *NXT*: Sasha Banks, Bayley, Becky Lynch, and Charlotte Flair. There is a cohort—whom I count myself among—who contend that all women involved in wrestling had a part to play in the evolution. And I wrote about the fans on social media who agitated for WWE to #GiveDivasAChance in 2015 in the prologue of this book.

WWE lore credits *NXT* showrunner, wrestler, and WWE executive Paul "Triple H" Levesque and his wife, heir to the WWE throne and an executive herself, Stephanie McMahon, with giving women's wrestling the credence it deserves. And some would say that this transformation didn't even originate in wrestling, that it was the achievements of sportswomen at large, such as Serena Williams and Ronda Rousey, that bled over into the wrestling ring.

While I will go into further detail in future chapters about Rousey and Nikki Bella, the two women vying for the *Raw* women's championship in the main event of *Evolution*, the troubling rhetoric surrounding their match proved that the physical act of women's wrestling may have evolved, but our biases toward it hadn't.

"Diva" was a relatively short-lived but extremely influential descriptor in the lexicon of women's wrestling history. It was introduced in the late 1990s/early 2000s as a catchall brand synonymous with the promotion of models and conventionally beautiful women over wrestlers.

Before that, women wrestlers such as Mildred Burke had spearheaded the sport, beginning in the 1940s. Women's wrestling fell by the wayside in the midtwentieth century in part due to The Fabulous Moolah's monopolization, but it was back with a bang—as was professional wrestling on the whole—in the eighties with the advent of the Rock 'n' Wrestling Connection.

The partnership between WWE and MTV featured women prominently, from Cyndi Lauper and her catalytic music video for "Girls Just Want to Have Fun" to "the female Hulk Hogan," Wendi Richter. Others in the entertainment industry also saw value in popularizing women's wrestling, such as producer David B. McLane and Jackie Stallone (yes, the mother of Sylvester!), who were behind the brainchild *Gorgeous Ladies of Wrestling.*

A cult classic perhaps better known now for being given the Netflix treatment with a prestige TV show of the same name, *G.L.O.W.* was a four-season program that was perceived as a joke when it aired between 1986 and 1990. Models and actresses rather than professionally trained wrestlers made up the bulk of the cast, arguably ushering in the mindset that looks and archetypal gimmicks were more important than in-ring ability, which the Divas era would later emulate.

Then came the Attitude era, with storylines deeply enmeshed in the sex, drugs, and rock 'n' roll ethos of the time. Standout moments include WWE women's champion Alundra Blayze taking the title to rival company WCW and throwing it in the trash on live television and Sable, who was by far the most popular woman in wrestling in the late 1990s and is often credited with creating the term "Diva," gyrating in the ring in hand-print pasties and not much else.

Sable (born Rena Greek in 1967) actually sued WWE (then known as the World Wrestling Federation) for more than $100 million for sexual harassment when she departed the company in 1999. The lawsuit[125] alleged that "men would routinely walk into the women's dressing room as if by accident; men would cut holes in the walls to watch the women dressing; extras were hired as WWF regulars to expose their breasts . . . . WWF produced catalogues and tee-shirts depicting Mrs. Mero [Sable's married name at the time] in a degrading fashion offering sexual favors; Mrs. Mero was requested to display affection to women to promote a 'lesbian angle'; Mrs. Mero was asked to have her gown ripped off repeatedly (notwithstanding promises to the contrary), and Plaintiff was asked to expose her breasts by 'mistake' on national television during a wrestling contest." She settled out of court several months later after being countersued by WWE.

Endemically, many of these things did eventuate on-screen with other female employees, such as the "Hot Lesbian Action" angle in 2002 and evening gown matches, where the loser is the first woman to have her frock torn off. Frequent participants in WWE's disdain for women were Trish Stratus and Lita, also two of the most iconic and beloved women wrestlers.

One of Stratus's biggest storylines in the company was in 2001 as owner Vince McMahon's mistress, during which she was forced to strip to her underwear, get on her hands and knees, and bark like a dog to prove

---

125 "Sable vs. the WWF," *Rajah.com*, n.d.

she was apologetic for stepping out of line. I started watching WWE only a few weeks after this segment, which was no doubt disgusting yet simultaneously par for the course at the time, but watching the complete footage while writing this book during the #MeToo era is yet another reason to question my fandom.

In the years following, fellow blondes Stacy Keibler and Torrie Wilson took up the mantle of McMahon's favorite playthings, placed in storylines in which they would act as his lovers.

Though she has some stiff competition, Lita seemed to bear the brunt of atrocious on-screen treatment. She was required to act out personal and traumatic storylines for the entertainment of the audience, such as a forced marriage to wrestler Kane, rape, and miscarriage. Though her in-ring talent and popularity among fans reached heights seldom seen by a female performer, her storylines always revolved around her personal life, never more so than when it was revealed in 2005 that she had left her real-life longtime partner, Matt Hardy, for her storyline lover, Edge. Lita was subsequently slut-shamed on screen, engaged in a kayfabe "live sex celebration," was ostracized from the locker room, and retired the following year with little fanfare other than the tag team Cryme Tyme auctioning off her used underwear. "It was very hard to come to work," she said on *Making Their Way to the Ring*.[126] "The fans were terrible. The majority of the locker room was terrible to me."

Lita's experience too takes a different form with our new understanding of the rigid portrayals of women in wrestling and their treatment backstage. As discussed in the previous chapter, for her return at the first women's Royal Rumble match in 2018, Lita wore "#TimesUp" on her ring gear and the names of Chyna and Luna Vachon, two women wrestlers who had challenging experiences in the industry and who died young, written on her wrist tape.

This is not to say that sexual harassment and assault haven't occurred behind the scenes in the days since Sable's lawsuit and didn't occur even earlier, but as social norms changed, women wrestlers were literally dressed down for entertainment in a sick mockery of workplace

---

126 Lilian Garcia, *AfterBuzz TV*, "Lita Interview | *AfterBuzz TV*'s Lilian Garcia's *Making Their Way To The Ring*," YouTube, April 10, 2017.

harassment.

Women's wrestling was commonly perceived as a bathroom break during this time, with hordes of fans emptying the arena to relieve their bladders and stock up on concessions; the ones who stayed emitted catcalls while the women tried to do their job, however far removed from professional wrestling proper it was. Although there were championships women wrestlers could compete for—the women's championship and the Divas championship, which, for a time, were defended separately, before being amalgamated in 2010—they were seldom defended,[127] and sportswomanship took a backseat to eye candy and melodrama. Don't get me wrong, there were bright spots, such as Jazz vs. Stratus vs. Victoria at *WrestleMania XIX*, Melina vs. Mickie James in the first women's falls count match anywhere in 2007, and the first women's tag team tables match, between LayCool (Layla and Michelle McCool) and the Divas of Doom (Natalya and Beth Phoenix), in 2010, but they stand out just as much for their quality as for the dearth of opportunities women got to do that on a regular basis.

After staggering toward serious women's wrestling, the industry took two steps back to what I call the *Playboy* era, which bridges the Attitude and Divas eras. Almost every year between 1999 and 2008, Sable, Chyna, Torrie Wilson, Torrie and Sable together, Christy Hemme, Candice Michelle, the late Ashley Massaro, or Maria Kanellis posed nude for the magazine, which, in turn, shot them to the top of the women's division regardless of their wrestling skills. LaToya Ferguson contends in *An Encyclopedia of Women's Wrestling* that "at the time, the crowning achievement for a Diva was a *Playboy* cover, not the gold."

The issue of the magazine coincided with *WrestleMania*, where the cover girl would be granted a women's championship match. In the myriad instances when a women's title wasn't defended at all, though, the cover girl wrestled in *Playboy* pillow fights and evening gown matches, ensuring peak publicity for both brands and further diminishing the perception of women's wrestling in WWE.

---

127 In the Divas championship's eight-year history, it was defended only once, at *WrestleMania 30* in a Vickie Guerrero—who was the *SmackDown* general manager at the time—Invitational match in which fourteen women competed for the title one-fall to a finish.

The focus on looks to the detriment of wrestling training has been spoken about by former women wrestlers, such as Massaro in her statement for the class-action lawsuit against WWE, and Sasha Banks, who said this attitude was still prevalent during her training in *NXT*.[128]

"When I first started out in *NXT* and the girls wanted to do certain moves in matches, and I remember our coach would tell us, 'You don't have to do that, you don't have to learn that. This is what is required of you.' And it was a lot of hair pulling, a lot of slapping," she said.[129]

The partnership between WWE and *Playboy* ceased in 2008 as the wrestling company moved toward a more "family friendly" product and, thus, the Divas era. While women wrestlers weren't getting their kit off as much, the division still wasn't a bastion of gender equality, which isn't family friendly if you ask me. But I digress.

The Divas era coincided with the period in which I largely stopped watching WWE, but I wasn't really paying much attention to it before then either. Can you blame me? The women's championship was retired in 2010, as previously mentioned, in favor of the Divas championship: a sparkly pink butterfly title that was at once a visual metaphor for female genitalia and had the visage of a cheap children's toy. And the storylines that did make it onto my radar positioned the women as beautiful trophies for men to win, fickle, jealous, or mentally disturbed, and all of those things.

The Bella Twins are no strangers to these stereotypes, which followed them throughout their career. During the early years of the Divas era, Brie and Nikki Bella flitted between male tag teams based on who had the gold, and in a particularly skeezy storyline, considering that Brie ended up marrying him in real life, they vied for the affections of Daniel Bryan.

128 Coaches such as Fit Finlay, Norman Smiley, and WWE's first female trainer, Sara Amato, worked to change this.

129 Jonathan Selvaraj, "Sasha Banks, Alexa Bliss at the Forefront of WWE History," *ESPN*, December 9, 2017.

Eve Torres's love triangle with John Cena and Zack Ryder, which spanned the early part of 2012, was peak wrestling soap operatics. Ryder had been pursuing Torres for months, though she was more interested in his best friend, Cena. Ryder caught the two of them kissing after Cena had rescued Torres from the back of an ambulance hijacked by Kane, who always seemed to find himself cast in the role of sadistic tormentor of women. When Torres confessed that she was only using Ryder, Cena admonished her with every slut-shaming epithet in the book—though all PG, of course. Cena said Torres was "sipping the skank juice," used her assets to further her career, and, when Torres tried to kiss him to smooth things over, accused her of having sexually transmitted diseases. "I lost a broski [Ryder's catchphrase] for a hoeski," Cena said, coining a term that would be chanted at Torres pretty much until she retired less than a year later. "The words you have called me have scarred me for life. I do not deserve this," she said in character.

Torres still does promotional work for WWE, and whenever she speaks about her time in the company she has a refreshing attitude regarding the treatment of women's wrestling in the Divas era compared with now.

"I'm happy to see how the women in WWE are getting more respect both in the show and off the show . . . " she said on an episode of WWE *Table for 3*.[130]

When challenged by fellow guests Maryse and Kelly Kelly, who countered that they felt left out of the women's wrestling evolution, Torres clarified:

"Everyone plays their part [in the evolution] and [they] chip away at [conventions of women's wrestling]. And the next generation chips away at it and eventually it breaks," she said. "And finally [WWE saw] that [women's wrestling] was worth investing in. I think it's fair to say that every generation did their part."

Kelly said she didn't like how the Divas championship has been erased from the record books.

"For me the Divas thing never landed," Torres, who won the Diva

---

130   "Divas Champions Club," *Table for 3*, WWE Network, June 19, 2017.

Search competition in 2007, offered. "It became part of my vocabulary because [we] were trained to [say] 'Divas, Divas, Divas, Divas, Divas, Divas Champion, Divas Champion,' but it never felt authentic to me."

Other women have expressed their dislike for the term.

"Who the hell are the Divas?" Lita recalls in her book, *Lita: A Less Traveled R.O.A.D.—The Reality of Amy Dumas*, upon hearing the word for the first time, while Stratus said she was "never really into the term Diva. I felt like, 'hey, just call us what we are, women wrestlers.' I worked my whole career for the right to be called a woman wrestler."[131]

Their compatriot Mickie James said on an episode of the *Ruthless Aggression*[132] documentary series on the WWE Network that "it was very frustrating for me to know that I had busted my butt for seven years and now I'm referred to as a Diva."

"It's a big deal for me to be called a Superstar, because for so long we were looked at as Divas, just eye candy. Being called WWE Superstars puts us on the same level as the men, and I am," said Naomi.[133]

And in her book with her father, Ric Flair, titled *Second Nature: The Legacy of Ric Flair and the Rise of Charlotte*, Charlotte Flair wrote:

> "I didn't have a problem with the term Diva, but to know that we were going to be called Superstars, just like the men, was monumental. . . . I understood that the term was a way to identify the participants, but the audience needed to know that the match they were going to see was part of a deep storyline, and the match was going to be as physical, as intense, and as compelling as a men's match!"

AJ Lee was perhaps the most emblematic Divas champion of the era

---

131 Pat Laprade and Dan Murphy, *Sisterhood of the Squared Circle: The History and Rise of Women's Wrestling*, 2017.

132 @AlexM_talkSPORT, Twitter, March 9, 2020.

133 "Total Superstars," *Total Divas*, E! Network, November 16, 2016.

(tying with Torres at three reigns apiece), defying expectations by being great both in the ring and on the mic. WWE capitalized on this, slotting Lee into the role formerly played by Torres as the romantic partner du jour of not only John Cena, but also Daniel Bryan, Dolph Ziggler, CM Punk (Lee's real-life husband), Primo, Hornswoggle, Paul Heyman, and Big E, sometimes simultaneously. Kane was also in the mix because of course he was. She likewise entertained a frenemy-lesbian subtext feud with fellow crazy archetype Paige.

What all of these storylines tell us is that as strong performers as Lee, Torres, and the Bellas were, the Divas era placed stock in women wrestlers' relationships to the men in their lives at the cost of all else. Lee has acknowledged as much:[134]

> "At the time, even being the champion wasn't a guarantee for television segments. . . . I was fortunate enough to still be embroiled in storylines that were prominent, because they heavily featured men."

Interestingly, the biggest indictment of the era came from Lee herself.

In 2013, WWE sought to increase its female customer base and give women wrestlers something to do other than being girlfriends and wives by creating *Total Divas*, a reality show whose first season chronicled the lives of seven women wrestlers: Brie and Nikki Bella, Natalya, Naomi, and former WWE wrestlers Arianne Andrew, Eva Marie, and JoJo. (However, most *Total Divas* cast members are in heterosexual relationships, which drives the storylines.)

Though Lee was no doubt asked to participate in *Total Divas*, she declined and in turn used the show to fuel her infamous "pipe bombshell" promo.[135] In it, she slut- and fame-shamed the cast of the

---

134   AJ Mendez Brooks, *Crazy Is My Superpower: How I Triumphed by Breaking Bones, Breaking Hearts and Breaking the Rules*, 2017.

135   WWE, "#PipeBombshell: AJ Lee Blasts the Stars of 'Total Divas'," YouTube, August 27, 2013.

show, asserting that "talent is not sexually transmitted." (This despite the aforementioned fact that Lee is married to wrestling darling CM Punk.)

Having cowritten that promo (something wrestlers used to be given the creative license to do, but is now entrusted to a writers' room lest wrestlers say something that doesn't toe the company line, costing it advertisers), AJ makes clear her distaste for the women of the Divas era— of which she was arguably the face.

Lee's memoir, *Crazy Is My Superpower*, positions her as not like those other girls who, at the time, were cast on *Total Divas*. At one point she wrote that she "didn't perpetuate girl-on-girl violence." What would you call the pipe bombshell then, AJ?

Despite her contempt for the women who used the Divas brand outside of WWE, AJ Lee was perhaps the biggest beneficiary of it. Would she be as exalted as she is had she faced as much competition as that which emerged after her departure and during the subsequent women's evolution? Similarly, other bastions throughout history, such as The Fabulous Moolah, Sable, Sunny, the Bella Twins, and even Chyna, were all trailblazers in their own right, but could be seen as self-interested as their prominence held back the division, not allowing other women to rise up to meet them.

AJ's internalized misogyny brings us back to *Evolution*. Listening to the bile spewed by Lee against her colleagues, it's not hard to recognize similar sentiments in the discourse between Ronda Rousey and Nikki Bella in the lead-up to their match at the event, which I write about further in the upcoming Rousey chapter. But here's a taste from one of Bella's promos:

> "We made the word 'Diva' mean something. We and other women made 'Diva' strong and powerful. Our hit reality show put more women and little girls in that crowd. . . . We made the world want to see women's wrestling even more."[136]

---

136 WWE, "Ronda Rousey Rips into the Bellas Before Destroying Their Private Security," YouTube, October 15, 2018.

Rousey responded by equating Bella's success with that of her ex, John Cena: "The only door you knocked down was the door to John Cena's bedroom," a line that made me die a little inside and yet another moment in which I wanted to throw in the towel on my fandom. (But by then I was already shopping this book around and had made WWE's women's evolution a focal point of my writing career. Everything is copy, as Nora Ephron would say.) It was rumored that Bella gave WWE her blessing to use her personal life in the build to her match with Rousey, who in turn wrote her own promos, as Lee did hers, but in interviews Bella was more contemplative about the retrograde marketing.

"I think we are taking some old ways and bringing it into [*Evolution*]," she said.[137] "I definitely hope it changes, and I think it will, because I think the women are better than that. I think we can tell empowering stories that have nothing to do with men or how men define us, because that's the point of *Evolution*."

In perhaps a nod to her evolving (heh) feminism and echoing the sentiments of Eve Torres, Kelly Kelly, and Maryse's *Table for 3* episode, Bella further unpacked the male-centric publicity for *Evolution* and, indeed, women's wrestling more broadly:[138]

"Because Triple H decided to make ['Diva'] a bad word, we were like, 'What do you mean? You taught us for years to make this an amazing word.' And that's what we did for years: we put our blood, sweat, and tears into this. . . . And when [credit] gets taken away from the Diva[s] era, that hurts me. . . . What those women represent—Michelle McCool, Beth Phoenix, Melina, AJ Lee, Paige, Brie Bella—they're strong, fierce women [who] cared and worked really hard, and I'm here to remind people of that history."

At the 2015 Slammys, Nikki Bella was crowned Diva of the Year. The

---

137 Joseph Staszewski, "Nikki Bella Has Real Problem with Ronda Rousey's Cena Taunt," *New York Post*, October 24, 2018.

138 Brian Campbell, *State of Combat with Brian Campbell*, "10/18 WWE: *Crown Jewel* Criticism, *SmackDown* 1000 . . . " Stitcher, October 17, 2018.

following year women wrestlers were renamed simply wrestlers (well, the WWE-branded Superstars) and the Slammy Awards done away with. It was a fitting end to an era, with the woman who largely defined it—or at least became emblematic of both its good and bad parts—going out with a bang.

Two other women who wrestled at *Evolution* with a semicoherent plot are the forenamed trailblazers Lita and Trish Stratus, the latter of whom was a fitness model in the late 1990s before busting her ass to become a legend in the industry. They took on Mickie James, herself an icon who enjoyed a major feud with Stratus in the mid-2000s and wrestled Lita in her retirement match in 2006, and Alicia Fox, replacing Alexa Bliss. Bliss, made in Stratus's image and originally scheduled to wrestle her one-on-one at *Evolution*, was unable to compete due to recurring symptoms of a concussion suffered at the hands of Rousey. Fox actually made more sense, with Stratus dubbing the match a "generational face-off":[139] she and Lita were icons of the Attitude era, while James and Fox were Divas era stalwarts.

We've already dredged up Stratus's and Lita's misogynistic treatment, but James and Fox were also collateral damage of wrestling's status quo: James burst onto the scene in 2005 as none other than Stratus's stalker, melding lesbian and mentally ill tropes that would inspire Paige and AJ Lee's future storylines. In an infamous moment at *WrestleMania 22*, James mimicked cunnilingus to the camera, a shot that has since been scrubbed from replays on the WWE Network, before winning her first women's championship from Stratus. Tying Stratus as a seven-time women's champion (six-time WWE Women's champion and one-time Divas champion), until that record was broken by Charlotte Flair in 2019, James, and her commitment to serious women's wrestling while its reputation in the popular consciousness crumbled, was a bright spot in a dark time. WWE repaid the favor by targeting James with a running

---

139 @WWE, Twitter, October 9, 2018.

fat joke that punctuated her career until she left the company in 2010 for the independent wrestling circuit and Total Non-Stop Action/*Impact*, WWE's biggest competitor for a time.

James made her return to WWE (via *NXT*) in 2016, when she teamed with Bliss, an alliance that carried itself to *Evolution*. "Team" is perhaps too strong a word, as James was relegated to Bliss's sniveling sidekick while Bliss racked up championships. A particularly troubling storyline, given James's prior predicament and Bliss's history with life-threatening eating disorders, saw the two targeting Bliss's former friend Nia Jax for her size.

Fox, although WWE's longest continuously contracted woman wrestler at the time, was often overlooked. She was not often seen on TV (though she did enjoy several seasons on *Total Divas*), and when she was, it was as the sassy best friend to the Bellas or Bliss. This is problematic for a Black woman, as is her apparent one-note character directive and subsequent tagline: crazy like a fox. Constantly underestimated and dismissed as an afterthought, Fox reacted to replacing Bliss in the *Evolution* match in a telling way: "This is the most monumental match of my whole career," she said,[140] dissolving into tears.

As encouraged by Lee, Rousey, et al., and despite Beyoncé's declaration that this book and chapter borrow their titles from, "diva" is now most often wielded as a slur, by fans and wrestlers alike, while others seek to reclaim it.

In a mid-2018 promo involving Charlotte Flair, Becky Lynch, and then-*SmackDown* women's champion Carmella, Flair spat that Carmella was a "Diva living in a women's era" in an attempt to diminish her in-ring skills.[141]

In a battle of the eras, Flair faced Stratus at *SummerSlam* in 2019 in a match for which the lead-up recalled reductive name-calling about

140 @WWE, Twitter, October 29, 2018.

141 WWE, "Charlotte Flair, Becky Lynch and Carmella Come Face to Face," WWE, YouTube, August 14, 2018.

Divas versus women akin to that of Rousey and Bella's feud at *Evolution*.

"The WWE has evolved, and [we're] no longer models shaking [our] assets; we are women changing the industry," Flair said.[142]

"You're being a bitch," Stratus retorted. "There would be no trail for you to blaze if it wasn't for me."

In case the contrast between serious wrestler and eye candy wasn't clear, what with all that name-calling, sexist commentator Jerry "The King" Lawler was there to moderate the proceedings.

But while many women wrestlers independently contracted to WWE are seasoned pros who have wrestled all over the world, others do have many traits of the Diva definition of old: models, dancers, or athletes in sports other than professional wrestling. Many of WWE's most iconic women wrestlers, from the Bellas to Flair and, indeed, Stratus and Carmella, began their careers in WWE without previous wrestling training. Shaming the women who experienced workplace harassment and were consistently underestimated and -utilized isn't standing against misogyny; it's putting them down for being at the mercy of a male-dominated industry and for doing what they had to to survive in it, further widening the gap between certain "types" of women, however arbitrary those designations may be.

As Beyoncé sings in "Diva," "I'm a diva, best believe her, you see how she gettin' paid?" Though *Total Divas* was the brainchild of male producers, the women of the show spun a sexist term that was conceived of to subjugate them into a brand that earned them a lot of money and success, just like Beyoncé did.

Author Kevin Allred wrote in his book *Ain't I A Diva: Beyoncé and the Power of Pop Culture Pedagogy*, which examines Queen Bey's work through a political lens, that the word "diva" "mark[s] who gets credit for what types of work . . . keep[ing] gendered associations of male hustler and female diva intact, but [in] a formulation that exposes the

---

142 WWE, "Charlotte Flair Challenges Trish Stratus to a *SummerSlam* Showdown," YouTube, July 30, 2019.

insidious ways that power works unidirectionally, from the top down. . . . Beyoncé equating the two illustrates that when it comes to work, women are always defined through men, never vice versa, and she thinks it's bullshit."

It could be argued, then, that the women of the Divas era and *Total Divas* have monetized and thus subverted patriarchal systems—professional wrestling, reality TV—that would prefer to see them as pretty but submissive.

"Diva," in all its iterations, carved out a space for women to exist in a male-dominated arena, using character traits previously derided, such as femininity and frivolity, to make their own mark. *Total Divas* provided a platform for women wrestlers to discuss issues like reproductive health, addiction, self-worth, ambition, legacy, motherhood, family, and love, which had never been done before. Even when they were infighting in typical reality-TV fashion about who was trying to get ahead and the manner in which they did so—Eva Marie was demonized by both her castmates and fans for being ambitious and angling to become "the best Diva ever" (she left WWE in 2017 after only a handful or two of matches)—*Total Divas* paved the way for other women-focused wrestling media such as Netflix's *GLOW*, *Fighting with My Family* (the Florence Pugh-starring biopic about *Total Divas* alum Paige), and Lita, Gail Kim, and Christy Hemme's scripted show about women in the industry, *Kayfabe*.

"These girls are extremely brave, because I realize how difficult it is to put your innermost thoughts and activities right on front street," John Cena said on a *Total Divas* aftershow.[143] "These girls are truly pioneers. We come from an industry where what you see in the ring is the show and what you see behind the stage is protected. These young ladies are the first to break down that wall in such a great way. I've loved filming this show, I've loved watching this show, but I also understand how hard it is to put their lives out there for all to see."

This allowed the women of the evolution to then smash through previous notions of what a women's wrestler could be.

---

143 "After Party," *Total Divas*, WWE Network, September 15, 2013.

Traditionally, their careers have had quick expiration dates. Though Stratus and Lita seemed to be beacons of the time period in which I first got into wrestling, in reality they were active as WWE wrestlers for only six years. Flair initially criticized Stratus for leaving wrestling for "mom duties," but for a long time that was all that was expected of women in the time of the Diva-to-motherhood pipeline.

Now, though, a good number of the women's roster are mothers. Becky Lynch relinquished her reign of the women's division when she revealed she was pregnant in 2020, while Brie Bella's whole brand hinges on her motherhood, proving that wrestling and being a *Total Diva* are not incompatible. (The Bellas have since left *Total Divas* to focus on their own spinoff, *Total Bellas*, and the Bella industrial complex more broadly.)

"Diva" isn't a four letter word but it is according to WWE. The slew of highly publicized firsts since the end of the Divas era indicate progress, but who enforced the inferior standing of women's wrestling that it had to progress from to begin with? (Hint: the acronym for the company that this book is about.) As we slowly march toward a place where WWE's women's division has matured from a petty, patriarchy-encouraged argument over which era allowed the women to do more stuff, those who are reclaiming or defending the term recognize that to be a Diva is to embody resilience and drive in the face of constant underestimation, to remember the journey women's wrestling has taken through a male-dominated industry, and to never stop evolving.

A version of this chapter originally appeared in Diva Dirt *as "The Evolution of the Diva."*

5. BAD TWIN:

The Empowerment Doublespeak of the Bellas

Content warning: *This chapter contains mentions of rape, fatphobia, intimate partner violence (IPV), and internalized misogyny.*

The Bella Twins, born Stephanie Nicole and Brianna Garcia-Colace in 1983, burst into WWE in 2008 not as twins at all, but as one wrestler, Brie. In a flamenco-inspired jumpsuit, Brie frequently won her matches against the likes of Victoria and Natalya with underhanded tactics that involved hiding under the ring and then reappearing to score the victory. Several months after Brie's debut it was revealed that in fact, she was a twin to Nikki Bella, and the move that became known as "Twin Magic"—where Brie and Nikki swapped places in the ring—was inserted into their repertoire.

I missed most of the Bellas' early reign in WWE. It was only when *Total Divas*, the E! reality show about WWE's women wrestlers with the Bellas at the fore, began airing in 2013 that I really became familiar with them.

The Bellas had stepped away from WWE for a brief period in 2012 due to their dissatisfaction over the lack of opportunities for women, but they were lured back in early 2013 with the promise of a marquee spot not only in the company's longest and most successful foray into mainstream reality TV, but in the women's division on WWE TV proper as well.

"I think WWE knew that we had never wanted to leave in the first place but that we were unhappy, and that they could get us to come back if they made the terms more fair," Brie wrote in the Twins' memoir, *Incomparable.*

WWE certainly made good on this promise, with the Bellas dominating much of the conversation around women's wrestling as it evolved from the Divas era, upon their return in 2013, to the current one. (The Bellas retired for good in 2018.) They both held the Divas championship, with Nikki's second reign consisting of a record-setting 301 days. The pipe bombshell promo by AJ Lee—who is believed to have a longstanding beef with the Bellas—and the #GiveDivasAChance movement were expressions from within and without WWE, respectively, of dissatisfaction with the Bellas' prominence in an underutilized division.

This is a valid argument, but like all polarizing women, the Bellas are often inextricable from the misogyny they seem to inspire.

Even though the Bellas, along with their Divas era peers, were coded as sexy and thus appealing to men, it's girls, women, and queer people who make up the biggest contingent of their fans, some of whom, such as Bianca Belair,[144] came to wrestling through *Total Divas* and *Total Bellas.*

"We have a really big female fan base, which is pretty incredible," Nikki wrote in *Incomparable.* "WWE used to be entirely dominated by guys in the audience, but *Total Divas* has really helped women connect. They're going through the same stuff in their lives as we are on the show, so they can relate on so many levels."

It's no coincidence that the disdain for the Bellas coincided with their meteoric rise via reality TV, as well as social media, another feminized realm. Just wait until the Bella haters hear about what they've been doing since retiring from the ring: running successful fashion, beauty, and wine companies; talking about their feelings on their podcast; and amassing nearly three million subscribers to their YouTube lifestyle

---

144 Lilian Garcia, *Chasing Glory,* "Bianca Belair—Defeating Depression and Eating Disorders with Physical and Mental Strength," Apple Podcasts, February 18, 2019.

channel at the time of this writing (and will likely well exceed that number by publication), all stereotypically feminine pursuits.

Their proximity to successful male wrestling stars further adds to their apparent illegitimacy, as AJ Lee insinuated in the pipe bombshell. Brie is married to Daniel Bryan, widely considered to be one of the best wrestlers in the world. By the time the Bellas returned to WWE in 2013, Nikki had begun dating the face of WWE, John Cena. Their stepfather is WWE executive John Laurinaitis (though he met and married the Bellas' mother after the Twins began working for the company).

Nikki summed this up on a 2019 episode[145] of her and Brie's podcast:

> "In the wrestling industry there's a section of fans called the 'smart marks,' which means they're smart to know the wrestling industry behind the scenes. We became hated by the smart marks. I always looked at it like we did a really good job as heels for so long, but the more successful we'd get with our reality shows and the men we were dating and married to and all that . . . [it was] very easy for people to create promos about us."

This is no doubt a reference to Lee's promo, Ronda Rousey's similar one about Nikki's relationship with Cena, and the storylines surrounding Nikki's return from injury in 2016, which were all on this topic, too.

"I gave thirteen years of my life," she continued. "I beat my body up. It was my world. It's so sad when I see the lack of respect [and] appreciation [for us, because] I wish I could go out there and wrestle again for the fans and for us. I have risked my life. I'm a human being; sometimes we like to be acknowledged or appreciated."

For this reason Nikki's return to the ring after neck surgery rubbed me the wrong way. Her two main storylines, with Natalya and Carmella, used her relationship with Cena to get cheap heat (wrestling vernacular

---

145 Brie and Nicole Bella, *The Bellas Podcast*, "You Can Be the In-Law or the Outlaw!" Apple Podcasts, July 3, 2019.

for a knee-jerk, negative reaction from the crowd, although in this case the storylines reinforced what the audience already felt about Bella, so it might be considered a cheap pop). Her third feud saw her partnering with her then-real-life beau, Cena, to take on fellow reality-TV couple The Miz and Maryse in a mixed tag team match at *WrestleMania 33*.

Fellow wrestling critic and Bellas fan Mira Adama wrote for Fightbooth[146] at the time:

> "Comebacks are for men. [Documentary] specials are for men. New t-shirts and revitalized gimmicks are for men. Titles are for men. Legacies are for men. . . . But hey, maybe Nikki and her neck will get proposed to at the end of the mixed tag and that's gonna be so fun on *Total Divas*, right?"

It's clear that the majority of the Bellas' careers occurred in the wrong era; today Nikki might have been heralded for twice returning to the ring after overcoming a career- (and life-!) threatening injury, while Brie's juggling of motherhood and rebounding to the fitness level she was prepregnancy would be eminent. Instead they're admonished for seizing opportunities that any self-respecting woman in the industry would take and for their romantic relationships. Instead of us criticizing individuals who fit a certain mold, how about we condemn the power structures that reward such convention while penalizing those who don't?

Part of the persistent rhetoric around the Bellas even in the midst of the women's evolution could be due to the fact that while WWE stopped calling women wrestlers Divas in 2016, *Total Divas* kept its original title.

"Being an executive producer of *Total Divas*, we've had so many discussions about changing the name of the show," Nikki, who obtained her producing credit on the show in 2017, said the following

---

146 Mira Adama, "Where's the Bellabration?" *Fightbooth*, March 23, 2017.

year.[147] "Unfortunately, it's on network TV, and you can't just change the name one day. [The other producers] have felt that people will still be connected with it even though it's called *Total Divas*. I feel the opposite. I feel like there's a huge disconnect because we've made that name so bad."

The cognitive dissonance that arises from half the WWE roster starring on a show with a title that is *sermo* non grata while others haven't been impugned with the moniker further contributes to the Diva-versus-"serious woman wrestler" divide.

It was fascinating if disappointing to watch the evolution of the Bella Twins—or the "Bellalution," as they called it during their comeback for the *Evolution* pay-per-view—from being perceived as the problem to part of the solution.

The seeds of the Bellalution seemed to have been sowed in 2015, as Nikki neared her record-setting Divas championship reign at 301 days.

"You all begged for a Divas revolution, and I gave you one," she said in the video package celebrating the milestone.[148] "This has been my story, my life, my revolution. I came into WWE eight years ago, and each and every one of you thought I'd be nothing more than arm candy. . . . I started a revolution and cemented a legacy."

Bella has long defended herself as breaking down doors for women in the industry, but her opponent at *Evolution*, UFC star-cum-wrestler Ronda Rousey, equated her success to that of her boyfriend's.

Bella, doing her damndest to promote *Evolution* as something other than a consolation prize for women wrestlers and their fans to offset the ill will caused by the all-male Saudi Arabian show *Crown Jewel* the same week, did the media rounds, saying[149] that she wanted to see WWE market women's wrestlers more creatively than purporting that they "slept their way to the top or [got there] because of a man that made a woman."

147 Anthony Alimondo, "ACE Comic Con WWE Panel The Bella Twins," YouTube, October 13, 2018.

148 Lunatic Boss, "WWE *Raw* Nikki Bella Divas Championship Promo," YouTube, May 22, 2017.

149 Joseph Staszewski, "Nikki Bella Has Real Problem with Ronda Rousey's Cena Taunt," *New York Post*, October 24, 2018.

Much of the Bellas' feminist awakening has taken place away from WWE TV, though, on *Total Divas/Bellas*, their podcast, and their memoir, *Incomparable*, where we get a better understanding of their personal motivations.

"Feminist awakening" is perhaps too strong a phrase, as I've only ever heard Nikki utter the word "feminist" twice on episodes[150,151] of *The Bellas Podcast*. For the Bellas, "women's empowerment"—feminism's "ugly stepsister," as podcasters and authors Aminatou Sow and Ann Friedman put it[152]—is a much more palatable phrase.

But what is empowerment? I wrote[153] in the halcyon days of 2016, when we still thought a Pantsuit Nation could elect a woman to the White House, about the propensity of celebrities to prefer empowerment over feminism, a trend I noticed partly thanks to the Bellas bandying about it on the *Total* franchise.

The dictionary definition of empowerment is to give power or authority to someone, but its watering down in popular parlance has made it almost devoid of meaning. Women's empowerment seems to have instead become shorthand for women doing things, regardless of how empowering they actually are. Women in government? Empowering[154] (even if their policies actually *disempower* women). Taking nude selfies? Empowering.[155] Defending Harvey Weinstein? Empowering.[156] As a 2003 headline in *The Onion*[157] declared, well ahead of its time, "Women Now Empowered by Everything a Woman Does."

---

150   Brie and Nicole Bella, *The Bellas Podcast*, "What's Your Truth?" Apple Podcasts, July 10, 2019.

151   Brie and Nicole Bella, *The Bellas Podcast*, "We're Pregnant!" Apple Podcasts, February 5, 2020.

152   Ann Friedman and Aminatou Sow, *Big Friendship: How We Keep Each Other Close*, 2020.

153   Scarlett Harris, "Why Celebrities Prefer Empowerment to Feminism," *Daily Life*, July 27, 2016.

154   Joanne Lu, "Ivanka Trump Launches $50 Million Program to Empower Women in the Workplace," *NPR*, February 13, 2019.

155   Hannah Meyer, "Kim Kardashian's Nude Selfies Might Break the Internet, But Are They Empowering?" *ABC*, April 11, 2016.

156   Anjelica Oswald, "Lindsay Lohan Lashes Out at Critics of Her Defense of Harvey Weinstein: I Am for Women's Empowerment," *Insider*, October 19, 2017.

157   "Women Now Empowered by Everything a Woman Does," *The Onion*, February 19, 2003.

The Bellas do this too. A season-five storyline on *Total Divas* saw Nikki inspired by hearing Maria Shriver talk at a charity event. "I want to empower women," Nikki said, as Brie expressed skepticism at the perceived disconnect between the way Nikki looks and what would be coming out of her mouth.

"When women are uncomfortable with the word 'power' . . . they say 'empower,'" said *Manifesta* author Jennifer Baumgardner, according to Andi Zeisler, cofounder of Bitch Media, in her book *We Were Feminists Once: From Riot Grrrl to CoverGirl®, the Buying and Selling of a Political Movement*, about feminism becoming a brand through which to sell empowerment.

While empowerment might have been well and good for the Bellas pre-women's evolution, power is what they now possess, running a multimillion-dollar conglomerate. What they don't seem to understand is that they've achieved this due in part, yes, to their hard work, but also their class and pretty privilege,[158] and how they can leverage that to empower other, less fortunate women.

"I became the longest-reigning Divas champion because I wanted to be equal to the men. I wanted to be like The Rock and John Cena. I wanted to be the first-ever woman to headline or for people to show up and buy tickets [for me] and not the men," Nikki said on *The Bellas Podcast*,[159] which is a trap she falls into constantly, because I don't think she's grasped the concept that just because she and women like her are succeeding doesn't mean it's a feminist act or that it's good for all women.

It's worth mentioning that the Bellas grew up biracial—their father is Mexican—in an abusive home. They have spoken about the racism they faced at times and how their mother struggled to raise them in an erratic environment. Like AJ Lee, also of Latinx descent, they are products of their own circumstances, at once influencing their desire to move beyond them and intertwined with the attitudes they now hold. As women of color, they rose to the top of a White-male-dominated industry, which is commendable. As White-passing women of color,

158 Janet Mock, "Being Pretty Is a Privilege, But We Refuse to Acknowledge It," *Allure*, June 28, 2017.

159 Brie and Nicole Bella, *The Bellas Podcast*, "#RelationshipGoals," Apple Podcasts, August 7, 2019.

they didn't face as many obstacles as others have.

Nikki, whose *WrestleMania* match was cut in 2013, expressed concern that something similar was happening again the following year. The lone women's match on the card was scheduled to take place in the same dead-zone slot before the main event. "Did anyone bring that up?" she asked on a season-two episode of *Total Divas* that chronicled that night. As the star of the reality show, the Divas champion, and romantic partner of Cena, Nikki had accumulated enough power to be the one to do so.

Empowerment and what Zeisler calls marketplace feminism are apparent in the rise of Facebook CEO's Sheryl Sandberg's "lean-in" theory (from her 2013 book, *Lean In: Women, Work, and the Will to Lead*); Gwyneth Paltrow's woo-woo wellness empire, Goop (the chief content officer of which ghostwrote the Twins' memoir); period panties company Thinx; and #Girlboss feminism, the brainchild of former Nasty Gal fashion maven Sophia Amoruso. All are White Feminist—a subset of feminism that prioritizes the interests of White women, such as equal pay and representation for women in executive positions when, as of 2019, there were no Latina CEOs of Fortune 500 companies[160] and Latinas in the rest of the workforce earned fifty-three cents to the dollar of White men, the largest pay disparity among women of color— versions of upwardly mobile women proffering their own empowerment to others through the purchasing of stuff. "To brand something as feminist doesn't involve ideology, or labor, or policy, or specific actions or processes. It's just a matter of saying 'this is feminist *because we say it is*,'" Zeisler wrote.

What these modes of trickle-down feminism,[161] a term coined by Black feminist writer Tressie McMillan Cottom, forget is that they're coming from an already-privileged position. Sheryl Sandberg was a billionaire when she published *Lean In*,[162] and Goop's $66 yoni egg,

160 Raquel Reichard, "The Fortune 500 Just Lost Its Second Latina CEO," *mitú*, January 16, 2019.

161 Tressie McMillan Cottom, "The Atlantic Article, Trickle Down Feminism, and my Twitter Mentions. God Help Us All," *Tressie McMillan Cottom*, June 23, 2012.

162 Lisa Goertz, "Sheryl Sandberg's Success Story," *Investopedia*, October 4, 2018.

which falsely[163] promotes vaginal wellness, might not seem that silly when you've secured health insurance and don't have a chronic illness. Amoruso and Thinx founder Miki Agrawal have been accused of less-than-feminist workplace practices, with Nasty Gal being sued for firing pregnant employees[164] and Agrawal allegedly sexually harassing her staff, which she denies.[165]

"A piece of the concern regarding the language of 'made by women' or 'female founded,'" as Nasty Gal and Thinx are, wrote[166] Zeisler's *Bitch* coeditor Rachel Charlene Lewis, "is that something being founded by a woman does not make that woman a feminist, or make the product itself feminist. Beyond the fact that a thing cannot be feminist (feminism is a lens and a goal, not a shoe), plenty of women have been the faces of businesses, products, and ideas that actively undermine feminist values and serve intrinsically sexist and disempowering agendas since the beginning of time. Women can found a company, and then abuse their workers; women can create a product, and harm their consumers."

Instead of agitating as a collective against the powers that be, as feminism was conceived to be, marketplace feminism throws some glitter on our problems and sells them back to us as personal failings instead of structural and political errors, not unlike the women's wrestling evolution itself.

Listening to an early 2020 episode[167] of *The Bellas Podcast*, I couldn't help but be reminded of the Twins' penchant for it. In a segment called "Matchup of the Week," Brie and Nikki debated FOMO (fear of

---

163 Julia Belluz, "Goop Was Fined $145,000 for Its Claims About Jade Eggs for Vaginas. It's Still Selling Them," *Vox*, September 6, 2018.

164 Anna Merlan, "Lawsuit: Nasty Gal's #GIRLBOSS Fired Employees for Getting Pregnant," *Jezebel*, June 9, 2015.

165 Noreen Malone, "Sexual-Harassment Claims Against a 'She-E.O.' Thinx Boss Miki Agrawal Wanted to Break Taboos about the Female Body. According to Some Employees, She Went Too Far," *The Cut*, March 20, 2017.

166 Rachel Charlene Lewis, "Patriarchy Proof: Thinx and the Perils of Emphasizing Female Founders," *Bitch*, January 16, 2020.

167 Brie and Nicole Bella, *The Bellas Podcast*, "She Likes to Wear the Big Hat," Apple Podcasts, January 1, 2020.

missing out) when it comes to business, a conversation that smacked of marketplace feminism and capitalism.

"I honestly believe that we here in America overdo it. We don't give ourselves days off," said Brie. Note that she puts the onus back on individuals to police whether they're overworked, not on a capitalist system that requires people to work themselves into the ground in the hopes of achieving the ever-elusive American dream.

"Some of us don't want days off," Nikki replied, which infers that people who work multiple jobs and have no time off do it because they want to, not because, oftentimes, they have to.

It's frustrating to examine the Bellas through a feminist lens, because they're always one step away from making a meaningful connection to intersectional issues (i.e., why are Americans workaholics? Because the minimum wage is so low and workers don't have paid sick days, maternity leave, social safety nets, labor unions, etc.), but they're seemingly so consumed by, and concerned with, their own stations that it's easier for them to just revert back to existing within their bubble.

The Bellas Podcast is littered with advertisements, which is annoying in and of itself, but their content and placement are puzzling at best and hypocritical at worst. For example, Brie's a vegan, yet she has allowed advertising for a meat-delivery service. An episode in which they interviewed an environmental activist who advocated for lowering consumerism over the holidays by eschewing bought gifts in favor of homemade ones was followed by a commercial for, you guessed it, Christmas gifts. And an ad for ThirdLove bras came right after a segment where the twins proselytized free boobin'.

It's not surprising that *The Bellas Podcast* is a wasteland of product endorsements given Nikki's habit of rewarding herself (or being rewarded by others) with stuff, a regular topic of consternation on *Total Divas/Bellas*.

"I've been a good girl so John got me [Christian] Louboutin [shoes] in three different colors," Nikki mused on a season-two episode of *Total Divas*.

"We deserve [this expensive bottle of wine]," she said in another episode.

"You think we deserve everything. Every time we wanna have dessert, you say we deserve it. Any time we go shopping, you're like, 'We deserve it,'" Brie replied.

"Is that a bad thing? I work right now five days a week, you work zero, so if I want to I'm getting [a bottle of wine]," Nikki retorted, referring to Brie taking time off to care for her injured husband.

Speaking of Bryan, who has strong opinions about Nikki's consumerism and her apparent influence on her sister: he admonished Nikki for this very thing on a first-season episode of *Total Bellas*, which caused a rift between them.

"I don't think you're humble, because you believe you deserve everything you have. Plenty of people work just as hard as you and don't have as much as you do," he said, demonstrating his understanding of capitalism in America.

Rachel Vorona Cote, in her book *Too Much: How Victorian Constraints Still Bind Women Today*, has a fascinating theory about women's hunger manifesting itself in material greed. She wrote:

> "Capitalism is defined by overabundance, set to a score of 'more and more and more,' a yen gurgling in its belly to create and destroy with the sloppiest strokes of greed . . . . Female hunger, when driven by consumerist fantasies that fill the coffers of the wealthy, is—sometimes, more palatable."

A *Total Divas* season-one storyline focused on Nikki's weight and eating habits and Brie's attempts to curtail them.

Nikki's repeated pronouncements of "deserving" things like a new bag or new shoes because she worked hard struggle to acknowledge the capitalist society they operate within, which perpetuates the confirmation bias that poor people—often people of color—don't have nice things because they don't work hard enough.

"Consumer empowerment dovetailed nicely with third-wave feminism, whose ideology was in part about rejecting what many young feminists perceived as inflexible dogma and embracing varied, intersecting identities instead," Zeisler wrote in *We Were Feminists Once*. "And this empowerment was certainly of a piece with the neoliberal ideal in which individuals operate independent of cultural and economic influence, proving that all you need to succeed—or, in liberatory terms, to achieve equality—is the desire and will to do so."

The Bellas talking about empowerment could be the spoonful of sugar through which they introduce their fans to feminist ideals without alienating them or inciting misogynists if they wanted it to. Through celebrity and marketplace feminism and empowerment, the political and ideological frameworks of gender equality have become bland and inoffensive enough that Nikki can feasibly call herself a feminist and advocate for women's issues without committing to anything revolutionary. In the women's evolution era of wrestling, only bigots holding on to nostalgia for the Attitude era—wrestling's equivalent of Make America Great Again—have a problem with that. It's kind of like Brie's concern for ~the planet~ but what does that mean exactly? With rising temperatures and an increase in natural disasters, most people are concerned with how the only planet we're sure can sustain humanity as we know it can continue doing so; therefore Brie is able to skate by without blatantly advocating for more drastic action on climate change and risk losing a portion of consumers of Birdiebee, the Twins' fashion company.

Not without controversy, Birdiebee launched its athleisure designs in sizes up to XL in the fall of 2017, with a view to introduce larger sizes in select styles, which it has since done, according to a now-deleted Instagram post addressing concerns from plus-sized customers about limited options.

Birdiebee marketed itself as an empowering and inclusive lifestyle brand with "something for everyone," but by neglecting the powerful consumptive force of plus-size women and positioning them as an afterthought, the company indicates that empowerment is only for thin women with disposable income.

Nikki addressed this on the podcast *Chasing Glory*:[168] "We thought it

---

168 Lilian Garcia, *Chasing Glory*, "Nikki Bella," Apple Podcasts, November 20, 2017.

would be fine to launch plus sizes in January even though we wanted to launch [them] in the beginning," she told host Lilian Garcia. "But what people don't understand is that it's not easy to get all this money and buy all these things. To spread our money out we had to wait for plus sizes in January. So we got attacked: 'You say you empower women, but you don't even have your plus size[s] out.' . . . Financially, we couldn't make it work."

If we've learned anything from the many feminist scholars and critics quoted here, it's that if we are being sold something, that something is inherently unfeminist. Say it with me: *there is no ethical consumption under capitalism.*

The Bellas had obviously preempted the backlash to their duplicity in marketing Birdiebee as "empowering," as Nikki goes on to say that "in those cases I was taught [that] you have to ignore the hate."

Valid criticism is not about "hate"; it's about responding to what consumers want. Presumably many of Birdiebee's customers were initially familiar with the brand through WWE, which has a long tradition of ridiculing and erasing plus-size women wrestlers. Tamina Snuka, Piper Niven, and Nia Jax are WWE's lone larger women at the time of writing, while others throughout history can be counted on one hand.

Jax was a model before turning to wrestling, and she has modeled Birdiebee designs—you know, *after* they launched plus sizes. The fact that Nikki was the first straight-sized woman to be invited to CurvyCon, a plus-sized fashion and lifestyle event held during New York Fashion Week, where she appeared on a panel with Jax called "Body Positive Besties," was galling considering Birdiebee's previous miscommunication around sizing. Body positivity is about accepting all bodies, and Nikki has had issues with her weight when comparing herself with her thinner sister. However, she is able to afford things like breast-augmentation surgery and Botox and is unlikely to have ever dealt with not being able to find fashionable, comfortable clothes in her size or being discriminated against due to her weight—issues that the body-positive movement aims to combat.

The Bellas have since acknowledged their misstep in *Incomparable,* writing, "It was a misfire. Knowing what [we] know now, [we] realize that it would have been a better message to be honest about the delay than to put up with Birdiebee leaving out a lot of our fans."

Nikki made reference in her interview with Garcia to Birdiebee being different from the offerings on her and her sister's previous employer's online shop.

"The WWE Universe [is] used to WWE Shop items. WWE Shop items aren't premium fabrics. We didn't want to make WWE Shop items. When we came out with Birdiebee I wanted it to be premium fabrics," she said.

By distancing itself from WWEShop.com, Birdiebee sees itself as more in line with a sporting/lifestyle brand such as Lululemon or Kate Hudson's Fabletics, which have their own problems with inclusivity[169] and ethics.[170]

What's also unclear about Birdiebee is what it is apart from Bella-branded clothing. Its "About Us" page in a previous iteration read:

"Birdiebee is a brand that combines philanthropy and beautiful products in support of women around the world. The Birdiebee brand mirrors this passion for life, women's health and wellness, all while celebrating Brie and Nikki's unique sense of style and individuality. Our mission is to help educate and inspire young women to be stronger, more confident, happier and to live their own lives on their own terms."

While there were no links as to how they did these things, this explainer has been scrubbed from the internet, and in its place reads the less-obtuse and more-in-line-with-their-brand three-word mission statement: "affordable, attainable + sustainable."

Brie and Nikki have spoken more often recently about their desire for Birdiebee to be an environmentally friendly and ethically produced line, demonstrating that they've recognized the need for transparency. "The

---

169 Kim Bhasin, "Shunning Plus-Size Shoppers Is Key to Lululemon's Strategy, Insiders Say," *HuffPost*, August 9, 2013.

170 Sapna Maheshwari, "Tons of People Have Gotten Screwed Over by Kate Hudson's Company Fabletics," *Buzzfeed*, September 25, 2015.

majority of our leggings are made out of recycled water bottles," Brie said on *The Bellas Podcast*.[171] "We are becoming more of a sustainable and recyclable company."

Nikki has also mentioned how they want the brand to expand into teaching young women about vaginal health.[172]

"Our long-term goal is to move into feminine hygiene products, to create organic tampons and wipes and lubes that are sex- and body-positive, and completely free from toxins. That are 100 percent safe or even actively good for you," they wrote,[173] which becomes particularly resonant upon Nikki's polycystic ovarian syndrome (PCOS) diagnosis, which she has been forthcoming about.

And so we ovate back to the yoni egg.

This crunchy ethos is obviously evident in Brie's whole demeanor, but Nikki often talks on *The Bellas Podcast* about affirmations and journaling, which offer varying degrees of success in terms of self-help[174] and mental wellness,[175] but what has touched a lot of Bella fans is Nikki's foray into therapy.

Initially resistant to the idea due to an experience in her teens, Nikki began counseling after enduring burnout from being on the road and managing (at the time) two companies. But Nikki really began to reveal things not often seen on reality TV or in pop culture as a whole when she expressed how therapy had helped her work through her disillusionment with her impending nuptials to John Cena.

"All of a sudden I wasn't . . . Nikki Bella, I was . . . John Cena's fiancée," she said in a *Total Bellas* season-three scene. "I think it's hard

171   Brie and Nicole Bella, *The Bellas Podcast*, "V-Day Double Date with Property Brothers' Drew & Linda Scott," Apple Podcasts, February 12, 2020.

172   Lilian Garcia, *Chasing Glory*, "Nikki Bella," Apple Podcasts, November 20, 2017.

173   Brie and Nicole Bella, *Incomparable*, 2020.

174   Sophie Henshaw, "Why Positive Affirmations Don't Work," Psych Central, July 8, 2018.

175   Catherine Moore, "Positive Daily Affirmations: Is There Science Behind It?" Positive Psychology, January 9, 2020.

when you're a hardworking woman and all of your accomplishments go away because of how successful the man you're with is."

In case it wasn't clear from my complex attitude toward her, Nikki is someone we project our feelings, both good and bad, onto. I've always identified with Nikki, from her having to overcome negative perceptions because of how she appears, to her guardedness, to her ambivalence about marriage and losing yourself in a relationship with a man. Nikki's self-professed aggression, drive and the way she and Brie describe their abusive father are things I've said almost verbatim about my own self and life.

The Bellas revealed further layers of themselves in their memoir, *Incomparable*. They wrote about Nikki being raped twice as a teen, stalking and sexually predatory behavior from strangers, backstage hazing and sexism, and their parents' abusive marriage, among other things. The new-look *Total Bellas* season five has a female showrunner (in comparison with *Total Divas'* production credits, which are top-heavy with men), which emphasizes the "reality" of their show and brand. Topics seldom tackled on TV, such as the profound sense of grief at the loss of a pet or not wanting to have more children (Brie has since had a second child)—a theme across the *Total* franchise—are depicted during the season, and the portrayal of urinating on a pregnancy test occurs several times.

People dismiss reality TV and platforms on which women in wrestling have told their stories, like memoirs and social media, but this is the way they've been able to carve out a space for themselves while they waited for the patriarchy to catch up. "We wanted a true memoir, that when you shut the book . . . [readers] felt like the hero of [their] own story," Nikki said.[176]

By showing the warts-and-all reality of what it's like to be a woman in a male-dominated industry—and, indeed, a woman whose persona is

---

176 Brie and Nicole Bella, *The Bellas Podcast*, "BTS of Nartem's First Fight!" Apple Podcasts, May 13, 2020.

dominated by the men in that industry—the Bellas remind us that they aren't ciphers for all of our complex feelings about women wrestlers. They are complex women wrestlers with feelings.

I wrote at the outset of this book that it's important to critique the things you love in order to make them better. I highly doubt the Bellas are reading this, but if they are, I hope they know that that is what I've tried to do here.

6. *COMING DOWN THE AISLE:*

The Wrestling Wedding Industrial Complex

Content warning: *This chapter contains mentions of forced marriage, rape, miscarriage, drugging, homophobia, economic and emotional abuse, intimate partner violence (IPV), and racism.*

Once upon a time, the traditionally feminized performance of the wedding ceremony was a staple of WWE, infiltrating the hypermasculine wrestling ring, where relationships were punctuated by violence, not by holy matrimony.

Randy Savage and Miss Elizabeth's 1991 pay-per-view wedding was not the first instance of in-ring marriage rites (the two had already married in real life years before), but it was perhaps the one that kicked off the glitzy shebangs that would follow into the late-nineties Attitude era and beyond.

Savage wore a white-and-gold tuxedo embellished with his signature streamers, while Elizabeth looked coy in traditional white. Like many of the wrestling weddings to follow, the nuptials were the main event of *SummerSlam*, and the reception was given a royal-wedding-esque video package, replete with a British voiceover. That is, until Jake "The Snake" Roberts and The Undertaker—who, along with his brother Kane, would become a frequent wrestling wedding infiltrator—broke up the festivities.

In the wrestling wedding heyday, the plot device was often used to seek revenge on the bride's male associates or punish and humiliate her for deigning to sully the blood, sweat, and tears of wrestling with rose petals and confetti.

Stephanie McMahon was left with egg on her face in all four of her wrestling weddings.

First, she was abducted by The Undertaker to be his Satanic bride and was subsequently rescued by Stone Cold Steve Austin, simply because she was a pawn in their feud and not because Austin had any sympathy for her.

Her second go-round was to her real-life boyfriend at the time, the late Andrew "Test" Martin, but it was revealed that she was already wed to her current real-life husband, Paul "Triple H" Levesque, who drugged her and married her in a drive-through Vegas chapel. Surely the bride being unconscious and unable to consent was grounds for an annulment. . . .

Several years later, McMahon was set to renew her kayfabe vows to Triple H in the ring; however, he left her at the altar when he found out she had been lying to him about being pregnant, a recurring theme.

The next-most-often-humiliated bride is Lita, who grew to heights of popularity among wrestling fans and in the general pop culture zeitgeist not normally seen by a woman wrestler.

For this she was cut down to size in both of her wrestling weddings, the first of which was forcibly to Kane, to whom she was pregnant by rape (she later miscarried within the story). Her second wedding, to Edge, was subsequently ruined by her fictional first husband, who came up from the depths of hell—in wrestling parlance, that means from under the ring and through the mat.

During both weddings, the theme music of Lita's real-life long-term partner Matt Hardy rang out through the arena. The first time, he tried to save Lita despite her agreeing to marry Kane in order to protect Hardy; the second wedding married storyline with reality.

During the course of Lita's on-screen alignment with Edge, the two had an affair that soon became public knowledge and was incorporated into a storyline. They both were deeply uncomfortable with this, but it allowed Hardy, who had lost his job due to his unprofessional behavior in the wake of finding out about it, to come back to work.

Lita said[177] that she "wanted to cry, scream, curse, and walk out at all times."

If it has not yet become apparent, wrestling weddings seldom go off without a hitch, so to speak. Aksana got fired and divorced; Krystal's much older groom, Teddy Long, had a heart attack in the middle of his vows; and Vickie Guerrero found out her husband, also Edge, was cheating on her with the wedding planner, Alicia Fox.

In the event that both parties say "I do" of their own volition, yet another certification that a wedding is taking place within kayfabe is that wedding crashers will inevitably show up without RSVPing. The aforementioned instance of Triple H crashing Stephanie's second trip down the aisle to reveal she'd be committing polyandry if she went through with her vows; pimp character The Godfather enticing the male guests away from Krystal and Teddy's wedding with the women he was trafficking; and The Undertaker and Jake "The Snake" Roberts assaulting Macho Man and Miss Elizabeth at their reception all exemplify this.

Perhaps the wedding that drew the most mainstream attention was the 2002 commitment ceremony (same-sex marriage was not yet legal) between tag team partners turned "lovers" Billy and Chuck, but for all the wrong reasons. Initially supported by the Gay and Lesbian Alliance Against Defamation (GLAAD) and promoted heavily in the media, the ceremony was unveiled as a publicity stunt, both inside and outside of kayfabe, when Billy and Chuck hesitated to say their vows. Turning to their manager—the coded-as-gay hairdresser Rico, who Billy and Chuck believed would put a stop to the vows before they said them— they were then attacked by the tag team 3-Minute Warning, a depressing metaphor for the treatment of gay people, even today.

GLAAD claimed it had been misled about WWE's intentions for a gay wedding, with media director Scott Seomin saying[178] that GLAAD was lied to even after the wedding was filmed:

---

177 Lilian Garcia, *AfterBuzz TV*, "Lita Interview | *AfterBuzz TV's* Lilian Garcia's *Making Their Way to the Ring*," YouTube, April 10, 2017.

178 Scott Seomin, "GLAAD: We Were Lied To," *OutSports*, September 13, 2002.

"I was told (lied to) the day after the show was taped in Minneapolis that the wedding took place and all was well. The WWE also lied to *The Today Show*, [*T*]*he New York Times* and other media outlets. Many have contacted me to express their disdain for the WWE's unprofessional marketing machine."

Almost twenty years later, shades of Billy and Chuck could be seen in Lana's wrestling wedding to Bobby Lashley, which was promptly— though not soon enough if the jeering audience members were any indication—crashed by Liv Morgan, which I will delve into later.

I can count only two in-ring unions that made it past the altar: that of Dawn Marie's 2002 "marriage" to Al Wilson, the father of fellow wrestler Torrie Wilson, whom Dawn was feuding with at the time (Al subsequently "died" on the honeymoon from a heart attack, so the wedding party's out on whether that could be considered a successful partnership); and Maxine and Johnny Curtis in 2012. And though AJ Lee's then-impending nuptials to Daniel Bryan, also in 2012, never eventuated, she was the lone woman to emerge triumphant from a wrestling wedding, jilting her groom to further her career and take on the role of general manager of WWE's flagship show, *Raw*. Prior to that, both in and out of kayfabe, wrestling and marriage had largely been incompatible for women in the business, with most of them retiring from the wrestling ring once they received a wedding ring.

Since the peak of the wrestling wedding industrial complex, wrestling underwent a "women's evolution," with more dedication professed to be given to women wrestlers. This was evident with the advent of *Total Divas*, the E! reality show charting the lives of some of WWE's female performers, in 2013, when WWE largely divorced itself from the wedding industry, which, it could be argued, inherently subjugates women.

Reality TV is widely considered to be fake, like professional wrestling, so it makes sense that wrestling weddings would take up residence in the highly feminized medium of reality TV.

WWE entered what it calls its Reality era around the dawn of the 2010s. Different from the Attitude and Ruthless Aggression eras (which arrived in 2002 and spawned the stars of your favorite action movies, John Cena and Dave Bautista), the Reality era acknowledges that fans have unprecedented access to wrestlers via social media and the WWE Network, the company's on-demand streaming service, and plays on that. So the relationship between Cena and *Total Divas* star Nikki Bella and the planning of their will-they-won't-they wedding (spoiler alert: they didn't) may have been a cornerstone of the *Total Divas* franchise, and its spinoff *Total Bellas*, but it wouldn't be out of place on WWE programming either. Especially since they simultaneously broke the rules of kayfabe while encapsulating the ethos of the Reality era with Cena's in-ring proposal to Bella at *WrestleMania 33*.

Like so many women's storylines, the feud germinated through The Miz's acrimony for Cena's position as the face of WWE, which The Miz believed Cena had obtained through backstage politicking. The Miz's wife and two-time Divas champion in her own right, Maryse, accused Nikki and her twin sister, Brie, of screwing her out of a job so that they could be the stars of *Total Divas*. Maryse then made it personal, saying that Nikki might have gotten the lead role, but Maryse got the ring, something Cena always claimed that Nikki would never receive from him. The feud, the highlight of which was The Miz and Maryse mocking Cena's robotic emoting and Nikki's pining for marriage in an entertaining parody of *Total Bellas,* called *Total Bellas Bullshit,* culminated in a mixed tag team match at *WrestleMania 33*.

The aftermath of the match, in which Cena gave Nikki an honest-to-goodness engagement ring in the ring, was the culmination of these aforementioned storylines and, furthermore, five years worth of plotting on *Total Divas/Bellas*, all while reducing Nikki to what she has purported not wanting to be: the product of, or sidekick to, a man's career.

The lead-up to the match and the increasingly likely proposal was centered on Cena, and Nikki wasn't even holding a microphone during the proposal, though traditionally all that's required of the person accepting is to say yes and/or look enthused. Given Nikki's well-documented preoccupation with her marital status for the previous half-decade, it was assumed she would say yes, and she did.

For anyone who watched the way Cena treated Nikki on *Total Divas* and *Total Bellas*, the fact that they broke up before they made it to the altar was unsurprising. Cena constantly withheld marriage from Nikki, despite the fact that she was willing to sign away her autonomy to be with him, demonstrating what could be perceived as emotionally and economically abusive behavior.

In season one of *Total Divas*, Cena presented Nikki with a cohabitation agreement that defined Nikki as a guest in his home with terms not dissimilar from the fine print in a hotel or Airbnb reservation.

"You make me feel so not a part of your life. When are you ever going to include me in your life . . . ?" she said. "I guess I'm always going to be that girl that signed a piece of paper, and I can be out of your life just like that."

Though Nikki had every right to be mad given that Cena had sprung the agreement on her after she'd already moved her things from one side of the country to the other (likely a plot decision made by the producers), she frivolously responded with her own prenup of sorts that stipulated a certain amount of physical affection, reinforcing the gender divide between pragmatic male concerns and emotional, feminine ones. Much was made of Cena's rules and controlling behavior, such as not allowing Nikki to keep her dog, Winston,[179] and even now Nikki can't legally say his name.[180] Perhaps that was why she was so hell-bent on having kids with Cena: so she'd have some company while he was away working all the time.

"John's always gone and now that I've lost Winston [when Brie and Bryan adopted him because Nikki was traveling so much] I'm just so lonely all the time," Nikki sobbed on a season-two episode of *Total Bellas*.

I personally enjoyed watching Nikki's evolution (heh) from desperately wanting to lock Cena down with marriage and children to sacrificing those things in order to be with the man she loves, partly

179 Michele Corriston, "John Cena and Nikki Bella Disagreed Over Beloved Dog Winston, Who She Called Her 'Baby,'" *People*, April 18, 2018.

180 Jen Ortiz, "How the Bella Twins Turned Your Fave Guilty-Pleasure Sport into a Feminist Empire," *Cosmopolitan*, October 10, 2018.

because they align with my own values.

That is until her family got in her head and invalidated her choices. Brie condescendingly tried to throw Nikki a "women's empowerment party"—you know how I feel about that term—because she'd never have a bachelorette party or baby shower. "I don't need a baby or a bridal shower to feel fulfilled," Nikki retorted. Women aren't empowered by parties; we're empowered by having our choices respected and affirmed.

But the key word there is sacrifice: Nikki always seemed to be giving pieces of herself away to fit into Cena's rigid ideal of what he wanted out of their relationship, which felt like a business negotiation (which I'm personally inclined to believe marriage should be instead of a public display of worthiness of conventional notions of love) rather than an equal relationship. Cena ultimately conceded that he would "give" Nikki marriage and a child, but by that point[181] Nikki was "over that word. I'm over that feeling."

Nikki took an extended leave from WWE for almost a year after the 2017 proposal due to lingering problems stemming from her neck surgery. But as far as WWE viewers were concerned, Nikki stopped wrestling because she got her happy ending. She'd reached "the marriage plot," a literary device that places a (heterosexual) marriage at the end of a tale and, thus, the end of a woman's story. Think Jane Austen, rom-coms, and Disney movies.

The cracks in the relationship were there for those who cared to see them: Cena didn't appear postengagement in *Total Divas* season seven in original footage at all, nor in half of the episodes of the preceding *Total Bellas* season two, in which Nikki moved to be closer to Brie during her pregnancy and Cena tried to make time to see his betrothed. Cena never participated in confessionals (it should be noted, Bryan and Artem Chigvintsev, Nikki's new fiancé and the father of her baby, are the only men to do so over the course of both shows, but more pointedly *Total Bellas*, of which they are a prominent part).

Fast-forward two and a half years and Nikki was officially retired from wrestling due to a cyst on her brain and engaged to, and pregnant

---

181 In *Total Bellas* season three.

by, Chigvintsev, her partner on *Dancing With the Stars*.

Given the way she and Brie spoke about Chigvintsev on their podcast,[182] I'm not out of line in deducing that the Bellas (and much of patriarchal society) subscribe to the notion of marriage being the ultimate goal a woman should aspire to, after which she is completely fulfilled.

"I wish Carrie Bradshaw did have the big wedding, and when she did the courthouse wedding and the diner I was bummed out," Nikki said. "I still want to have the big wedding . . . but do I showcase that on TV? Are there things that I should keep private in my life?"

"What's hard [about] being a reality star and taking people on [the journey of] the last seven years of your life is it's kind of like if you don't give them the ending, everyone would hate that. Could you imagine watching a movie and there's no ending?" Brie responded.

"I felt that the first time around," Nikki replied. "People were very upset at me not just because of my breakup [with Cena] but because I didn't give them their fairy-tale ending. They were on this journey of something I wanted for six years, and then they didn't get that."

The Reality era ensures we know that many of WWE's women wrestlers are married (with many of their weddings having taken place on *Total Divas*) or in committed, long-term (heterosexual, it is not insignificant to point out) relationships, usually with their fellow wrestlers, which obviously makes the work of marriage that much easier. In that way, *Total Divas* and *Bellas* are helping to portray an alternative depiction of the wrestling wedding. For example, Nikki stated that she wanted to walk herself down the aisle because it's—here's that word again!—"empowering" and referred to wrestling as "the thing I wanted more than the love of my life."[183]

In another way, though, *Total Divas* is in the same vein as much of highly curated reality TV that perpetuates conservative relationships. Shows such as *The Bachelor*, *Bachelor in Paradise*, and *90 Day Fiancé* primarily focus on straight relationships between White people. On the

---

182 Brie and Nicole Bella, *The Bellas Podcast*, "Cat's Out of the Bag," Apple Podcasts, January 8, 2020.

183 Brie and Nicole Bella, *Incomparable*, 2020.

rare occasions that queer, non-White, or nonmonogamous (but only in the case of the women) contestants are featured, they're routinely shamed for it.

It's for these reasons that I find more problems in Brie and Bryan's marriage than in Nikki and Cena's doomed relationship. It's unclear how much of their wedded woes are manufactured for the medium of reality TV; however, Bryan's constant putting down of Brie for dressing in her free-spirited manner and drinking alcohol is upsetting regardless. In a season-one episode, Brie tries to covertly activate "Brie mode" (getting wasted) during a trip to Las Vegas for Nattie's bachelorette weekend so as not to upset her then-boyfriend. And in season four, Bryan admonishes Brie for "showing too much skin" and "giv[ing] all these men [in the restaurant] erections."

"I wish Bryan would rejoice in my body and say, 'You look good,'" Brie complains, and she conspires with Nikki to borrow some of her clothes in an attempt to prove that Brie's clothes are not that revealing.

"You think [Nikki] looks nice?!" Bryan exclaims when he uncovers their ploy. In true Bella-beau fashion, Bryan is shown engaging in economic abuse by shutting off the plumbing to his and Brie's house in order to teach Brie a lesson.

In another episode, Bryan stalks Brie by monitoring her bank accounts because he believes she spends too much.

Lest we think Bryan's misogyny is reserved for his wife (he and Brie were married at the end of season two of *Total Divas*), he constantly insults Nikki for being materialistic, "too selfish to have a baby,"[184] and not on his intellectual level. (It's fitting that he condescendingly hosts the quiz-show segment of their YouTube channel and podcast, "Bella Brains," where he gets to lord his knowledge over them.)

Though the Twins often take this in jest, the cracks in Brie and Bryan's marriage started to show in season five of *Total Bellas*, when they weighed whether to have another child. Bryan wanted a boy, to carry on his family name, not understanding that their daughter, Birdie, might be the one to do it by not changing her name when she gets married

---

184 WWE, "The Bellas Discuss Their Plans for the Future with Daniel: *Total Divas* Preview Clip," YouTube, July 27, 2015.

or—shock horror!—not getting married at all. Brie felt this pressure, having a minifeminist awakening as she pondered whether she could manage two kids and a career while Bryan's on the road wrestling. "I would never in a million years ask [Bryan] to stop his career . . . but because he's the man he never once has to ask me, 'Is it OK if I leave every week to go out of town for my job?' because it's just assumed," she said.[185]

It's not a "traditional" wrestling wedding that exemplifies the dichotomy of the wrestling wedding industrial complex at all, but rather one that occurs in the scripted Netflix show *GLOW*.

In the final episode of season two, Rhonda Richardson (Kate Nash), who wrestles as Britannica, The Smartest Woman in the World, is about to be deported back to Britain. Her fellow wrestlers suggest she should marry her stalker fan Toby, who previously proposed to her. Somewhere along the way, the decision to televise the nuptials on the season, and what becomes the series, finale of the show *Gorgeous Ladies of Wrestling* (*G.L.O.W.*) within the show *GLOW* is made, and Rhonda is set to become an honest woman.

Rhonda's wedding is a welcome exception to the trope of wrestling brides being humiliated. This time, it's Toby who's left out in the cold ("Love is fake—just like wrestling!" he spits), with *G.L.O.W.* announcer and financial backer Bash (Chris Lowell) coming to Rhonda's rescue. Apparently they'd been sleeping together, unbeknown to their colleagues and to viewers. Carmen (Britney Young), who wrestles as Machu Picchu, is visibly taken aback by this development (no doubt inspired by the late original *G.L.O.W.* star Emily Dole, who played Mount Fiji and confessed in the 2012 documentary about the show that she was in love with IRL Bash, Matt Cimber). This, coupled with Bash's inability to come to terms with the death of his best friend and butler, Florian (Alex Rich), from AIDS-related complications, foretells

---

185   E! Entertainment, "Brie Tells Nikki She Doesn't Want to Give Up Her Career | *Total Bellas* | E!," YouTube, April 2, 2020.

that Bash and Britannica's union can only result in disaster, as with so many other wrestling matrimonies.

But doomed marriage isn't the only prophecy *GLOW* espouses when it comes to wrestling weddings. The fact that male wrestlers in *GLOW*, *Total Divas*, and the wrestling industry proper are so willing to participate in wrestling weddings speaks to the industry's involvement in capitalism, with reality-TV wrestling weddings being just another arm of that.

As Zoya the Destroyer (Alison Brie) said on *GLOW*: wrestling weddings are a "bourgeois capitalist scam for huge TV ratings."

During the battle royal for Rhonda's bridal bouquet and, in turn, the *G.L.O.W.* championship tiara, Carmen's brother Kurt (former WWE wrestler Carlito) and his wrestling buddy Chico Guapo (fellow former WWE star and *GLOW* trainer Chavo Guerrero, Jr.) make a surprise entrance, à la the wedding-crashers plot device. Pissed that Carmen stole their moves to use on the show, Kurt and Chico are willing to call it even if she can "get [their] face[s] on TV."

Say what you want about weddings and reality TV more broadly sullying the sport of professional wrestling *insert spit take gif here,* but Tyson Kidd is arguably better known for being Nattie's husband (as the fans were wont to chant at him prior to his early retirement due to injury) than he is for wrestling.

WWE messed with its previously perfected method of melding wrestling weddings with reality TV by staging the interracial wedding of Lana and Bobby Lashley on the final episode of *Raw* for the 2010s.

Lana, a former cast member of *Total Divas* who had two weddings on the show (one in Malibu, one in her real-life husband Rusev's home country of Bulgaria) and another ceremony on WWE TV in 2016, is perhaps the Reality era's equivalent of Stephanie McMahon in wedding count alone.

The union between Lana and Lashley had been problematic from the get-go.

Lana, Lashley, and Rusev all returned to WWE TV after a several-month absence in October 2019 as part of a storyline between Ric Flair and the formerly disgraced-but-apparently-forgiven Hulk Hogan. Too decrepit to wrestle, Hogan and Flair were issued younger, more virile wrestlers to stand in for them in a ten-man tag team match to take place in Saudi Arabia as part of WWE's controversial deal with the autocratic state. Lashley, a Black man, was on Flair's team, while Rusev was with the racist-but-by-wrestling-logic-babyface (wrestling parlance for good guy) Hogan. There were also parallels between Lana's blonde-bombshell appearance and that of Hogan's daughter, Brooke, whom Hogan said he didn't want dating Black men in the viral Gawker tape.

Later in the storyline, Lana took out a restraining order against her ex, Rusev, whom she claimed was stalking her in her new relationship with Lashley. When Rusev showed up, the cops arrested the Black man instead of the person violating the order because of course they did. "This is the state of Tennessee and we do things differently," said the officer, a representative of the state in which, as of 2018, African Americans were incarcerated at three times the rate of Whites.[186] Lana then mouthed off to the police officers, resulting in her own arrest.

Though Lana was clearly fabricating her need for a restraining order, her arrest is representative of police misidentifying and charging IPV victims. According to a study by Women's Legal Service Victoria, Australia (the state in which I wrote this book), 57 percent of women initially thought to be perpetrators were actually victims.[187]

The following week, sometimes-tag-team-champion, sometimes-court-jester (one of the few stereotypical roles available to Black men in WWE) Angelo Dawkins made a connection to the 2017 horror film *Get Out*, in which a White woman behaves frighteningly similarly toward the police in the company of her Black boyfriend, to illustrate how systemically White people have little regard for Black bodies.

By the time the nuptials had finally arrived, on the day before New Years Eve 2019, Lana and Lashley's wedding incorporated all the

---

186 Adrian Mojica, "Tennessee's Incarceration Rate Above Average, African Americans Have 3x Rate of Whites," Fox17.com, October 11, 2019.

187 Emma Younger, "When Police Misjudge Domestic Violence, Victims Are Slapped with Intervention Order Applications," Australian Broadcasting Corporation, August 15, 2018.

hallmarks of the wrestling wedding industrial complex, including a faked pregnancy, gatecrashing by former lovers, and the redebuting Liv Morgan confessing her feelings for her ex-girlfriend Lana. These feelings didn't appear to be of love, though, as the two broke out into a fight, with Lana's storyline-former-husband Rusev bursting out of a cake to attack Lashley to top things off.

WWE had been promising queer representation for years. It arrived in the lipstick lesbian affair between Liv and Lana that recalled HLA (a blip on the Attitude era's radar in which scantily clad women would come to the ring and performatively engage in acronymic Hot Lesbian Action until the previously mentioned 3-Minute Warning beat them up) and, for those who cared to see it, inferred IPV. Taking into account the problematic nature of, and negative response to, WWE's first foray into queer storylines in nearly two decades, which is unlikely to have included any input from actually queer writers or wrestlers, we will probably be waiting just as long until the company attempts it again.[188]

It is for this reason, along with the wealth of wrestling weddings listed here, that WWE cannot be trusted to portray marriage as the life-affirming partnership that it is for so many who choose to put a ring on it. And until things old, new, borrowed, and blue stop being synonymous with femininity, it's unlikely we'll see wrestling weddings treated as anything other than a sideshow.

A version of this chapter originally appeared in VRV *as "The Wild World of Wrestling Weddings." Republished with permission.*

---

188   Sonya Deville, WWE's first out lesbian wrestler, was working on a queer storyline with her tag team partner, Mandy Rose, with input from GLAAD, earlier that year, according to an interview with *Uproxx.* A clip from *Total Divas* season nine shows Deville and Rose's storyline getting cut in order to put more emphasis on the first women's main event of *WrestleMania.* At the following year's *WrestleMania,* Deville and Rose's inevitable feud revolved around two heterosexual men fighting for Rose's affections. Elle Collins, "Sonya Deville on Finding Her Activist Voice on WWE and Wrestling through the Coronavirus," *Uproxx,* March 18, 2020.

7. DADDY'S LITTLE GIRL:

Stephanie McMahon & Toeing the Company Line

Content warning: *This chapter contains mentions of forced marriage and sexism.*

February 2015 was a big month for gender equality.
Patricia Arquette, upon winning the Academy Award for Best Actress in a Supporting Role for her performance in *Boyhood*, gave the following speech:

> "To every woman who gave birth to every taxpayer and citizen of this nation, we have fought for everybody else's equal rights. It's our time to have wage equality once and for all, and equal rights for women in the United States of America."

"It's time for all the women in America and all the men who love women and all the gay people and all the people of color that we've fought for to fight for us now," she continued in the press room after her win.

While on the surface this speech was a rallying cry for feminism, it ignored several things. First-wave feminism was largely a racist movement that was built on White women getting the right to vote and excluding women of color for fear that it would convolute the message. Social-justice movements such as Stonewall and #BlackLivesMatter were started and supported by queer people of color and Black women, with little support from the presumably straight, cisgender, White women Arquette meant when she called for pay parity. Intersectionality—the term coined by critical race theorist Kimberlé Crenshaw that posits that oppressed people exist at the intersections of many identities (i.e., person of color, woman, disabled, queer, etc.) and thus experience many different kinds of discrimination—wasn't present in Arquette's speech. If it were, she perhaps would have mentioned that the pay gap experienced by women of color in service jobs far outpaces that between successful White women in Hollywood such as Arquette and men in her industry, whom she was presumably talking about. Also, not everyone who gives birth is a woman.

But it certainly piqued the interest of Stephanie McMahon, chief brand officer of WWE.

She tweeted a meme of Arquette's speech and praised the actress for "having the courage to fight for #WomensRights on such a grand platform.

"#UseYourVoice," she ended the tweet.[189]

This, in turn, rankled AJ Lee. She replied to McMahon's tweet with two of her own (these were the days when Twitter was still offering only 140 characters per tweet): "Your female wrestlers have record selling merchandise & have starred in the highest rated segment of the show several times, [a]nd yet they receive a fraction of the wages & screen time of the majority of the male roster," Lee wrote across the two tweets, finishing with the same #UseYourVoice hashtag.[190,191]

McMahon curtly replied in a standalone tweet, thanking Lee for her opinion.[192]

Like Arquette, McMahon probably wasn't expecting to get called out for seemingly innocuously supporting wage equality, as she was by both Lee and an increasingly vocal fan base—women's wrestling fans

189 @StephMcMahon, Twitter, February 24, 2015.

190 @TheAJMendez, Twitter, February 25, 2015.

191 Ibid.

192 @StephMcMahon, Twitter, February 25, 2015.

had realized the power of their collective voice that same day with the hashtag #GiveDivasAChance, which urged WWE to invest more time (and, it would suggest, more money) in the women's roster.

Stephanie McMahon's tweets illustrate the hypocrisy of her as the figurehead of the women's wrestling evolution: if McMahon was so moved by the fight for gender equality, why didn't she push for Paige, Emma, and the Bella Twins to get more than thirty seconds of airtime that very same day?

I understand that overhauling a division that had been subjugated— and, if we look back over the events discussed throughout this book, since women's wrestling began—takes more than a day. In fact, for WWE it would take five months for the company to instigate its Divas Revolution™.

McMahon was at the forefront of this marketing plan, "set[ting] the table of opportunity"[193] for some of the existing women on WWE's main roster (Paige, the Bellas, Alicia Fox, Naomi, and Tamina) and the fresh faces of Charlotte Flair, Sasha Banks, and Becky Lynch, who were launched onto the scene.

The three teams that these nine women were divided into—Team Bella, consisting of the Bellas and Fox; Team PCB (formerly the Submission Sorority, before someone realized the faction shared its name with a porn series), which stood for the first initials of Paige, Charlotte, and Becky; and Team B.A.D., which was made up of the Beautiful and Dangerous Naomi, Tamina, and Banks—competed in different formations for several months, but they never really reached the expectations that #GiveDivasAChance and the resulting Divas Revolution had laid out for them.

There was a clear disconnect between *NXT*—the WWE developmental brand from which Banks, Flair, and Lynch all came, and where Paige and Emma tore it up for twenty minutes in one of the nascent moments

---

193 Season twenty-three, episode forty-five, *WWE Raw*, USA Network, July 13, 2015.

of the women's wrestling evolution in 2013—and WWE proper.

This was never more evident than during *SummerSlam* weekend, the August pay-per-view that is second only to *WrestleMania* in terms of size and influence. The year 2015 marked the first time *NXT* held a marquee event, titled *NXT Takeover: Brooklyn I*, outside of its Florida base camp, and it was also the first in a four-year residency for the event at Brooklyn's Barclays Center.[194]

That year, *NXT Takeover: Brooklyn I* hosted the *NXT* women's championship match between Banks, in one of her last *NXT* matches before she graduated to the main roster for good, and Bayley, in an instant classic, considered one of the best wrestling matches ever.

The following night at the main *SummerSlam* show, Banks was set to face off with her Team B.A.D. members against Team PCB and Team Bellas in a three-team elimination match. We all thought, after Banks's hell of a performance the previous evening, that she would be the MVP; however, she and the rest of her team were eliminated first, in a lackluster match that illustrated this separation between the organic evolution of women's wrestling on *NXT* and the convoluted marketing scheme of the main roster.

Perhaps in an attempt to get the rub from *NXT*'s game-changing division, McMahon was there before the women's championship match to introduce it (though, curiously, she did not make the same appearance as an on-screen authority figure before the match that she put together the following night on *SummerSlam*) and was met with a lukewarm reaction from the notoriously fickle New York crowd.

"We are all making history, right here, right now," she said. "And speaking of making history, a few weeks ago on *Raw* I said that I wanted a Divas revolution. But make no mistake about it, that Divas revolution started right here in *NXT* with some extraordinary women who give it their all and leave everything in this ring night after night. Triple H said earlier today that he doesn't just put them in the main event, they are the main event. So it is my honor to introduce to you tonight's first main event for the *NXT* women's championship."

---

194 I attended *SummerSlam* weekend at the Barclays Center in 2017.

The fans were right to be skeptical of McMahon's involvement, as her empty words about the match being the main event (which has traditionally been the last match of the night; this was the second to last) were indicative of how WWE's flagship brands, *Raw* and *SmackDown*, had fumbled women's wrestling, rather than the grassroots evolution of *NXT*.

More likely, McMahon was there to support her husband, Triple H (real name Paul Levesque).

Some backstory on the woman who became known as "The Billion Dollar Princess" and "Daddy's Little Girl":

Stephanie McMahon was born to Vince and Linda McMahon in 1976. Vince took over the World Wide Wrestling Federation from his father, Vince McMahon, Sr., in 1983 and turned it into the conglomerate better known as WWE (and, before that, World Wrestling Federation, until losing a lawsuit to the World Wildlife Fund in 2002). Linda, whom Vince married in 1966, became WWE's president and chief executive officer as well as an on-screen presence as—you guessed it!—Vince's wife, before pursuing a career in politics. Linda was named the head of the Small Business Administration (she has experience in running the territories and small, independent wrestling companies out of business, you see) in the Donald Trump administration, which she left in 2019 to run the super PAC for Trump's reelection that promised to spend $18.5 million in Florida in exchange for allowing WWE's workers there to perform during the COVID-19 pandemic.

Stephanie McMahon's older brother, Shane, is also involved in WWE, as a wrestler, on-screen authority figure, and behind-the-scenes executive.

McMahon herself began performing secretarial and modeling work for WWE as a teen while she completed her communications degree at Boston University. She then graduated to an on-screen role, playing the undead bride to The Undertaker, an innocent bride to Test, and an unconscious one to her future on-air and real-life husband (with whom she has three daughters), Levesque, who revealed that he was actually already married to "Daddy's Little Girl" in a nonconsensual drive-through Las Vegas union.

As Triple H and Vince feuded over the love of Stephanie, she revealed herself to be in on Triple H's surreptitious marriage and subsequently "turned heel," a role that she has largely occupied ever since, in such positions as the storyline owner of Extreme Championship Wrestling (ECW, an independent company that WWE purchased in its takeover of the industry), the general manager of both *Raw* and *SmackDown*, and figurehead of the women's wrestling evolution.

McMahon was perhaps one of the first women to prove she could go toe-to-toe with men on the mic, and for that she was rewarded with her first and only women's championship, in 2000. This was rumored to be not only a gift from her father, but the reason the women's division continued at all, since, if you'll remember from earlier chapters, this was during the bane of the Attitude era. The esteem the women's title was held in at the time was reflected in McMahon's gear for the match: bike shorts, a white T-shirt, and trainers, as if she was off for a morning stroll, not a competitive championship match.

Behind the scenes, McMahon worked her way up the ranks, becoming WWE's chief brand officer in 2013, while Triple H has worn many executive hats and is responsible for turning WWE's training facility into the third brand of WWE, known as *NXT*.

Of McMahon's binary role, wrestler Chris Jericho, a frequent foe, said, "She does a great job of the duality of what a WWE Superstar has to do and what a WWE top executive has to do."[195]

McMahon and AJ Lee's on-screen interactions were few and far between, but when they did encounter each other, it was a metaexploration of their apparent personal issues. For example, in a 2013 promo, McMahon told Lee that she didn't "get why you'd rather perpetuate stereotypes about women. That we're vicious, conniving, manipulative, that we'd rather

---

195 "Women's Evolution," *WWE 24*, WWE Network, August 16, 2016.

tear each other down than build each other up." (Perhaps someone saw an early draft of Lee's memoir . . . .)

"Instead of dating Superstars, maybe I should marry one," Lee shot back. "And let's not get started on your daddy issues; now that's a whole other can of worms."

"You're not disappointed in me . . . because I am you," she continued. "Except younger."

While Lee was clearly the heel here, McMahon shifted into a lawful evil gear, reminding Lee that "if I want to, I can take [your Divas championship] away from you. If I want to, you won't have a job anymore." This was particularly biting given that WWE would fire Lee's real-life husband, CM Punk, on their wedding day.

McMahon made a similar threat in her biggest feud and her first match in more than a decade against Brie Bella in 2014. McMahon and Triple H, in their faction The Authority, had an ongoing vendetta against Bella's husband, Daniel Bryan. The two wielded their power over the Bryan-Bella family by forcing Bryan to relinquish his world title, firing Bella, and turning her twin sister, Nikki, against her.

By 2018, the women's wrestling evolution was well underway, and McMahon had cemented herself as its spokeswoman. She was always going on about how MMA star Ronda Rousey had proved that women could be a draw in UFC and thus had helped the women's evolution along. In real life, McMahon was close with Rousey, and most people thought it was only a matter of time before she appeared in WWE.

That time had come, and you can be damn sure the fictional McMahon was going to take credit for it, just as she had the women's evolution, leading to Rousey's debut match with fellow Olympian Kurt Angle against McMahon and Triple H at *WrestleMania 34*.

The following year, in an attempt to capitalize on Becky Lynch's surging popularity and re-create the Attitude era dynamic between the corrupt boss, Vince, and beleaguered everyman Stone Cold Steve Austin, Stephanie and Triple H, as well as Vince, insinuated themselves into many of her storylines as obstacles in her way to Rousey and the main event of *WrestleMania 35*.

LaToya Ferguson wrote in *An Encyclopedia of Women's Wrestling: 100 Profiles of the Best in the Sport* that many of McMahon's storylines, especially her involvement with The Authority, "represent[ed] what wrestling fans already felt about the McMahons and their particular corporate choices," a major element of WWE's 2010s Reality era, as these storylines will attest.

To his credit, Triple H has done a lot in *NXT* to help change the perception of women's wrestling within WWE as a whole.

"My husband started recruiting elite-level athletes from all over the world, and he started training the women the same as the men," McMahon said on Lilian Garcia's *Chasing Glory* podcast. "He started giving them the same match times, the same opportunities within the show, so they had the same opportunities to get the same number of rep[etitions] as the men. As we all know, repetition and practice is how you learn. That's how you grow. If you're not ever given that opportunity, you're not going to learn and grow at the same rate."

McMahon has also been a big proponent of women's wrestling behind the scenes, according to numerous wrestlers.

"There would have been no career, there would have been no opportunity, there would have been no revamping of the women's division if Stephanie wasn't behind it all," legendary women's wrestler Trish Stratus said.[196] "She is always supportive of showcasing a strong, powerful woman. There would have been no division, and none of the women would have got the push that we needed or the encouragement we needed without her."

But where it gets trickier is on the main roster, which is where McMahon primarily works and which is ruled with the iron fist of her father. No matter how many progressive ideas or writers are hired to make a more inclusive and representative product, the elder McMahon has final say and will often rewrite storylines the day of and even during the show!

As the CBO, then, she should know better than to write verbal

---

196 Pat Laprade and Dan Murphy, *Sisterhood of the Squared Circle: The History and Rise of Women's Wrestling*, 2017.

checks that her ass can't cash.

Which brings us back to AJ Lee and the disconnect between what McMahon says and what actually eventuates.

McMahon is a mouthpiece for the women's wrestling evolution in WWE. She rarely strays from the company line, repeating terms such as "first ever" and "history making" as well as the fabled story of WWE's first match in the Middle East.

WWE held its first women's match in Abu Dhabi in late 2017, between Sasha Banks and Alexa Bliss. McMahon has repeated numerous times in the mainstream media that the crowd chanted "This is hope" during the match, when in reality only a few people could actually be heard chanting that.

She also said in mid-2016 that WWE would begin incorporating queer storylines. At the time of writing there have only been two: WWE's first out lesbian wrestler, Sonya Deville, sabotaging the heterosexual love life of her best friend and tag team partner, Mandy Rose,[197] out of jealousy—because what other emotions do women, particularly queer women, have?—and Liv Morgan crashing Lana's (straight) wedding to Bobby Lashley because Morgan was in love with Lana.

Eric Shorey, a wrestling critic and host of the *Nobodies Watching Wrestling* YouTube show, tweeted[198] that WWE's hollow progressivism is "a perpetual rhetorical catch 22 of pretending to be progressive by hiring and featuring diverse talent but also as a company actively supporting politicians who are working towards the elimination of the civil rights of those same performers. It manifests symptomatically in moments like last night's already-infamous promo[199] in which a star can discuss 'breaking barriers' while strategically not mentioning which barriers

---

197 The two were originally supposed to have a lesbian storyline with input from GLAAD; however, that was scrapped.

198 @eric_shorey, Twitter, April 24, 2020.

199 Openly gay wrestler Jay Atlas said he wanted to "break barriers."

and for who: because doing so would inevitably call attention to the company's conservatism."

McMahon's silence when AJ Lee called her out for not practicing the gender equality she preached was stark.

As I mentioned, this was the same day #GiveDivasAChance was hatched, which McMahon failed to acknowledge on social media.

What she did boost on Twitter was the renaming of the Fabulous Moolah Memorial Battle Royal to the *WrestleMania* Women's Battle Royal in 2018, which McMahon made sure included the SEO terms "historic" and #WomensEvolution.[200]

As CBO, McMahon committed the rare faux pas when, in 2015, she tweeted a quote attributed to Twitter cofounder Biz Stone: "philanthropy is the future of marketing, it's the way brands r [sic] going 2 [sic] win."[201] Not unlike her Patricia Arquette tweet, it drew controversy, as it positioned WWE's copious charity endeavors as cynical marketing opportunities. The tweet was sent out on the same day as *WrestleMania* weekend's Hall of Fame induction ceremony, where the first-ever Warrior Award (named in honor of the homophobic Ultimate Warrior, who had passed away just days after his own induction the year prior) would be presented to the family of wrestling fan Connor Michalek, who inspired WWE's pediatric cancer charity, Connor's Cure, after succumbing to the disease at the age of eight. McMahon did not express her own feelings toward the quote (retweets are not endorsements, etc.).

Another questionable charitable partnership is that between WWE and Susan G. Komen, which reaches a candy-colored sugar high during Breast Cancer Awareness Month in October. Komen has courted controversy by pulling (and then reinstating) funding to Planned Parenthood because it provides abortions, and because the amount of its annual contributions to breast cancer research have remained the same

---

200 @StephMcMahon, Twitter, March 15, 2018.

201 @StephMcMahon, Twitter, March 29, 2015.

despite a surge in donations and revenue.[202] Komen is one of the main perpetrators and beneficiaries of "pinkvertising": branding everything from fracking equipment[203] to products that contain known carcinogens[204] to wrestling ring ropes. Every October WWE and other male-dominated industries, such as the NFL (which donates 5 percent of the proceeds from its breast-cancer-branded merchandise toward finding a cure),[205] come out with all manner of pinkwashed paraphernalia in an attempt to raise awareness of the second-most-common cancer in women, which I personally think we're plenty aware of at this point. And because in the hetero-normative world of WWE breasts (and breast cancer) equal women, the company puts a particular focus on women during this time. For example, the first all-women pay-per-view *Evolution* occurred during October in 2018, and half of the questions in a WWE Fan Council (a collective of fans who are surveyed on their opinions about WWE) questionnaire about the event were about Komen.[206] And the range of Rise Above Breast Cancer merchandise has far more in women's sizes than it does in men's.[207]

In view of everything I've written about in this chapter and, indeed, the rest of this book, one cannot be surprised that WWE and the people who run it might see charity work as good press and nothing more. On the other hand, does it matter if WWE has ulterior motives if those in need of charity are benefiting from it? I can imagine McMahon's answer to that question.

---

202   Sharon Begley and Janet Roberts, "Insight: Komen Charity Under Microscope for Funding, Science," Reuters, February 8, 2012.

203   Jilly Daly, "Women's Health Advocates Denounce Komen Foundation's Partnership with Baker Hughes," *Pittsburgh Post-Gazette*, October 24, 2014.

204   Karuna Jaggar, "Komen Is Supposed to Be Curing Breast Cancer. So Why Is Its Pink Ribbon on So Many Carcinogenic Products?" *The Washington Post*, October 21, 2014.

205   Erin Gloria Ryan, "The NFL's Campaign Against Breast Cancer Is a Total Scam," *Jezebel*, October 11, 2012.

206   @newageamazon, Twitter, October 30, 2018.

207   Scarlett Harris, "Rise Above Pink," *Cageside Seats*, October 16, 2015.

I've been hard on AJ Lee throughout this book, but by using her voice in an attempt to enact change she undid some of the damaging rhetoric she spewed toward her female colleagues.

Lee wrote in her book, *Crazy Is My Superpower*, that she had tried to get more merchandise for women wrestlers, so it's obviously a sore point for her.

"I tried to pitch for my own merchandise, [but I was told] that 'women don't sell,'" she wrote, confirming that she was indeed the first woman wrestler to get her own merchandise since Trish Stratus at least as far back as the mid-2000s. "When they had considered giving a girl a hat as merchandise a few years earlier, the other women on the roster had complained so much, they scrapped the idea," which is symptomatic of the desire for the division as a whole wanting more: more opportunities, more money-making ventures, and more exposure, which it eventually received with the advent of *Total Divas* and the several fashion and beauty lines many women wrestlers are involved with now. "Since then they hadn't wanted the trouble and didn't think it was worth the backlash. Because 'women don't sell.'"

Indicative of the "there can only be one" mentality that governed wrestling, and many other male-dominated industries, until recently, those starving for opportunity of course are going to fight over the scraps thrown to them. Thanks in part to Lee, now most women on the roster have their own merchandise, but there are still problems, such as limited sizing, insufficient supply at live and international shows, unimaginative designs, and opaque production policies.[208,209]

Lee's tweet was one of her parting shots to the company, as she left WWE less than two months later, having achieved all that she could at that point, before the #DivasRevolution, and due to personal issues.[210]

---

208 Scarlett Harris, "A Dearth of Women's Merch for WWE Fans," *Paste*, February 22, 2017.

209 Harris, "Is WWE Finally Recognizing the Buying Power of Women and Girls?" *Racked*, September 11, 2017.

210 Lee's husband, CM Punk, had left WWE about a year prior and had been very vocal about his disdain for it.

She said she wanted to leave WWE having made it better for the women who came after her.[211]

"It was widely thought that not only did women not sell, but they couldn't get ratings either," Lee continued in her book.

Lee bucked that apparent trend, with her segments with Kaitlyn gaining some of the highest ratings in years. Nowadays, as traditional-television ratings trend downward because more people are watching on demand after the live broadcast, online, and on the WWE Network, women's wrestling segments routinely get millions of views on YouTube.

Given the monopoly her character held over the women's division during her tenure, Lee arguably couldn't have been a part of the women's wrestling evolution.

But that wasn't necessarily Lee's fault, as merely a player in a game[212] run by McMahon's family. Lee, along with sportswomen such as Ronda Rousey, Serena Williams, and the US women's soccer team, showed WWE that women could indeed sell.

Wrestling is built not on the natural athleticism of its sportspeople, but on implementing all the tools at the disposal of a juggernaut such as WWE to catapult them to stardom. Roman Reigns and John Cena are prime examples of this: WWE wanted them to be the face of the company throughout varying eras, so that's what they were going to be, whether the fans liked it or not.[213]

With this in mind, WWE shouldn't have needed a women's wrestling evolution or a women's sports evolution more broadly to invest in female performers; if it really wanted to, it could have made it a priority from the get-go.

Which is why it's so frustrating when McMahon says things like,

---

211　AJ Mendez Brooks, *Crazy Is My Superpower: How I Triumphed by Breaking Bones, Breaking Hearts and Breaking the Rules*, 2017.

212　Triple H's wrestling nickname is The Game, and his theme song has lyrics such as "It's all about the game, and how you play it."

213　Sometimes this happens organically and the fans' response is so loud that WWE has no choice but to give them what they want, as is evident in the meteoric rises of stars such as Stone Cold Steve Austin, Daniel Bryan, and Becky Lynch.

"We're pushing for *Evolution 2*."[214] Who's "we"? The people who run the company, of which you are one? Great, then make it happen.

Film and television critic Angelica Jade Bastién wrote[215] that corporate feminism like that exhibited by McMahon "isn't so much feminism but a shield that women of privilege use to hold on to the power they've garnered—even if it means undermining other women's concerns . . . to retain that power." Though McMahon wields far more power than her onetime foils and stars of *Total Divas*, they seem to subscribe to similar schools of feminism, such as marketplace and individual feminism.

But maybe it goes back to the ultimate power monger, McMahon's father, calling the shots at the end of the day.

McMahon said in a 2016 promo,[216] upon the return of Shane after a seven-year absence from WWE, that he was able to step in where he left off because he was a man, ignoring all the hard work that she had put in while he was away. Shane had talked about how his sons were the heirs to the family business, and McMahon reminded him that her three daughters, whom she frequently says in interviews are so lucky to see the women's wrestling evolution happening before their eyes, will have just as much right to be involved if they choose to. Though how much truth there was to the promo remains unclear (rumors of a rift between Shane and the rest of his family have persisted), it served as an affirmation of who controls WWE at the end of the day—Vince McMahon—and who is poised to take it over—Triple H, who, as a man, gets more credit for the women's evolution than the most powerful woman at the organization, despite her protestations—when Vince retires or dies, whichever comes first.[217]

Then again, maybe not.

---

214   Alex McCarthy, "Stephanie McMahon EXCLUSIVE: 'Pushing' for *Evolution 2*, WWE's Move to BT Sport in the UK and More," *Talk Sport*, December 18, 2019.

215   Angelica Jade Bastién, "*The Good Fight*'s Most Scathing Episode Yet," *Vulture*, April 14, 2020.

216   WWE, "Stephanie McMahon Finally Delivers Her Legacy of Excellence Award Speech" YouTube, February 29, 2016.

217   Vince McMahon is seventy-five years old at the time of publication and shows no signs of slowing down.

Rightly or wrongly, Stephanie McMahon has successfully branded herself as the fairy godmother of the women's wrestling evolution, calling to mind parallels to another controversial matriarch of the industry, The Fabulous Moolah.

This is never more evident than in Pat Laprade and Dan Murphy's book, *Sisterhood of the Squared Circle: The History and Rise of Women's Wrestling*, which, in its final sentence, describes McMahon thusly:

"The future of women's wrestling might very well be in her hands."

If nothing else, she's earned the title of chief brand officer.

8. WHO'S AFRAID OF INTERGENDER WRESTLING?

Content warning: *This chapter contains mentions of intimate partner violence (IPV) and transphobia.*

Women in WWE have come a long way, baby, from bra and panties matches to the main event of *WrestleMania*. But there can't be an examination of gender equality in WWE without discussing intergender wrestling, a controversial topic that never fails to divide fans.

An intergender wrestling match takes place between two or more people of different genders, usually someone who identifies as a woman and another who identifies as a man. It thrives on the independent wrestling scene and has enjoyed periods of popularity in WWE, mostly during the Attitude era of the late 1990s and early 2000s. Most wrestling fans within my progressive bubble are in favor of the match type, claiming that in a predetermined display of athleticism there should be no reason why people of different genders can't wrestle each other, and I agree. (I would even go so far as to say I don't see a reason for gender segregation in legitimate sports either if the competitors are of similar physical skills.) People on the other side of the argument believe that in a kayfabe world where supernatural dead men, leprechauns, and a literal Boogeyman exist, women holding their own against men in a wrestling ring is unrealistic and that intergender wrestling promotes intimate partner violence (IPV). The latter argument I will return to later. But if

Daniel Bryan is a credible threat to Brock Lesnar, surely Charlotte Flair can hang with Cesaro and Io Shirai can mix it up with Rey Mysterio.

While WWE has flirted with intergender wrestling again in recent years, it has usually been for one-off spots, such as Ronda Rousey manhandling Triple H in her debut wrestling match at *WrestleMania 34* or Zelina Vega surreptitiously pulling a hurricanrana on the male opponents of her client Andrade behind the referee's back.

In perhaps the biggest example of WWE's dalliance with intergender and a simultaneous callback to the Attitude era, when men and women would regularly face each other in the ring, Nia Jax became the first person to enter both the men's and women's Royal Rumble matches on the same night in 2019, attacking R-Truth and taking his final spot in the match. While sexist commentators Jerry "The King" Lawler (alleged statutory rapist[218] and intimate-partner batterer, though the charges were dropped[219]) and John "Bradshaw" Layfield didn't imbue Jax's entrance with the resonance it deserved, she held her own against the likes of Randy Orton, Dolph Ziggler, and Mysterio, all of whom are unequal to her in size and arguably strength.

It was then rumored that Jax would face Dean Ambrose in his final WWE match at *WrestleMania*, a version of which was floated for a house (nontelevised) show following their post-Rumble interactions; however, it and the subsequent '*Mania* dream match were quietly canceled, amid little fanfare.

Only three other women have entered the men's Royal Rumble match: Beth Phoenix, Kharma, and Chyna, who was the first woman to do so. Chyna was also the first woman to enter the King of the Ring tournament and to challenge for WWE's world (read: men's) title, as well as being the first and only woman to capture the Intercontinental championship, in a "good housekeeping match" that was rife with controversy and a telling example of the carny roots of wrestling.

The Intercontinental champion at the time was Jeff Jarrett, whose

---

218   David Bixenspan, "Jerry Lawler Wrote a Really Dumb Letter to Prosecutors in His 1993 Rape Case," *Deadspin*, February 13, 2018.

219   Maane Khatchatouria, "Jerry Lawler Suspended by WWE After Domestic Violence Arrest," *Variety*, June 17, 2016.

contract had apparently already expired prior to his scheduled defeat to Chyna. She wrote in her book that in agreeing to "do the job" (lose), Jarrett had politicked his way into a $300,000 payday for the match.[220] Jarrett's character had been growing increasingly misogynist in the lead-up, abusing his valets, Debra and Miss Kitty, as well as The Fabulous Moolah and Mae Young, who were seated at ringside during a *SmackDown* taping and got into an altercation with him.[221] Though Chyna eventually delivered Jarrett his comeuppance, the match actually fed into the regressive notions that surrounded it, in which household paraphernalia such as an ironing board and a kitchen sink—items synonymous with women's work in the home—were used to gain the victory.

This feminization of violence continued in women's matches. For example, Lita and Jacqueline—who was a cruiserweight (read again: men's) champion in her own right—pummeled each other with hair dryers and baking sheets alongside ladders and trashcans in a hardcore match for the women's championship in 2000. The hardcore match two years later between Trish Stratus and Victoria also featured the use of an ironing board, and a gilded mirror. A 2010 match was dubbed an "Extreme Makeover," which really says it all, doesn't it? It was as if WWE was letting these women compete against men or in traditionally male matches, but only if their rightful place in the home was signposted by such stereotypically feminine items.

Chyna's Intercontinental championship win was her last gender-barrier-breaking achievement, after which she was relegated to the women's division amid efforts to "feminize" her persona, like pairing her with Eddie Guerrero as his love interest and having her pose for *Playboy*. Furthermore, though women have always been sexualized in wrestling, the Attitude era presents a cognitive dissonance in which women wrestlers were sexually degraded on a regular basis but were also physically able to challenge their male colleagues.

After the Attitude era, efforts were made to separate women wrestlers

---

220 Joanie "Chyna" Laurer with Michael Angeli, *If They Only Knew*, 2001.

221 Pat Laprade and Dan Murphy, *Sisterhood of the Squared Circle: The History and Rise of Women's Wrestling*, 2017.

from men. Although previously male factions often had a female valet or sidekick, such as Lita to the Hardy Boyz and Ivory with Right to Censor, women were seldom seen interacting with men unless in a romantic storyline and were regularly pushed off the card altogether, resulting in scores of television shows and pay-per-views that had no women's matches at all.

Whereas the intergender matches of yore often crossed over into the bounds of exalting IPV (there's a horrific match from 2001 in which domestic batterer[222,223] Stone Cold Steve Austin relentlessly hits Lita with a steel hair, leaving her prostrate on top of her boyfriend, Matt Hardy, whom she was trying to protect), the one full-blown intergender match that has taken place in WWE in recent years was quite the opposite.

James Ellsworth was an unfortunate blight on women's wrestling history (he was later accused of sending nude photos to an underage girl, though never charged[224]). As manager to Carmella, Ellsworth had ingratiated himself into the first women's Money in the Bank match in 2017, climbing the ladder to retrieve a briefcase that held a championship contract for his client in yet another example of WWE's fumbling of the women's wrestling evolution. So much controversy ensued that WWE had to restage the match two weeks later, which resulted in Carmella rightfully capturing the briefcase herself.

Later that year, it seemed that the women of WWE—Becky Lynch especially—had had enough of Ellsworth, to the point where the first bona fide intergender match in five years was scheduled, in which Lynch wound up making quick work of Ellsworth.

The repeated digs at Ellsworth's manhood—and, in some cases, personhood, since he was referred to as an "it" and "not human" (calling

---

222 Gary Susman, "Stone Cold Surrenders on Wife-Beating Charge," *Entertainment Weekly*, August 14, 2002.

223 "Stone Cold Steve Austin Roughs Up Girlfriend," *The Smoking Gun*, March 29, 2004.

224 Shane O'Sullivan, "Exclusive: Evidence of James Ellsworth's Contact with Accuser," *Ringside News*, November 16, 2018.

to mind the dehumanization of another intergender competitor, Nicole Bass, whom I wrote about in Chapter 3)—were also counterintuitive to the women's wrestling evolution. If Ellsworth wasn't a "real man," did Lynch's victory over him mean anything?

In early 2018, WWE appeared to be making a push toward bringing back intergender wrestling. The *Mixed Match Challenge* was strictly mixed-gender wrestling, which is different from intergender in that although men and women team up, the wrestlers in the ring at any given time must be of the same gender; once a member of a different gender is tagged into the match, the opposing tag team's partner of the same gender must enter. It's clunky, but the *Mixed Match Challenge,* which took place on Facebook Watch instead of traditional WWE TV, was a way for WWE to test the intergender waters.

While many of the teams consisted of real-life romantic couplings, the relaxed format allowed wrestlers from the men's and women's divisions to collaborate in ways they normally wouldn't, including in intergender sequences. Charlotte Flair showed off her physical prowess by chest-chopping Rusev and putting the figure eight submission hold on Jimmy Uso. Uso's wife and partner in that match, Naomi, has said[225] that she thinks intergender wrestling is the next frontier in the women's evolution:

> "At this point, with the women being where they are and proving ourselves and wanting to be considered as equals in the company, you can't hold back in some areas and not in others. It would really make things equal. I think we can handle ourselves against the men."

Similarly ungainly to the *Mixed Match Challenge* was the mixed-gender match at *Extreme Rules* in 2019 between real-life couple Becky Lynch

225 So Catch by Hal 2, "Interview with WWE Superstar Naomi—I Have More to Prove [EN/FR]," YouTube, January 12, 2020.

and Seth Rollins and Baron Corbin and Lacey Evans. The bout was contested under the extreme rules from which the event took its name, which essentially means there are no rules . . . except when a person of a different gender tags into the match and their opponent is required to do the same. Makes (absolutely no) sense, right? But when Corbin violated these rules and pulled his finishing move, End of Days, on Lynch, the rapturous boos he was met with meant the sequence served its purpose: establishing Corbin as a heel, garnering sympathy and admiration for Lynch, and getting the fans invested in the match. Perhaps a little too invested, judging by the death threats Corbin[226] received.

These bright spots aside, intergender wrestling in WWE has mostly subsisted as it always has: as an occasional treat, not the main course. Due both to its move toward a more family-friendly product than that of the Attitude era and to the corporate sponsors that need placating, WWE is unlikely to bring back fully fledged intergender wrestling anytime soon.

Another reason could be that as the women's wrestling evolution continues, and women's wrestling receives more prestige, the women don't need to compete with men to prove their worth.

Paul "Triple H" Levesque, Ronda Rousey's sparring partner at *WrestleMania 34* and showrunner of *NXT*, where the women's wrestling evolution arguably began, has said as much:[227]

> "WWE's women Superstars don't need a man to make them successful in the ring. They don't need a man to step in the ring with them to make them have a spectacular match. . . . You know what makes a female empowered? When she is so good with another female in that ring that no man on that card can stand up to them."

I really enjoy being mansplained as to what women's empowerment is,

---

226 Felix Upton, "Baron Corbin Talks Death Threats After Hitting Becky Lynch with an End of Days," *Ringside News*, September 17, 2019.

227 Manny Tsigas, "Triple H: Will WWE Ever See Men and Women Wrestle Each-Other?" YouTube, October 4, 2018.

but I can see his point. However, isn't the ultimate equity of gender that which doesn't segregate by gender at all? If a man and a woman have similar skills and abilities, shouldn't they be able to compete against each other? No one wants to see a man twice a woman wrestler's size beat her bloody, but I don't really want to see two wrestlers of the same gender go at it like that either. However, when it comes to technical wrestling, there's no reason why wrestlers of different genders can't compare their skills in an athletic bout.

Jacqui Pratt, Ph.D, agrees. She wrote in the anthology *Women Love Wrestling*[228] that "gender-segregated wrestling may best be understood as a contemporary iteration of separate but equal: the false assertion of equality in a segregated environment," using the example of *Pro Wrestling Illustrated* magazine's yearly power rankings, for which male wrestlers have five hundred spots while women wrestlers get one hundred.[229]

Furthermore, professional wrestling is fake. It's a mutually agreed upon—between the wrestlers and, by extension, between the wrestlers and the audience—simulation of violence that in essence *can't* contribute to IPV. By breaking kayfabe and breaking down the elements of consent that go into a wrestling match, we are better able to understand, identify, and prevent IPV.

Claiming that intergender wrestling glorifies IPV further solidifies WWE's cis- and hetero-normativity, ignoring the existence of gender-diverse relationships and the reality that IPV occurs therein. As of this writing, WWE does not employ anyone who openly identifies as transgender or nonbinary. Apart from its ill-fated Billy and Chuck union and the hot-potato love affair between Lana and Liv Morgan, WWE is yet to have an empowering, realistic, and explicitly queer storyline.

Conveniently, anti-intergender proponents are rarely concerned with preventing *actual* intimate partner and gendered violence, as is evidenced by the number of wrestlers listed in this chapter who've perpetrated it. Unfortunately, the common consensus still seems to be that IPV is a private matter, and traditionalist fans sweeping it under the rug further

---

228 Jason Norris (ed.), *Women Love Wrestling: An Anthology on Women and Professional Wrestling*, 2020.

229 *The PWI Female 50* list was created in 2008, and renamed the *PWI Women's 100* with an additional fifty spots added in 2018.

perpetuate these damaging attitudes.

There are people within wrestling shining a light on IPV, though, and how it differs from intergender wrestling.

WWE and *NXT* wrestler Mia Yim has spoken about her time spent in an abusive relationship and how, because she had wrestled her partner before, she wasn't sure where wrestling ended and the abuse began. She told *HuffPost*[230] in 2016 when she was wrestling under the name Jade in *Impact* about how her partner had put her in a headlock. "When he finally let go, my then-boyfriend just left me there, and I'm wondering what the hell just happened. Was he legitimately trying to hurt me? Because it was a headlock, and we're both wrestlers, I justified it as maybe it was him trying to playfully end [the argument]," she said.

Yim is quick to point out how IPV and intergender wrestling, which she is a big proponent of and a participant in, are dissimilar, and to comment on the role of consent in wrestling overall.

"We choose to get in the ring. We're trained to keep ourselves and our opponents safe. But when someone brings it back home, that's not wrestling anymore. That is not entertainment. That is just straight abuse," she continued.

"I just wish that, as wrestlers, when we claim that this is going on, that we're not second-guessed, that we're believed. The minute we mention it, it's sensitive and we want some support."

As an ambassador for Safe Horizon's #PutTheNailInIt campaign to raise awareness of IPV by painting a fingernail purple, Yim further elaborated[231] on the struggle for women in sports such as wrestling to speak up about being victimized. "It's never easy to just leave. Once I finally got the strength to leave, I would talk to my close friends about what to do. Talking to them, I realized a lot of my friends had been

230 Brian Pacheco, "This Popular Female Wrestler Is Shattering the Silence Around the Domestic Abuse She Endured," *HuffPost*, August 1, 2016.

231 Byron Saxton, "Exclusive Q&A: How Mia Yim Overcame Hardships Inside and Outside the Ring," *Safe Horizons*, November 29, 2018.

through similar situations, but they never wanted to speak out because as female wrestlers, it made them feel that they need to have a strong image or that people wouldn't believe them because of the sport they are in," she said. "I wanted to tell the survivors that they are not alone and that it's [OK] to speak about it."

Yim's story conjures the notion of women's bodily autonomy. Abusers seek to take away the gains women have made in the last fifty years, by tampering with birth control, limiting contact with the victim's outside support network, and committing economic abuse such as controlling bank accounts and credit cards, just as examples. Physical violence is the most obvious example of this, and is something society is beginning to understand and take action against. For women wrestlers and other sportswomen, their bodies are their livelihood, and their abusers weaponize that against them.

Another woman wrestler and Safe Horizon ambassador is Charlotte Flair, who wrote about being in an abusive relationship in her book, *Second Nature.* She wrote about how her first husband exhibited what she now realizes were warning signs of the physical violence that would ensue, such as drug,[232] animal,[233] and economic abuse and possession of a firearm.[234]

"I acted like a 1950s TV housewife except that I was in my early twenties in the 2000s," Flair wrote. "I had my whole life ahead of me. I became a servant to my fiancé. There was never anything done with me in mind. My needs were never a concern. How did I end up in this environment filled with physical, emotional, and verbal abuse?"

Seeing that a pillar of the women's evolution and an outspoken advocate for gender equality such as Flair was a victim of IPV serves to shed light on the fact that anyone can be.

---

232 Jeffrey Juergens, "What Is Domestic Violence?" Addiction Center, June 18, 2020.

233 "The Link Between Cruelty to Animals and Violence Toward Humans," Animal Legal Defense Fund, n.d.

234 "Guns and Violence Against Women: America's Uniquely Lethal Intimate Partner Violence Problem," Every Town, October 17, 2019.

Many of Yim's and Flair's fellow *NXT* wrestlers are well-known for their intergender work on the independent wrestling scene. One such wrestler who comes to mind is Candice LeRae.

The legend of LeRae began in 2007 in the independent wrestling promotion Pro Wrestling Guerilla (PWG). The wrestler she had been valeting, Human Tornado, had been abusing her in storyline. They engaged in a feud that saw her simultaneously gain back her autonomy and her intergender wrestling chops, which she continued to sharpen over the next few years. In 2011, she challenged her future intergender tag team partner Joey Ryan—with whom she began partnering in 2013 as The World's Cutest Tag Team—for the PWG world championship.

Perhaps the most enduring image of LeRae's time on the indies is that of LeRae's crimson mask as she scored the winning pinfall to capture the PWG tag team titles in 2014, blood staining her blonde hair and white gear.

Since arriving in *NXT* in 2018, LeRae has been relegated to the role of concerned wife of Johnny Gargano, discouraging him from fighting his battles instead of fighting them for him: a far cry from the fearless intergender warrior described above who routinely outwrestled her real-life husband. Only after he left with an injury in late 2019 was she allowed to show just how tough she is. WWE and *NXT* likely won't let LeRae get as down and dirty with male wrestlers as she was once accustomed to, but portraying her as more than a wife and as the skilled (perhaps more so than her celebrated husband) wrestler she is will be a step in the right direction for gender equality.

In June 2020, LeRae put out a statement on Twitter[235] that read:

> "I am mortified. I absolutely DO NOT and never have condoned such horrible actions. I have zero tolerance for it."

---

235 @CandiceLeRae, Twitter, June 23, 2020.

She wasn't talking about the debate surrounding intergender wrestling but rather her former intergender tag team partner, Joey Ryan, who had been accused of rape by multiple women as part of the #SpeakingOut movement (he denies the charges).

#SpeakingOut was wrestling's #MeToo and it was a long time coming. Many of the people who were outed as abusers and predators were no surprise; their names had circulated throughout the whisper network in the industry by survivors who sought to keep others safe, and power brokers who swept their actions under the rug. Others were gut-wrenchingly disappointing revelations of people who hid in plain sight under cloaks of Nice Guy™ progressivism.

One such person was Ryan, with whom I was acquainted from my time working in an Australian wrestling company. Ryan was a big proponent of intergender wrestling—so much so that this chapter had originally included a quote from him—and I often maintained that he was one of the only wrestlers I've worked with who treated me like an actual human being and not a novelty, an inconvenience, or a novice. While I was initially perturbed by his sleazy wrestling character (a Facebook memory from exactly five years prior to allegations against Ryan broke in June 2020 shows me visibly unimpressed as I interviewed him in my on-screen role), his seemingly real personality couldn't have been further removed. Since then, Ryan continued his ascent, going viral later in 2015 with his move "the dick flip," in which he forced his opponent to grab his penis and used it to flip them. He also patented a move called "the boob plex," which entailed him grabbing his frequent female opponents' breasts from behind and suplexing them over his head. Many of these encounters were scripted to be nonconsensual within kayfabe.

You know what they say: when someone shows you who they are, believe them.

As mentioned above, wrestling is fake, and any risky moves have been agreed upon by the participants beforehand. They know that by stepping through the ropes they're putting their bodies, livelihoods, and sometimes their lives in the hands of their opponents. Therefore trust and consent are huge factors in professional wrestling, just as they are in relationships. More power to adults who consensually engage in BDSM, rough sex, and the like, but what Yim and Flair describe is unwanted, nonconsensual, and abusive. Good wrestling, like good relationships, is none of those things.

When wrestlers violate these rules they are met with swift repercussions, as happened in 2017 when Sexy Star allegedly deliberately injured her opponent, Rosemary, with an armbar at a AAA event in Mexico. " . . . if you take liberties with someone's body when they are giving it to you and trusting you to keep them safe . . . [y]ou are an asshole. And you don't belong in this business," Rosemary tweeted[236] after the incident. Star was rightfully ostracized from the industry for violating the chief tenet of wrestling, but it's interesting how many of her peers spoke out about her while they still work with people (mostly men) who violate consent outside of the ring.

If I can diverge from WWE for a moment, perhaps the best example of intergender wrestling in a modern, televised product is Yim's former *Impact* colleagues Tessa Blanchard and Sami Callihan's rivalry on the show.

In mid-2019, Blanchard came to the rescue of Scarlett Bordeaux (now also contracted to *NXT*), who was being victimized by Callihan and his merry band of henchmen, Madman Fulton and Dave and Jake Crist, who together make up the faction oVe (Ohio Versus Everything). When Callihan subsequently came looking for Blanchard in the women's locker room to settle the score, Blanchard told him he didn't belong there. "Kind of like [how] you didn't belong in the ring sticking your nose in my business," he retorted.

"In the ring, kicking your boys' ass is *exactly* where I belong," Blanchard said, providing a metacommentary not only on the women's

---

236 @WeAreRosemary, Twitter, August 28, 2017.

wrestling evolution but also on how, contrary to Triple H's comments earlier, intergender wrestling is the sport's logical next step.

"You want me to treat you as an equal?" Callihan taunted Blanchard as he and oVe attacked her with a baseball bat.

I was conflicted about this storyline, which became only messier as it went on. It established Blanchard as a viable threat and contender for the world championship, which she eventually won in her retribution match against Callihan. This was overshadowed by accusations of bullying and racism[237] against Blanchard on the eve of her win, which she has not apologized for, and has only doubled down on, sullying her historic achievement. And like many of the men mentioned here, Callihan has been accused of IPV outside of the ring.[238] In this instance, the lines between IPV and intergender wrestling are blurred: if Callihan doesn't treat his intimate partners with respect and, indeed, the equality he professed to Blanchard, why would he extend such a courtesy to a coworker whose job it is to get beaten up by him?

To posit another question: is this feud—and, by extension, intergender wrestling as a whole—damaging if the people involved are empowered by it? Blanchard's roster mate in *Impact* and fellow intergender performer Jordynne Grace has told me[239] that she finds intergender wrestling to be empowering to "both men and women." And, hearkening back to Yim's survival from IPV, Bolivia's *cholita* wrestlers are reclaiming their empowerment after escaping abusive relationships by wrestling men. Blanchard and Callihan's feud illustrates why intergender wrestling is so important: by normalizing it, we are less likely to see people of marginalized genders as fragile, in need of protection, and incapable of exacting violence ourselves. Instead, society begins to accept us in roles we're rarely allowed to occupy and thereby treat us with respect. And that's how we get gender equality: through society's realization that we can do anything men can do, for better or for worse.

---

237 Alfred Konuwa, "Tessa Blanchard Under Fire Amid Allegations of Racism, Bullying," *Forbes*, January 11, 2020.

238 "Sami Callihan Accused of Domestic Abuse," Reddit, 2017.

239 Scarlett Harris, "Intergender Wrestling Empowers Women by Pitting Them against the Guys," *A Beautiful Perspective*, November 1, 2018.

9. *HAIR BODY FACE:*

How Women Wrestlers
Use Their Appearance to Tell a Story

Content warning: *This chapter contains mentions of racism and intimate partner violence (IPV).*

There's a scene in the first episode of *Total Divas* in which "rookie Diva" Eva Marie is asked to dye her brown hair—accented with red highlights because it was the mid-2010s—blonde. Like in an act from a makeover installment of *America's Next Top Model*, Eva is unimpressed, as are her castmates.

"WWE wants everyone to stand out," Natalya reasons. "Eva Marie can't have dark brown hair because the Bellas have dark brown hair. But, hello? Natalya's blonde. I'm here, I'm right here; you have a blonde girl already."

Natalya's—Nattie for short—insecurities about her appearance are well documented throughout the series.

"I'm in a career where I'm in the spotlight and I feel like I have to look good at all times. There is this pressure to keep up with the Joneses in the beauty department," she said in an early episode.

More recently, Lana dyed her blonde hair pink in an attempt to stand out from the growing pool of flaxen-haired women wrestlers.

This hearkens back to a time in WWE when there were so few women vying for an elusive, pre-women's evolution spot on WWE TV that each was prescribed her very own number on the hair-color scale (which notably goes up only to ten).

Just as *Total Divas* was a driving force behind many aspects of the women's evolution, here the show served as the genesis of WWE's move from more naturally occurring hues to the rainbow that currently exists in the women's division.

Eva Marie ultimately eschewed blonde and went fire-engine red, a look that better exemplified her personality. "This is heat, this is fire, just like me," she said.

Since then, the majority of WWE's women wrestlers have followed in her footsteps, flirting with all manner of hues, from Becky Lynch's flame-evoking orange to Naomi's neon-green glow to Sasha Banks's wig reveal from purple to blue, which I will write about later.

In a rapidly expanding landscape, it makes sense for women wrestlers to try to differentiate themselves by any means necessary, and hair seems to be the most striking choice.

One could argue that in WWE, as in wider culture, there has always been an agreed-upon look. Women's wrestling gained mainstream attention in the 1980s through WWE's Rock 'n' Wrestling partnership with MTV, and *G.L.O.W.,* or *Gorgeous Ladies of Wrestling* (which inspired the Netflix series of the same name), which brought with it the gravity-defying tresses of the time. This gave way to the interchangeable blonde bombshells of the 1990s Attitude era and into the Divas era, with emphasis placed on how good they looked in a bikini rather than their wrestling skills or character development.

Perhaps one of the only women who managed to maintain individuality during this time was Lita, who wrote in her book, *Lita: A Less Traveled R.O.A.D.—The Reality of Amy Dumas,* that the Divas era "[took] away the individuality of the girls by lumping us all into one group. Everybody is their own character, but by making us all Divas, then the more people are going to look for similarities. Since the idea of Divas first started, I think the girls have gotten less unique . . . "

It is only since the women's wrestling evolution that the majority of women in WWE have had clearly defined characters. Previously women wrestlers' motivations would fluctuate from week to week, creating an interchangeable roster of wrestlers whose primary personality trait was being a woman. Gradients of hair color aid in differentiating female characters in the most stacked women's roster in WWE history.

Scott Lowe, in the *Hair* installment of the Object Lessons book series, wrote about hair as a dialect:

> "Human hair rules can be compared to languages, in that each option—shaving, trimming, styling, covering, dyeing—functions like a phoneme . . . [d]ifferent languages favor different phonemes and combine them in distinctive ways to form words and sentences that convey meaning . . . "

Some wrestlers have used this apparent hair-color mandate as part of their character work, such as Lynch and her orange hair reflecting her fiery fighter persona, Naomi's "glow" being incorporated in everything from her hair (she experimented with colors you would find in a packet of highlighters) to her light-up shoes, and Eva Marie's dye job turning her "evil and bitchy" according to Nikki Bella on *Total Divas*. Yet more often than not it's a case of stand out or fall behind.

There are some women who've beat what I like to call the "WWE Hair" trend. As far back as the 1990s, Luna Vachon and Bull Nakano challenged women's wrestling conventions. Nakano's gravity-defying mohawk of the time is an instantly recognizable iconography of wrestling. Vachon, meanwhile, experimented with shaving the sides of her head.

In the early 2000s, Molly Holly took this to the extreme. As a babyface, Holly sported blonde ringlets, but in 2002 she reinvented herself by chopping them off and going for an unassuming brunette bob, with a surly attitude to match. Furthermore, in 2004 Holly went so far as to volunteer to have her head shaved by her *WrestleMania XXX* opponent, Victoria, if it meant a women's championship match could get on the show. (One women's match—a *Playboy* evening gown match involving blonde quartet Sable, Torrie Wilson, Stacy Keibler, and Jackie Gayda, with Sable and Wilson teaming up against Keibler and Gayda— was already scheduled, and the consensus of the time was that that was more than enough women's wrestling for one night.)

"I was really devastated [about not being booked for *WrestleMania*], so I thought, 'I've got to come up with something that makes them change their minds," Holly said.[240] "I presented [my idea] to some of the writers and I said, 'I'm willing to shave my head. Can I please be on *WrestleMania*?' And sure enough they came back to me a couple of days later and said, 'Alright, we're gonna let you get your head shaved at *WrestleMania*.'"

It's a pretty searing indictment of WWE's attitude toward women's wrestling at the time (which continues today) that those who didn't fit the mold were given opportunities only by humiliating themselves at the altar of beauty that worships blondeness and curses all others.

In similar fashion, the short-lived on-screen[241] WWE career of Serena (who cites Molly Holly as inspiring her to get into wrestling[242]) began in 2010 when she posed as an audience member willing to pledge allegiance to the Straight Edge Society faction by having her head shaved in the ring.

While a woman with a chrome dome has yet to be seen in WWE since,[243] some women wrestlers have attempted to subvert the WWE Hair trend that has permeated the company since Holly and Serena.

One such wrestler is Ruby Riott, formerly Heidi Lovelace on the independent wrestling circuit. As Lovelace, she sported a punky, masculine undercut on one side and a sort of grown-out pixie cut that she let flop in her face on the other. This, matched with her copious piercings and tattoos and her unconventional wrestling gear of one long pant leg and one short, created a sort of haunted-rag-doll look. "I've tried to use makeup . . . as a form of expression . . . from tattoos to makeup to hair," she said.[244] Since signing with WWE in 2016 and

---

240 *Ring the Belle*, "Victoria and Molly Holly on WWE Return, Pitching WWE to Shave Head and Bleed | Top 5 Moments," YouTube, January 23, 2019.

241 She later became a trainer in *NXT*, between 2018 and 2020.

242 Pat Laprade and Dan Murphy, *Sisterhood of the Squared Circle: The History and Rise of Women's Wrestling*, 2017.

243 A Hair vs. Hair match between Sonya Deville and Mandy Rose was scheduled for *SummerSlam* in 2020; however, the stipulation was changed so that the loser, Deville, left WWE after her home was broken into by a stalker and she took time off.

244 WWE, "WWE Superstars Remove Their Makeup for a Candid Conversation," YouTube, March 12, 2020.

making her main-roster debut the following year, Riott has grown her hair to similar lengths and levels of lustrousness to her colleagues' (or has employed extensions), reinforcing her femininity.

Sarah Logan, Riott's former teammate in the Riott Squad, adopted a Viking-esque character and lifestyle, which extended to her hair. Vikings were believed to wear their hair in dreadlocks, as did Logan. Controversially, she turned her nose up at some fan art that depicted her, along with third Riott Squad member Liv Morgan, with long, flowing tresses in the style of most of her comrades. "My hair looks nothing like that," she commented on Instagram. While many were quick to condemn Logan, the wrestler has gone to great lengths (heh) to appear in a way that contravenes WWE Hair (and makeup, but more on that later).

Nikki Cross, also from the indies, who spent time in *NXT* as a deranged, one-dimensional asylum escapee as part of the group Sanity, let her mousy brown hair hang straight and wet. Since Cross debuted on the main roster and filled out her character development by tagging with Alexa Bliss, her tresses have appeared lustrous. Cross could never be described as ugly, but because the focus was on her crazy character and willingness to do daring stunts in *NXT* rather than on her looks, she was coded as such, or at least as existing outside the realm of beauty. Conversely, she now "takes care of herself"—that backhanded compliment plenty of people of marginalized genders who aren't conventionally attractive and/or thin have been on the receiving end of—and takes pride in her appearance; hence Cross is now presented as beautiful.

Sonya Deville's catchphrase is "put your hair up and square up," and she is one of the few women to do just that, tying her hair up to wrestle most of the time. She was also the first open lesbian in WWE. While the way Deville wears her hair is one method by which she demarcates herself from her colleagues, especially her former tag team partner Mandy Rose, who looks like she was created in a lab using the DNA of Divas of Wrestling's Past (and uses this to assert her dominance, putting down anyone who doesn't subscribe to this ideal), it could also be seen as a way of othering her due to her sexual identity.

Shayna Baszler, also a queer woman, favors a minimalist look that doesn't get in the way of her decimating her opponents.

Becky Lynch said[245] of her one-time opponent:

"It's not about looks. Yes, you need to have a unique look, and, of course, Shayna has that. And you have to have something about you—and Shayna has that, too. There is not a mold to fit into. Maybe that happened for a period of time in wrestling, but hiring people on how they looked was an unsuccessful period of time in wrestling."

Rhea Ripley, the Australian rising star who bested Baszler for her *NXT* women's championship in 2019, debuted as a fresh-faced, sun-kissed blonde in 2017. Ripley didn't find her niche until the following year, when she chopped off all her hair and took on a more gender-neutral disposition.

Lynch too began to wear her hair up to wrestle, since adopting the moniker of The Man. Lynch calls herself this because she has reached a level of fame and accomplishment previously achieved only by men. In a way, her alignment with masculinity could be perceived as supporting the age-old theory that being concerned with femininity is frivolous, while masculine pursuits are akin to success.

The rarity of women wrestlers putting their hair up and squaring up begs the question: why *aren't* the vast majority of women wrestlers in WWE doing this?

In a piece[246] for *Vox* about superheroines also wearing their hair down, Rebecca Jennings wrote that "to anyone with longer than shoulder-length hair who has played on a recreational soccer league as a kid, [this] seems nuts. Aren't these people, like, *fighting* each other? While doing flips and jumps and stuff?"

Christina Dokou, an assistant professor of American literature and culture at the University of Athens, Greece, is quoted in the piece as

245 Justin Barrasso, "Empty-Arena *WrestleMania* Doesn't Diminish Becky Lynch's Feud with Shayna Baszler," *Sports Illustrated*, March 30, 2020.

246 Rebecca Jennings, "Superheroes Don't Wear Ponytails, and Yes, It's Sexist," *Vox*, May 4, 2018.

boiling Jennings' observations down to the male gaze.

"The physical attributes and feminine beauty of superheroines are exaggerated to make them look like, well, frankly, porn stars at worst, and sexy female athletes at best," she said, which evokes WWE Hair.

This dichotomy between sexy hair and physical work is evident in the comic book character Harley Quinn, specifically her depictions in the films *Suicide Squad* (2016) and *Birds of Prey* (2020). In the former, male-directed film, her signature Bomb Pop pigtails are a tool of the male gaze, inferring both infantilization and pornification. In the latter, directed by Cathy Yan, she hacks them off as a postbreakup reclamation of self. In *Birds of Prey*'s instantly classic scene, Quinn hands her fellow *Bird of Prey* Black Canary a hair tie during the climactic fight sequence. Dr. Megan Mooney Taylor, an adjunct professor at Swinburne University of Technology in Melbourne, Australia, called[247] it an "act of support and understanding and, magnificently, sheer bloody practicality," while *Birds of Prey* screenwriter Christina Hodson said[248] she "wouldn't even consider eating a sandwich with [my] hair untied. So, yeah, it had to go in there."

It's something I wish I saw in wrestling more often.

If Deville, Lynch, et al. are subverting WWE Hair, then Bianca Belair leans so far into the notion of having a standout style that she fashions it as a weapon. Piling her hair high onto her head, Belair weaves it, with the help of extensions, into a plait that possesses the regalia of Rapunzel and the animation of Beyoncé's almost sentient braid, which Belair said inspired her.[249] (Google Queen Bey flicking it over her shoulder during one of her Formation World Tour shows, with it perching perfectly

247   Dr. Megan Mooney Taylor, "*Birds of Prey* (And the Fantabulous Emancipation of the Female Gaze)," *Overland*, February 24, 2020.

248   Brian Davids, "How *Birds of Prey* Writer Christina Hodson Crafted That Hair Tie Moment," *The Hollywood Reporter*, February 11, 2020.

249   Lilian Garcia, *Chasing Glory*, "Bianca Belair—Defeating Depression and Eating Disorders with Physical and Mental Strength," Apple Podcasts, February 18, 2019.

on the other side.) Flowing almost the length of her five-foot-seven frame and doing double duty as a whip, Belair's hair demonstrates the importance of creating a unique look (she sews her own ring gear) to underscore her incredible athleticism.

Belair is Black, and it's worth mentioning the enormous pressure Black women are under to wrestle (pun intended) their hair to fit Western beauty norms. One only has to look at Black women's hair in the news, from the US Army banning such hairstyles as Afros, twists, and dreadlocks in 2014 (although the restriction was lifted in 2017) to Black girls getting sent home from school for wearing their hair in these ways.

Naomi, who returned from a six-month absence in the third-annual women's Royal Rumble match in January 2020 sporting a bountiful Afro, has felt this pressure to conform.

"When I first started [wrestling] I had natural hair," she said.[250] "I was told, 'Hey, we want you to look like this,' and I was shown a picture of Naomi Campbell, a supermodel, who I look nothing alike [sic], but had contacts in and long hair, thirty-inch hair, you what I mean? And so, at the time I was so hungry and eager to not give anyone any reason not to book me, for me not to be on TV. So I feel like I had to conform, and I did for many years. When I came in [it] was the Divas era, and what we looked like was so much of our job at the time. That was focused on more than our actual talent at times."

Naomi's weave process has been documented on *Total Divas*.

It would appear that Black women wrestlers in WWE are *required* to adhere to the WWE Hair decree more so than non-Black women. Of the other Black women wrestlers on WWE's roster, few wear natural hairstyles on WWE TV. (A Black History Month photoshoot in 2020 of the Black women of *NXT* featured several women with natural hair, so this might be changing as young Black women challenge the status quo.) A roll call of those who have hair colors not their own supports this theory: Ember Moon (who's gone from silver to blue to red to purple hair), Sasha Banks (who has been vocal about her distaste for this

250 *AfterBuzz TV Wrestling & Sports*, "Women's Wrestling Weekly: Naomi Interview," YouTube, February 19, 2020.

process and frequently draws the ire of racist and sexist wrestling fans for not always having her roots done and edges laid), and Mia Yim (blue). Alicia Fox was perhaps the biggest proponent of this theory, seeming to have a different hairdo every week!

White and White-presenting women wrestlers such as Mandy Rose, Lacey Evans, and Taynara Conti have criticized Black women's hair, resulting in an uproar among woke wrestling Twitter. The system upholds their attitudes, being that they are three women afforded the ability to slot into the blonde wrestler archetype without having to conform to WWE Hair to stand out. Others, such as Alexa Bliss (who does wear the slightest of colored tips on the ends of her pigtails, in a style invoking Harley Quinn) and Charlotte Flair, who just happen to be two of the winningest women wrestlers of the evolution, indicate that despite there being a wider variety of women wrestlers—and, thus, hair colors—than ever before, the standard largely remains the same.

Though Black women—and non-Black women who've adopted the same Black traditions of extensions, weaves, and wigs that are the cornerstones of WWE Hair—spend a lot more time and money maintaining their looks (a Nielson study reports that Black consumers pay nearly nine times more for hair and beauty products than their non-Black counterparts[251]), most of these blondes achieve it from the bottle. This, plus time spent in the makeup chair and nail salon, adds hours to the extracurricular activities that are required of women wrestlers as compared with men. The only men I can think of who have donned anything close to what the women have to endure are Kofi Kingston, Xavier Woods, R-Truth, and No Way Jose (yes, that's his actual wrestling moniker). Not coincidentally, all of these men are Black. This "pink tax"[252] should be taken into account in the argument for equal pay, which is still sorely lacking in the wrestling industry.

---

251 Stephenetta (Isis) Harmon, "Black Consumers Spend Nine Times More In Hair & Beauty: Report," *Hype Hair,* February 26, 2018.

252 "Pink Tax," Wikipedia, last updated April 19, 2020.

If Eva Marie's rebellious red tresses heralded the beginning of the women's wrestling hairvolution, then Sasha Banks's wig reveal the night after *SummerSlam* in 2019 managed to parlay the superficial pastime of getting our hair did into one of the most iconic moments of the year. Not only that, but she also deconstructed WWE's apparent directive of women's hair color equaling archetypal personalities to signal her own change in personality and the importance of hair in the performance of wrestling overall.

As discussed in the following chapter, Banks was absent from WWE for four months, living her best life outside of the ring, traveling, relaxing, and trying out a multitude of hairdos.

It first appeared that Banks had decided to keep the grape-Jolly Rancher hue that saw her through the majority of her time in WWE when she burst back into the wrestling stratosphere that night in Toronto to interrupt Natalya tearfully talking about both her loss to Lynch the night before and her dad, wrestler Jim "The Anvil" Neidhart, who'd died suddenly a year prior and was also a Canadian hero.

But after surreptitiously hugging Natalya, Banks ripped off her purple wig to reveal a new blue 'do underneath while smashing a forearm into Nattie's face. The flame-haired Lynch came out to stop Banks's steel-chair attack on Lynch's opponent from the night before. After all, blue is the opposite of orange on the color wheel. Banks's wig reveal managed to fuse the deep roots that wig reveals have in drag culture (brought to the mainstream by *RuPaul's Drag Race*) and high-camp femininity with the wrestling staple of the heel turn.

Banks's former tag team partner Bayley wasn't far behind in her heel turn. It took a little longer for Bayley to match her facade—going from side ponytail to severe, blunt bob—to her comportment.

"As our storylines changed, our gear kept evolving too," Brie Bella wrote in her memoir with twin sister Nikki.[253] "When Nicole was out with her

---

253 Brie and Nicole Bella, *Incomparable*, 2020.

broken neck and Bryan was out with a concussion, I got into a storyline against Charlotte Flair, and I started to wear their clothing. I brought in Bryan's kickpads and Nicole's shorts, just to inject the whole thing with a little more emotion, to heighten our matches with everything that I had at stake—because Nicole and Bryan couldn't be there to fight too.[254] People knew I had their gear, and they would look for it out there in the ring. . . . Surprising, delighting and changing it up are key—in wrestling, you always have to evolve, whether that means a new look or becoming a heel."

Or sometimes both.

As Bella suggests, changes in style, not just of the hair variety, have long been the easiest way to visually signify changes in character or motivation.

For example, Lita got rid of her cool-girl cargo pants and fishnet tops in 2005 for attire better suited to the Vegas Strip and the "live sex celebrations" she was forced to participate in, as discussed earlier. Ivory adopted a white shirt and tie for her role in the conservative group Right to Censor. Mickie James got some actual wrestling gear—the questionable flared pants and halter tops she still wears today—instead of mall fare when she leveled up from Trish Stratus's stalker to serious wrestler in 2007. AJ Lee switched up her ring gear as often as she did her character, cycling through a tartan two-piece and a pantsuit for her role as general manager and denim cutoffs and Hot Topic-esque tees during her final run in WWE. We saw the beginnings of Alexa Bliss's current-day look when she ditched the glitter and tutus for Freddy Krueger cosplay in *NXT* in 2014. Kairi Sane went from a Harajuku kinderwhore-style—one that is popular among the sexualized *joshi*, or Japanese women wrestlers—pirate costume to a horror-movie villain in 2019, while her former tag team partner Io Shirai switched up her monotonous red shorts and top to a black Lycra bodysuit that conjured a sexy acrobat. Rhea Ripley competed in the first *Mae Young Classic* (*MYC*)—a wrestling tournament featuring women wrestlers from all over the world hosted by WWE—in 2017 wearing black booty shorts

---

254 Due to their respective neck injuries.

and a red top that showed off her cleavage, her frequent attire on the Australian independent scene. The *MYC* the following year saw a markedly different Ripley, in both demeanor and looks. In place of the shorts were black leather pants accented by jangling chains and a matching crop top that took the emphasis off her femininity. And though the beginning of Becky Lynch's storied style evolution wasn't to accompany a heel or 'face turn, it did signify an ascension of sorts. Lynch's match in *NXT* against Sasha Banks for the women's championship—for which she debuted her orange hair and an accompanying steampunk look—forced fans to see Lynch on a par with her Four Horsewomen stablemates, Banks, Charlotte Flair, and Bayley. Lynch explored versions of that gear for the next several years while simultaneously finding her footing on WWE's main roster, settling on variations of black pleather shorts and matching tops with fluctuating sleeve lengths.

She is perhaps best known, imagewise, for the moment she stood with her arms outstretched, broken nose streaming blood onto her generic blue *SmackDown* T-shirt, having led an invasion onto the opposing show *Raw*'s turf in late 2018.

Some women wrestlers were lucky enough to find their look early on. Banks's rotation of utilitarian boot covers and armbands made by her seamster husband gave her an edge. Flair adopted the iconic feather robe of her father, Ric, pretty soon after arriving on WWE's main roster. Bianca Belair makes her own gear. The bejewelled geisha mask and brightly colored, fur-lined kimono sported by Asuka is influenced by her Japanese heritage.

Banks and Bayley take the use of gear to chart their story to a whole different level, with Bayley switching to raggedy flags on her pants when she turned heel, in contrast to the carnivalesque blowup men and streamers that had accompanied her babyface veneer. Their gear as a tag team combined aspects of what each wore to face the other in their iconic match at *NXT Takeover: Brooklyn I* in 2015. As their relationship progressed to a feud once more, they wore variations of Bayley's victorious color scheme: silver and gold, making it that much more meaningful when Bayley inevitably turned on Banks. The two share a costume designer in Banks's husband, Sarath Ton, whose knowledge of their personal relationship injects a greater level of symbolism and foreshadowing into their gear, which can also be seen in Banks's army-print getup during her first two stints in the Hell in a Cell match, both of which she lost.

Less cryptic are Lacey Evans's boots and Dana Brooke's gear, both of which have been spoken about in backstage vignettes.[255,256,257] Evans puts letters from fans in her boots, which she had Lynch's face emblazoned on for the first women's match in Saudi Arabia, honoring the women's wrestling trailblazer, while Brooke wears a dumbbell embroidered on her top to memorialize her late boyfriend, bodybuilder Dallas McCarver. And Natalya and Ronda Rousey have paid tribute to Jim "The Anvil" Neidhart (Natalya's father) and "Rowdy" Roddy Piper, respectively, by wearing their jackets to the ring.

There also appears to be a burgeoning trend of wrestlers integrating superhero and other pop culture ephemera into their gear for special occasions such as *WrestleMania*, perhaps in an attempt to forge a connection with fans of those characters, or to go viral as real-life superheroes flying through the air, as those characters can only do in CGI. Alexa Bliss has cosplayed as Buzz Lightyear, Banks wore Wonder Woman's colors for the first women's Royal Rumble match, and Lana and Tegan Nox have both vied for Captain Marvel's attention.

On the other side of the looking glass, wrestling gear can be seen in mainstream media anywhere from Netflix's *GLOW* to *Project Runway* to *Dancing with the Stars*, where Nikki Bella finished a dance—replete in a red ball gown with cutouts that recalled her early wrestling gear—by body slamming her partner. As I wrote in Chapter 6, Nikki and her twin sister, Brie, are stars of the reality TV franchise *Total Divas* and *Total Bellas* and have their own clothing line, Birdiebee.

Others still are experimenting with their looks and their characters, but one thing's for sure: with the women's wrestling evolution comes a women's wrestling *gear* evolution.

---

255 WWE, "Lacey Evans Shows AJ Styles What She Keeps in Her Ring Boot: *WWE The Day of: Royal Rumble 2020*," YouTube, February 14, 2020.

256 *WWE The Day Of*, "Crown Jewel 2019," WWE Network, November 29, 2019.

257 WWE, "Dana Brooke Honors Her Late Boyfriend on *WWE 24*—Monday After *Raw* on WWE Network," YouTube, March 17, 2018.

The Attitude era was a dark time for women's wrestling. When women wrestlers were permitted to physically compete, actual wrestling gear made of television-ready materials that would support bodies and show off moves was rare. Instead the women were relegated to bikini competitions and lingerie, evening gown, and bra and panties matches, all of which involved wrestling in some form of undress.

But it wasn't always like that. Women's wrestling became popularized in the mid-1900s, with women such as Mildred Burke, June Byers, and the controversial Fabulous Moolah showing their physical prowess in the ring in the boy shorts and one-piece halter-cut styles of the time, into which they would sew shoelaces to tie around their thighs to keep them from riding up. (So maybe there's not that tenuous of a link between the sexualization of women's wrestling in later years . . . .)

It enjoyed another boom in the 1980s with the Rock 'n' Wrestling Connection period, the outrageous characters and outfits of women's wrestling fitting perfectly with the era. Picture Cyndi Lauper, who was a central figure in bringing wrestling to the masses, meets body slams.

The original *G.L.O.W.* also put focus on women in the industry and could be seen as the genesis of today's partnership between character and look. On the other hand, the cartoonish hijinks and lack of skilled wrestling arguably led to the cheapening of women's wrestling in the decades that followed.

Several women were able to break out of the mold as much for their unique style as for their wrestling ability. Chyna's dominatrix gear, encasing her rippling muscles, always strikes a chord with both wrestling fans and non. And Lita's initial fly-girl style, consisting of fishnet armbands and visible thong peeking out from her baggy pants, resonated with teen girls just as much as her top rope maneuvers and the fact that she could hang with the guys in the ring.

There's still a fraught relationship between the ghosts of women's wrestling's sexualized past and the present. Women may have main-evented *WrestleMania* in 2019, but storylines that same year saw Mandy Rose and Alexa Bliss in compromised positions regarding their clothes, or lack thereof. (Rose appeared in a towel, seducing another wrestler's husband, while Bliss was filmed getting dressed in a backstage segment.)

While that was going on stateside, WWE was preparing its first women's wrestling match in Saudi Arabia, between Natalya and Lacey Evans, in November of that year, as part of the kingdom's Vision 2030 partnership with WWE.

Natalya, who usually sports a latex bodysuit with sheer cutouts and sequins, and Evans, who favors a 1950s pinup getup, wore long-sleeved black tops and black leggings underneath oversized T-shirts, as mandated by the host country.

For the second women's match in Saudi Arabia, at 2020's *Super Showdown*, Bayley defended the *SmackDown* championship against Naomi in the company's first title match to take place in KSA. The competitors were still required to have their limbs covered; however, Bayley got away with a regular-fit T-shirt. Naomi's voluptuous figure was hidden by an even larger T-shirt, which Bayley used to tuck Naomi's legs under and secure the victory, in perhaps a covert statement against their rigid dress requirements.

Though Islamic dress stipulates that men also be clothed "modestly in loose garments that do not reveal what is between their navel and knees,"[258] male wrestler Ricochet decided to switch up his gear the same night that Naomi was put in a neon green sack, debuting trunks instead of his usual long tights.

Women's wrestling and women's wrestling gear are experiencing a twin evolution, fighting to be taken seriously in an industry that would prefer women look pretty, no matter how impractical, and, in the case of Saudi Arabia, like an unidentifiable blob if they must be there at all.

Wrestling gear needs to be able to complement the character and showcase the moves the wrestler is performing. For this reason, the majority of women wrestlers are still scantily clad. What's different from the bra and panties matches of yore is that though women's body parts may still be on display, it's for athleticism and functionality as opposed to simulated titillation, slaps, and hair pulling.

---

258   Abu Khadeejah Abdul-Wahid, "Understanding the Muslim Dress Code: Modesty for Men and the Hiba for Women (Islamd 4.5 & 4.6)," *Abukhadeejah.com*, October 19, 2017.

In September 2017, the corner of the web known as the Internet Wrestling Community (IWC) was abuzz when a male fan posted a photo with a makeup-free Alexa Bliss.[259] He captioned the picture with this little ditty: "For those who think Alexa Bliss is so hot is what she really look like [sic]."

Not only is this exemplary of the ugliest aspects of the IWC—not to mention the fact that he's plain wrong and Alexa Bliss is stunning with or without cosmetic enhancement—it also highlights the importance of makeup in wrestling. Wrestlers need to be able to emote so that fans seated in the rafters can understand what's going on in the ring just as well as those in the front row and watching on TV, and makeup serves to amplify this.

Though makeup has long been paramount for both male and female wrestlers, long before HDTV and brand endorsements, its presence was really felt in the 1980s, when WWE programming became syndicated and exploded into living rooms across America and the world. Wendi Richter wore the candy-colored eye shadow of the day, extending all the way up to her eyebrows. Larger-than-life Sensational Sherri Martel found inspiration in nature for the butterflies and spiderwebs on her lids. Japanese wrestler Bull Nakano sported blue lips that splintered down her face, mimicking the presence of veins under the skin. Nakano's former tag team partner Luna Vachon, who wouldn't have been out of place in the *Mad Max* Thunderdome, favored Lichtenberg figures across her cheek and up into her undercut, while maintaining more traditional makeup on the other side of her face, no doubt inspiring Chelsea Green's "Hot Mess" Jekyll and Hyde look thirty years later. Many of these women seemed wholly unconcerned with being sexually appealing, which was partly why they were all escorted out of WWE by the late 1990s and replaced with Sable and her aforementioned blonde-bombshell affectation.

Those who participated in the Attitude era were primarily positioned as beautiful, cosmetically (and often surgically) enhanced trophies. Occasionally women such as Chyna and Lita broke out of that mold.

---

259 @oldathers, Twitter, September 1, 2017.

While each had her own iconic look, they shared a penchant for the overplucked eyebrows and the chola lip look (despite neither being of Latinx descent) that littered my high school yard and the fashion magazines we traded therein.

Today, women wrestlers take to social media and *Total Divas* (which tag teamed with Total Intensity cosmetics for a co-branded partnership in 2016[260]) to share their makeup looks, realizing how a strong brow, lined eye, and bright lip can heighten the action and emotion in the ring. In the early days of the show, it was clear that none of the cast members knew how to do their makeup. (Eileen Sandoval is credited as a makeup artist in *Total Bellas* and later seasons of *Total Divas*.) Throughout the seasons, as the airbrushed faces of *Total Divas*'s E! channelmates the Kardashian-Jenners permeated culture, the Bellas, Nattie, et al. started to appear more like they do today. Scenes from the show portray Nattie, in particular, taking joy in experimenting with makeup on herself and others, whereas the COVID-19 pandemic exposed just how heavily others rely on professionals to maintain their look.

No fewer than four former *Total Divas* stars—Brie and Nikki Bella, Paige, and Eva Marie—have tried their manicured hand at being beauty entrepreneurs. Paige has her makeup line, Saraya Jade, and the woman mentioned at the outset of this chapter for ushering in the hairvolution, Eva Marie, was a one-time hair-extension mogul, selling a replica of her red hair through Bellami. The Bellas, in addition to running their fashion line, Birdiebee, are seeking to take over the wellness space with their beauty line, Nicole + Brizee, which sells hair, body, and pet products. Like Birdiebee's, Nicole + Brizee's website is spare when it comes to the ingredients they use and just how the line "empowers" women.

Their podcast[261] provides a little more information: "Our products are sustainable; some of them are recyclable. They help make a good change," said Nikki.

"The biggest goals I want for my companies . . . is to keep them

260 Gabi Duncan, "*Total Divas* Teams Up with Total Intensity to Launch a Cosmetics Line: Get the Scoop on Nikki Bella and Eva Marie's Makeup Looks," *E! Online*, February 3, 2016.

261 Brie and Nicole Bella, *The Bellas Podcast*, "V-Day Double Date with Property Brothers' Drew & Linda Scott," Apple Podcasts, February 12, 2020.

going more and more green," Brie continued. "You bet your ass that I'm going to try to get Nicole + Brizee . . . to have refillable [shampoo and conditioner] stands [in pharmacies]."

Just as there seems to be an edict for WWE Hair, the faces—or at least what they put on them—of women wrestlers have become increasingly homogenized, with most everyone sporting the same contoured cheekbones yet Vaseline-lens visages of what is known as "Instagram face."

New Yorker writer Jia Tolentino, who authored *Trick Mirror*, defines Instagram face thusly:[262]

> "It's a young face, of course, with poreless skin and plump, high cheekbones. It has catlike eyes and long, cartoonish lashes; it has a small, neat nose and full, lush lips. It looks at you coyly but blankly, as if its owner has taken half a Klonopin and is considering asking you for a private-jet ride to Coachella. The face is distinctly white but ambiguously ethnic—it suggests a National Geographic composite illustrating what Americans will look like in 2050, if every American of the future were to be a direct descendant of Kim Kardashian West, Bella Hadid, Emily Ratajkowski, and Kendall Jenner (who looks exactly like Emily Ratajkowski)."

Some women wrestlers, such as Paige and Carmella, have been open about getting injectables in their faces; however, the sameness of much of WWE's women's roster can likely be attributed to the Glam Squad, the collective name for WWE's backstage hair-and-makeup team. As of this writing, the Squad's Instagram page, where this assimilation could be seen in all its glory, had been deactivated.

On the other hand, a few women wrestlers have taken pains to distinguish themselves. Ronda Rousey frequently wore heavy—and

---

262 Jia Tolentino, "The Age of Instagram Face," *The New Yorker*, December 12, 2019.

heavily criticized—eye makeup akin to war paint during her one-year tenure with WWE. Bayley seemed to be saddled with Rousey's makeup artist upon her departure. Since she did away with her ponytail, which couched her in innocence and therefore made her immune from a lot of looks-based judgments, her severe bob and experimental eye makeup have coded her as ugly, like some of the aforementioned WWE Hair-abstaining women.

In addition to flaunting a maverick hairstyle, Sarah Logan bucked the system by refusing to wear makeup on TV, likely a first in WWE.

"I walked into Vince McMahon's office . . . and I said, 'I don't want to wear makeup anymore,'" she said.[263] "I don't think I need it. I don't think it adds to my character. I don't think it helps me as a talent in this company. And I don't like it on my face."

Conversely, others gain confidence for performing in the ring by wearing makeup, as Io Shirai has said.[264]

During her time in WWE, Logan[265] managed to win the zero-sum game that makeup can often be. "You're beautiful without makeup" and "What are you hiding under there?" are common refrains heard by people of marginalized genders who favor a more dramatic look. Yet when we do go au naturel—sans the makeup we wear to appear natural, resulting in a look that straight cisgender men so often think is makeup free—many of us are met with the ridicule Bliss faced.

Cosmetics have long been marketed to subjugate women and appeal to our insecurities, so there is some validity in the argument that makeup distracts from the athleticism in the ring.

My eye has certainly been drawn to the smudged red lipstick of Sasha Banks, Bianca Belair, and Lacey Evans during their time in *NXT*, indicating that the stay-put skills of the Glam Squad are a privilege reserved for the main roster. In other highly sexualized women's sports, such as the Legends (formerly Lingerie) Football League, flawless foundation,

---

263 Stefi Cohen, "Powerlifter Turned WWE Wrestler?! Ft. Sarah Logan," YouTube, March 8, 2019.

264 WWE, "WWE Superstars Remove Their Makeup for a Candid Conversation," YouTube, March 12, 2020.

265 She was let go from WWE in early 2020.

feathery lashes, and lined lips are of paramount importance, even at the expense of adequately protective headgear. (Competitors wear hockey helmets,[266] which obscure their faces less than a football helmet might.) In contrast, members of the US Women's National Soccer Team wear makeup on the field[267] not because their sport demands it, but because they want to.

Take a look at any woman wrestler in her element and you'll find she often has flawless claws to go along with her punches. As I wrote in Chapter 9, Mia Yim used her nails to make not only a statement in the ring, but also a political one, pairing beauty with activism as part of the #PutTheNailInIt campaign to end domestic violence.

"I started getting more and more support from people who knew what the campaign meant or asked why my nail was painted," she told *The HuffPost* in 2016.[268] "So, painting my nail became my secret way of telling the world 'I'm a survivor.'" Charlotte Flair is also a supporter of the cause.[269]

Through the perceived frivolity of clothes, makeup, and hair, women wrestlers are both subverting and conforming to long-held and evolving conventions about how they look doing what they do in the ring.

Some portions of this chapter appeared as part of "What Gear Can Do" in Contingent Magazine *and "In Professional Wrestling, Makeup Doesn't Just Make You Look Good" in* Racked. *Republished with permission.*

---

266   Jordan Ritter Conn, "The Lingerie Football Trap," *Grantland*, July 23, 2015.

267   Renee Jacques, "We're in Awe of the U.S. Women's Soccer Team's Sweatproof Makeup," *Allure*, June 26, 2015.

268   Brian Pacheco, "This Popular Female Wrestler Is Shattering the Silence Around the Domestic Abuse She Endured," *The HuffPost*, August 1, 2016.

269   @MsCharlotteWWE, Twitter, October 25, 2017.

10. THE FOUR HORSEWOMEN OF THE EVOLUTION

It's hard to pinpoint the exact moment in wrestling herstory when Sasha Banks, Bayley, Becky Lynch, and Charlotte Flair were crowned the Four Horsewomen of the industry.

Taking equal inspiration from the original 1980s stable the Four Horsemen, headed by Flair's father, Ric, and the group of mixed martial artists turned wrestlers consisting of Ronda Rousey, Shayna Baszler, Marina Shafir, and Jessamyn Duke, the Four Horsewomen of *NXT* seem to be first mentioned in mid-2015, when women's wrestling really started to experience its evolution.

"They were doing an article on us, and they were taking a picture, and I remember we all just put up the four [fingers] symbol, and we were just like, the Four Horsewomen," Banks said in a WWE Network documentary about the stable, which is no longer available.

"The reason this meant a lot to me was because this was real," Flair wrote in her 2017 memoir with her father, titled *Second Nature: The Legacy of Ric Flair and the Rise of Charlotte*. "No one said, 'let's package these women from *NXT* together and call them "the Four Horsewomen."' It was something that happened naturally through the fans admiring our work and contributions to wrestling. When I realized that, I couldn't have been prouder to hold up my hand with that familiar symbol with three women I admired. We all fought hard every night for the progression of women's wrestling and for it to be featured and appreciated in the same light as the men's."

Lynch, however, identifies the genesis of the Four Horsewomen as earlier that year. "I think the Four Horsewomen came about after our Fatal Fourway at *NXT Takeover* back in February," she said in the same documentary. "I think that was when we really cemented our place on the card."

For a roughly two-year period between 2013 and 2015, the Horsewomen honed their characters and helped *NXT* get to a level it is unlikely to reach again. They put on a series of barn-burning matches that punctuated their interconnected feuds.

Banks and Flair first encountered each other as part of the faction BFFs—Beautiful Fierce Females. Along with former WWE wrestler and *Total Divas* cast member Summer Rae, the two terrorized *NXT* in 2013, particularly Bayley. Later, Flair became a kind of mentor to Bayley, who proved herself to Flair as a worthy, if unsuccessful, contender to her *NXT* women's championship. Flair won the title in a tournament in May 2014 after it was vacated by Paige, who had graduated to the main roster of WWE and won the Divas championship on her first night! Simultaneously, Banks and Lynch were joining forces, and the four met in the aforementioned Fatal Fourway match at *NXT Takeover: Rival* in February 2015, a barometer-setting match in which Banks won the *NXT* women's championship from Flair by the skin of her teeth. As Lynch said, this is the match against which all the Horsewomen's subsequent bouts in *NXT* would be measured.

After Banks's championship win, relations between her and Lynch broke down, culminating in yet another match-of-the-year contender when Lynch challenged Banks for the title at *NXT Takeover: Unstoppable*, where Lynch debuted the fiery orange hair that has become synonymous with her relentless spirit. Ultimately, though, Lynch was unsuccessful in her quest to obtain gold. She remains the only Horsewoman to never hold the *NXT* women's championship, but as you will see, she has arguably become the most successful member of the group.

Next, Bayley tried her hand at Banks's title, challenging her at the first *NXT Takeover* to be held outside of the show's home base at Florida's Full Sail University, this time in Brooklyn as part of *SummerSlam* weekend in 2015.

Banks was coming into her own as a cocky heel, taunting Bayley for her role-model status among children and, thus, for being childlike herself. "I'm going to show all of these little girls [who look up to you] that fairy tales don't have a happy ending," Banks said.

Bayley was establishing herself as the ultimate underdog, sick of being underestimated by her peers, especially Banks. "I am going to prove to Sasha Banks that she was wrong about me, and I will defeat her," she said.

It's perhaps for these intertwined reasons, along with the real-life friendship between Banks and Bayley elevating the passion of the feud, that the match had that je ne sais quoi, signaling its specialness before it started.

It's also for these reasons that WWE made the wrong move in patronizingly billing it a "co-main event" (read: not the final and thus most important match), with the ladder match between Kevin Owens and Finn Bálor for the *NXT* men's championship hanging above the ring going on last, as was tradition. Owens acknowledged the mistake, calling the women's match a "tough act to follow" on a WWE Network documentary about the event.[270] Though he went on to say that he thought his match with Bálor couldn't have been better, it was clear that Owens was disappointed in his position on the card, with an emotionally spent crowd struggling to stay invested in the main event. By staging an inferior men's match last, what with their "women's evolution" and all, WWE executives seemed to be admitting they were scared women's wrestling wouldn't be a drawcard. They were wrong, with the match being named the best of the year by WWE.com, the first time a women's match ever ranked so highly. Many, myself included, call it the best match ever, regardless of gender, and frequently point to it as a beacon of the women's evolution and a clinic in in-ring psychology and storytelling in general.

The stakes were elevated even further when the rest of the Four Horsewomen came to the ring to congratulate Bayley as Banks skulked back into the squared circle to hug her successor and best friend. The four triumphantly raised their arms and four fingers in a bittersweet

---

270 "*WWE NXT Takeover Brooklyn*," *WWE 24*, WWE Network, October 5, 2015.

gesture that symbolized the end of their reign in *NXT*. Flair and Lynch advanced to the main roster the next night in a three-team elimination match that also featured Banks, who stayed in *NXT* another month to finish her feud with Bayley and challenge her to a rematch.

In a sportswomanly gesture on a following episode of *NXT*, Banks acknowledged that in Brooklyn, Bayley was the better woman. "That night, you were great," she said. "But that night only." The two contended that they now had even more to prove. For Bayley, it was that she could stay on top of the *NXT* women's division and retain her title, while Banks needed to earn back her title and her respect, the latter of which was the subtitle of the next *Takeover*, where they were scheduled to meet again for the women's championship in a thirty-minute Ironman match, with the wrestler with the most falls within that timeframe crowned the victor. This time, it would be in the main event.

The lead-up to *NXT Takeover: Respect* gave Banks and Bayley's match the credence it deserved, with promo videos of each woman upping her workout regimen and discussing her strategy. Or, as Banks said, "I don't need to tell you my strategy: you'll see it."

It would seem that Banks's blueprint was to combine ruthlessness with her continued mocking of Bayley's apparent innocence, this time through Bayley's young fan, Izzy, whose idolatry of the wrestler became an emblem of her fan base more broadly.

Izzy wore Bayley's purple "I'm a Hugger" T-shirt and her hair in a side ponytail, replete with a signature headband, as she cheered the new women's champion on from ringside. Given Izzy's prominent position, both physically and symbolically, Banks pulled an instantly iconic heel move by ripping the headband from Izzy's small skull and wearing it to taunt both Bayley and Izzy as the tween cried in her father's arms.

Banks apologized after the show, tears streaming down her face. She then made her ascent to the main roster, leaving Bayley to work on her legacy and lead the next generation of *NXT* women to greatness for the next year while Banks and Flair blazed a trail on the main roster.

Flair captured the Divas championship from Nikki Bella within the first two months of her main-roster tenure, subsequently turning heel and obtaining the services of her father and hype man, Ric.

Meanwhile, Banks and Lynch had fitful debuts in WWE proper, with Lynch feebly orbiting around Flair (which would later form the basis of their feud and Lynch's meteoric rise) while Banks was a blip on WWE TV until the *Royal Rumble* in early 2016. A series of matches and minifeuds among the triumvirate set up their triple-threat match for the new women's championship at *WrestleMania 32*, which Flair won, marking the change from calling women wrestlers Divas to, well, women wrestlers.

In mid-2016, WWE underwent a brand extension, meaning the roster would be split and wrestlers would work for only one of the company's two weekly shows: *Raw* or *SmackDown*. This turned out to be the best thing for Lynch, who was the first woman drafted to *SmackDown* and its first women's champion, while Flair and Banks headed up the *Raw* women's division. They traded back and forth the previously lone women's title (since renamed the *Raw* women's championship) in falls count anywhere and Ironman matches, as well as the first women's match inside the Hell in the Cell structure, which was also the first time women main-evented a main roster pay-per-view.

The brand extension also allowed other women wrestlers, such as Carmella, Alexa Bliss, and Nia Jax, to excel, widening the focus beyond the Horsewomen.

Shine theory[271] is a concept created by the cohosts of the podcast *Call Your Girlfriend*, Aminatou Sow and Ann Friedman. It posits that women are better as collaborators than competitors, and that there's more than one seat at the table. When one of your female friends is thriving, it inspires others to up their game too.

This might initially seem counterintuitive to the world of wrestling, especially in WWE, which has a hard time portraying women's friendships, which ultimately devolve into jealous cattiness (Alexa Bliss's

---

271 Ann Friedman and Aminatou Sow, *Shine Theory*, n.d.

mean-girl shtick is an example of this). As Lynch often says, "We're in the conflict business." But wrestling is also a counterfeit business, in that the fights are predetermined. It's not so much about who emerges the winner after the bell, but how the wrestlers involved in the match work to tell the story, thus elevating the performers.

"I came from team sports. And I knew what it meant to work together and the bond and dedication to sport," Flair, who had in 2017 begun calling herself "The Queen," said at "The Female Quotient" panel at 2019 SXSW Festival. "And being able to work with everyone, I think, is my gift. Being able to adapt to each player in the game. And go from there and hopefully lead by example in the ring. The ones that don't work with the others, they will fall off. This is a team effort even though it looks like individual Superstars. It takes an entire women's roster to get where we are."

That's why the Four Horsewomen work as a cohesive unit. When one excels, they all do.

Lynch echoes this sentiment. Though she wasn't familiar with the term when I interviewed[272] her in early 2019, everything she has said about her ascent is the apotheosis of shine theory.

For example, in late 2018[273] Lynch talked about feeling like she had to placate people for her achievements:

"The first time I won the *SmackDown* women's championship, I remember wanting everyone to be the champion. I want[ed] to build the division and I want[ed] everybody to do well. I was almost apologetic for my success."

Lynch went on to say that subsequent champions took their opportunities without concession or hesitation regardless of whether they'd earned it, which illustrates the struggle to balance reveling in your success with using it to inspire others, as shine theory encourages.

When I told her about this, she said that the Four Horsewomen are

---

272 Scarlett Harris, "No Apologies: A Conversation with Becky Lynch," *FanByte*, April 3, 2019.

273 Adam "Edge" Copeland and Jay "Christian" Reso, *E&C's Pod of Awesomeness*, "Becky Lynch Comes Around…," Omny, December 14, 2018.

all about shine theory:

> "Everybody wanted to see better from the other, instead of being competitive, you know? Everyone wanted to step up their game. Everybody wanted to have the best match, everybody wanted to have the best reactions, and that helps everybody step up, because nobody wants to be left behind. And that's the thing I say now—I think for a long time I used to dumb myself down because I didn't want to rock the boat or outshine anyone or make anybody feel uncomfortable. And then once I stopped doing that and was like, 'No, you wanna get on my level, come meet me up here,' I think it sparked a bit of a fire in everyone. And I think it's great! I love it."

This at once emphasizes celebrating others' achievements, which has been an emblem of the women's evolution, and expels the notion that the Four Horsewomen's position at the center of the women's wrestling evolution is exclusionary to others.

Alexa Bliss, who fell by the wayside during the Four Horsewomen's tenure in *NXT* and has since found more success on the main roster of WWE as a multitime triple-crown champion (winning all three women's belts), takes umbrage at the fact that the Horsewomen's contemporaries have been overlooked. "I wasn't featured as one of the Four Horsewomen; I wasn't chosen for that opportunity. I wasn't highlighted like the other women, but I was still there with all of them," she said on a WWE Network documentary about her in 2019.[274]

What Bliss gets wrong is that the Four Horsewomen were a natural formation, not a manufactured marketing tool. The only time before mid-2019, some four years after their configuration, that they were featured as a WWE-sanctioned cohesive unit in a storyline was during

---

274 "Alexa Bliss," *WWE 365*, WWE Network, June 23, 2019.

the "curtain call" after Bayley's *NXT* championship win at *Takeover: Brooklyn*. Though obviously Flair and Lynch were given the blessing to go to the ring to congratulate their friends, the reason why it was so emotional was because it was organic. "There are four girls who just have this undeniable chemistry," Flair acknowledged in the documentary about the group.

Their adulation is warranted. Flair is a natural athlete, taking to the wrestling business with the quickness. Bayley was one of the first women to emerge as a bona fide hero to children, in the vein of John Cena before her. Banks was perhaps the first woman in WWE to really break out with not only a deep character, but with the heel tactics and intense knowledge and appreciation of, and knack for, wrestling. And Lynch, well, I'll get to her.

What Bliss does accurately hit on, though, is a tendency to pit certain "kinds" of women against each other. In this case, it's the gifted women who make up the Four Horsewomen against most of the rest of the women's roster in WWE. "Serious wrestlers" versus those who came up through other industries, such as modeling, dance, and other sports. Never mind that Flair herself was one of these "other" women, having had experience in gymnastics, cheerleading, and college volleyball, and that she worked as a personal trainer prior to being signed to *NXT*. (On the other hand, Flair cops an equal amount of flak for being the daughter of one of the greatest wrestlers of all time, and thus having things "handed" to her, which I'll return to.)

This attitude is rampant online. In one corner are misogynist blank-avatar Twitter accounts spewing bile about how women's wrestling will never be on par with men's, and in the other is the group that represents toxic women's wrestling stan Twitter.

For those unfamiliar, "stan" comes from the 2000 Eminem song of the same name, in which the titular character loves the rapper so much he kills his pregnant girlfriend and then himself, inspired by Eminem's lyrics about abusing his own wife. Now the term is popularly recognized to mean loving a celebrity so much you would do anything for them, even kill—or, in the case of the late Japanese woman wrestler and *Terrace House* star Hana Kimura, encourage them to kill themselves.

Wrestling stan accounts often have handles and profile pictures consisting of the woman wrestlers they stan, and are in a constant battle with anyone who speaks ill of them. Think Beyoncé's Beyhive, or Nicki Minaj's Barbz. But this group also consists of people who want to take the opportunity to talk up their fave at any opportunity, often at the expense of other women wrestlers. For example, when a longtime champion finally loses her title, her stans will jump in to assert that she should always be on top of the division, despite the reality that such a monopoly would prevent other women from being given a chance. And when those other women are given a shot to run with the ball, stans of yet other women wrestlers pipe up with their reasoning why *their* favorite wrestler should be in that position, not yours, and so on and so forth. It's exhausting and perpetuates the idea that there can be only one or a handful of women wrestlers worthy of recognition.

A lot of these reactions are valid responses to what can be monotonous booking, but I think where stans go wrong is that they often direct their criticism at an individual woman wrestler rather than widening their argument to take aim at the patriarchal system of wrestling within which they operate. It is unlikely that frequent female champions keep racking up title reigns because of their politicking; more likely, they subscribe to a certain look that has mass-market appeal, or they are eloquent and toe the party line at press events. Just because a woman wrestler possesses these attributes doesn't mean she should be demonized for her prosperity.

But as the Horsewomen's somewhat unconventional characteristics— such as Lynch's Irish accent, which was rumored to be a barrier to her getting a push[275] (being a prominent character in a storyline/getting a title shot) and Bayley's and Banks' identities as women of color—attest, success in a primarily looks-based industry like professional wrestling can be attained by other methods, which may contribute to the chagrin of people like Bliss.

---

275 *PWMania* staff, "Becky Lynch Reacts to Rumors About Her Accent," *PWMania*, October 19, 2016.

Lynch has gone through many physical incarnations during her time in WWE, from a tartan-sporting Irish dancer to an orange-haired steampunk. Lynch's most iconic visage occurred by accident, leaving her bloody, bruised, and with a broken face.

The image of Lynch with her arms outstretched as she smugly surveyed the damage she hath wrought when she and her fellow *SmackDown* women wrestlers invaded *Raw* in the lead-up to 2018's *Survivor Series* event, blood streaming down her face and onto her blue, *SmackDown*-branded T-shirt was an instant classic. So much so that it launched a thousand memes, as Lynch became the talk of the business.

Much has been made about whether Lynch's rise was thanks to Nia Jax, whose stiff punch to Lynch's face caused Lynch to miss her scheduled match against Ronda Rousey at *Survivor Series*. "I just don't like her, to be honest with you," Lynch told me. "If she wants to sucker punch me, that's fine, but she's gonna get a receipt."

Or maybe it was the fact that, in Lynch missing the match, the anticipation for something that we couldn't have increased, almost immediately propelling it into the *WrestleMania* main event conversation, even though that show was five months away. "I was gonna find a way to get myself in the main event of *WrestleMania* one way or another," Lynch told me. "I'm out here making people actually care, actually give a damn, so that [women] have to be the main event at *WrestleMania*, that it's warranted, to make people want this as the main event more than anything else."

Either way, Lynch saw an opening to continue to be the most-talked-about thing in wrestling and did everything she could to remain in that position. "When I came [to WWE], that's what I said. I said I wanted to make *women's wrestling* cool," she admitted to me.

It all began in August 2018, when Lynch, who was riding a several-months-long undefeated streak, secured a match against Carmella for her *SmackDown* women's championship at *SummerSlam*. Flair had been out of action for several months by this point, tending to her sick father and getting her breast implants replaced. But she came back on the scene around that time and wanted what her best friend was having. By winning a nontitle match against Carmella, she was inserted into the *SummerSlam* title picture, making it a triple threat, with all three women competing at the same time. Flair emerged that night as a seven-time champion (tying the record with Trish Stratus), and Lynch embraced her in the ring before snapping and attacking Flair to raucous cheers from the crowd. Though this was supposed to be a heel turn for Lynch, fans including myself identified with her discontent at always playing second fiddle to Flair.

"There's always one at work . . . [who] gets handed absolutely everything," Lynch said to me. "There's folks here that are grinding and scratching and clawing, but she's always gonna get it, always gonna get the big matches, the press opportunities, the things that I have begged for for years. And of course she was fine with me being in the background and me not getting all those things, and then when I broke out, when I said enough is enough, then she had a *huge* problem with it, and then everything changed."

For the next several months, the two embarked on a feud for the ages, resulting in a Last Woman Standing bout at WWE's first all-women's pay-per-view, *Evolution*, in October 2018, a match that rivaled Bayley and Banks for best women's contest.

Like Bayley and Banks's initial *NXT* feud (their subsequent, main-roster feud, in 2017, was a disaster best scrubbed from our memories, but which I will write about later), Flair and Lynch's quarrel resonated so much because they have such a strong connection behind the scenes. It's easy to push the buttons of someone you know and love, which, in turn, adds passion to a feud.

The messaging surrounding Lynch's motivations for attacking Flair and ending their friendship echoed what she had said earlier about finally stepping up and taking her place in the spotlight. Lynch was ultimately able to vocalize some of her deep-seated resentments about her previous place in the women's wrestling canon, and it struck a nerve with fans who agreed. "I think everybody has that one friend, or that one person, who's just leeching, just taking everything they get, just leave you the scraps and expect you to be grateful," she mused. And thus, Lynch's trajectory from one of the underdogs of the Horsewomen (the other being Bayley, who has struggled to find her footing as a pure babyface on WWE's main roster) to arguably its most successful member was set in motion.

Though Lynch's one-on-one feud with Flair was all tied up at *Evolution*, Lynch just couldn't shake Flair, who found herself taking Lynch's place in the aforementioned match with Rousey at *Survivor Series*. Flair challenged for Lynch's *SmackDown* women's championship, along with Asuka, in a triple-threat TLC (tables, ladders, and chairs) match at the December 2018 event of the same name. The following month, Flair and Lynch emerged as the final two in the women's Royal Rumble match, which Lynch ultimately won and which put her in the *Raw* title picture against Ronda Rousey at *WrestleMania*. WWE kept insisting that you can't have a women's main event at *WrestleMania* without Flair, who was anointed a competitor in the match by Chairman Vince McMahon, while Lynch had to fight her way back into it at *Fastlane* in March 2019 in a desperate attempt to keep the storyline going till April. Finally, on March 25, it was confirmed that, for the first time, a women's match would close *WrestleMania 35*.

"You had this division by the neck for four years and you did nothing with it," Lynch said to Flair in the lead-up.[276] "Then I came along and now we're the main event of *WrestleMania*. So I don't think we need a Queen, never did. What we need is The Man."

Who's this "Man" Lynch is referring to? In mid-October of 2018, Lynch took to Twitter, where many of her best barbs take place, and simply wrote "I am the man,"[277] which later became her official, capitalized byname. "The Man" has historically been the person (usually of male

---

276 @KingNj90, Twitter, March 13, 2019.

277 @BeckyLynchWWE, Twitter, October 19, 2018.

gender) at the pinnacle of the industry, which she clearly was at that time, so why wouldn't she call herself that, Lynch's reasoning went.

And by that logic, she's absolutely right. Lynch is confronting the notion of who can be considered the best in a male-dominated industry and, thus, questioning gender norms more broadly.

"It make[s] people's minds explode, which is hilarious," she told me. Chief among them was Rousey.

"I certainly didn't pour my heart and soul into changing the meaning of 'fight like a girl' so the leader of the women's revolution could call herself The Man," Rousey seethed.[278] Though Rousey has long had an obsession with other people's gender identity and expression, this idea is worth unpacking.

Lynch has indisputably been the biggest name in wrestling, being the first woman to main event *WrestleMania* and make the cover of a WWE video game, as well as the first WWE wrestler ever to be the cover star of *ESPN* magazine. She was the first woman to step away from the ring due to pregnancy while being on top of the industry. Wouldn't it be even more subversive to challenge the power structure by coming up with a new sobriquet entirely? To take it a step farther, gender could also be taken out of the equation, with nonbinary nicknames taking the place of "The Man," "The Queen," and "The Goddess" (Alexa Bliss's appellation). As Lynch asserts, "It's not about gender; it's about being the top dog." But because professional wrestling operates within our White supremacist patriarchy, the best will always be a White man by default. Lynch has been known to pronounce that "The Man makes history every time I step into this ring." Except "The Man" doesn't, because there's little history left to be made by men. It's *been* made. If we consider Lynch the leader of the women's evolution—The Woman—she has made history. Discussions around Lynch's epithet *should* be about gender and changing the perception that the best is always going to be a White man and that assuming so buys into the very gender binary Lynch believes she's busting.

Lynch disagrees. "It's not about gender and it's not about belittling

278 WWE, "Ronda Rousey Rips into 'The Man,' Becky Lynch," YouTube, November 12, 2018.

women. I've been an advocate for women's wrestling since I started, since I was fifteen. I've always wanted to change the game; that's what I've been trying to do, and that's what I've *been* doing," she continued in our conversation.

It's also interesting that Lynch chose to call herself The Man when she is one of the few women wrestlers without a connection to famous men in the industry. Women such as Nikki Bella, AJ Lee, Nia Jax, Flair, and even Banks (whose cousin is frequent WWE collaborator and Hall of Fame member Snoop Dogg) have all had their male family members or romantic partners used against them as the reason for their success and have wielded it as a weapon themselves. Lynch (who has since become engaged to fellow wrestler Seth Rollins, who has things like "Mr Lynch" and "Becky's husband" chanted at him in a refreshing role reversal) was able to reclaim "The Man" as empowering, rather than the reason for her power.

This alignment with men—or The Man—has allowed Lynch to be one of the few women to bask in her accomplishments as a man would his: i.e., standing singularly and triumphantly in the middle of the ring at the close of *WrestleMania*. Tellingly, many of the defining moments of the women's evolution have been punctuated by public displays of shine theory—the curtain call, Bayley and Banks getting their flowers after their Ironman match, the whole women's roster coming out at the end of *Evolution* to congratulate one another—whereas men's accomplishments have not, which inherently others women's wrestling. On the other hand, celebrating the progress of women in an industry that encouraged infighting for the top spot because it detracted attention from the systemic inequality that claims that there could only be one is part of the evolution. It does beg the question, though: if the Four Horsewomen were four men, like Flair's father's faction before them, would I be exalting their friendship in this way?

"To be the man, you've got to beat the man" is Ric Flair's famous catchphrase, no doubt inspiring Lynch's adoption of the handle. Despite Charlotte Flair's enviable accomplishments (which I'll get to), she will always fall victim to the nepotism argument because of the success of her father.

For this reason and others, Flair exemplifies everything women's wrestling stans rally against: conventional beauty, didn't work the indies, famous lineage, copious title shots and exposure. Flair was the second woman ever to hold the *NXT* women's championship after only two years of wrestling experience, to which her Horsewoman compatriot Banks took exception.

Flair wrote in *Second Nature* that she and Banks connected over their shared dissatisfaction with their standing in *NXT*. "Sasha and I became close friends away from the cameras," she wrote. "The BFFs worked very well because it was real. We were both disappointed with where we were in the developmental program. That frustration created a bond between us. We felt that if we didn't do something, we'd be confined to being enhancement talent."

Like Lynch, Flair and Banks "both wanted to be the best," which Banks let get the better of her when it appeared that the powers that be thought Flair was worthier of that distinction.

"Sasha felt that she should've been crowned the *NXT* women's champion because of her talent and dedication and because she was more experienced than I was," Flair wrote. Banks used her feelings to fuel their subsequent feuds for both the *NXT* and *Raw* women's championships, the latter of which Flair prevented Banks from holding any longer than two weeks. (A wrestler who receives criticism akin to Flair's, Alexa Bliss, ended Banks's fourth *Raw* women's championship reign in similar fashion.)

It's often the best friends who make the best rivals, because they know each other so well—their insecurities, but also their strengths—as seen in the other variations of singles feuds between the Horsewomen. The opposite of love isn't hate, it's apathy, and judging by Banks's reaction to Flair's success, there are still a lot of feelings there that make wrestling magic between the two.

The rest of Flair's résumé reads thusly: she retired the Divas championship and was the first holder of the brand-spankin'-new WWE women's championship after the company transitioned out of the Divas era. She ended Asuka's two-and-a-half-year undefeated streak. She won the 2020 women's Royal Rumble match. She was the first woman, along with Lynch and Ronda Rousey, to main event *WrestleMania*, and as of this writing she is a twelve-time women's champion,[279] likely to usurp the record of sixteen world championships set by her father (yet another instance of a woman wrestler's legacy being tied up in that of a man's).

"I am the queen of selfishness. People say a lot about me, but what you see is what you get," Flair acknowledged.[280]

Flair might come from a privileged background, and she happens to look a lot like many of the women who came before her and those around her who continue to get pushes, but she backs it up. But again, even if she didn't, instead of castigating an individual woman who is wielding all the tools at her exposure to gain an upper hand in a patriarchal industry where she's unlikely to have any real power, we should be trying to dismantle the power structure that says there can be only one and even then she probably doesn't deserve her success.

I think that's why "The Man" grates on me. There's nothing progressive about endorsing a power structure where men are automatically the best and women never can be.

Lynch might have said that the women's wrestling evolution never needed a Queen, but out of character, Flair is never one to shy away from talking up her real-life best friend.

"Imagine a friend who has something that you have dreamed about your entire life, but you still give her advice and want her to have that position and success. That's true friendship. Even if I was getting pushed and Becky wasn't, she was there for me. I can't wait for the day when I get to repay her," Flair wrote in her book in 2017, before Lynch catapulted to the top of the industry.

"I cannot emphasize enough how important it is for women to support each other. Because when one of us succeeds, we all succeed,"

---

279 There is some consternation about this number, as she has won main-roster women's championships ten times and the *NXT* women's championship twice. WWE wasn't counting her first *NXT* title until Flair used the title shot she obtained by winning the Royal Rumble to challenge for the *NXT* women's championship, which she won at *WrestleMania 36*, and her record quickly jumped by two reigns.

280 AJ Brie Larson, "720pHD WWE *Smackdown* 09/03/19 Sasha Banks and Bayley Attack Charlotte Flair," YouTube, September 4, 2019.

she reiterated on the Quibi show *Fight Like a Girl.*[281]

Whereas Banks wasn't able to separate professional envy from personal resentment, Lynch and Flair combined their twin ambitions to support the theory of shine.

Shine theory is also at the root of Bayley and Banks's friendship. When Bayley ended her *NXT* women's championship run, dropping it to Asuka in 2016, she advanced to the main roster as Banks's surprise tag team partner against Flair and her partner, Dana Brooke, also an *NXT* rostermate of the Four Horsewomen, at the *Battleground* pay-per-view. Bayley did double duty in *NXT* for a few more months attempting to win her title back from Asuka, who was in the middle of her 914-day winning streak. Needless to say, Bayley was unsuccessful in her quest.

But this meant she was able to join Banks, Flair, and Lynch as the final Horsewoman in WWE's big leagues. Like Banks, Bayley challenged Flair for the *Raw* women's championship for the first few months of her tenure, winning it with an assist from bestie Banks in February 2017. The three then faced one another in a Fatal Fourway, along with Nia Jax, for the title at *WrestleMania 33*, Bayley's debut at the Super Bowl of wrestling.

Enter Alexa Bliss, who proceeded to make Bayley look like a juvenile fool in their subsequent feud while handing Banks her fourth women's championship defeat, within two weeks of winning it. Contrary to her above protestations, Bliss, though a fine athlete, is nowhere near the level of Banks and Bayley, but was scripted as superior to the two friends and holds the second-longest-combined *Raw* women's championship reigns, after Lynch, as of this writing.[282]

What was different about Bayley and Bliss's feud and Bayley and Banks's *NXT* storyline was that Banks took aim at Bayley's status as a hero to children and wrestling fans, perhaps out of jealousy, whereas Bliss

281 "Charlotte Flair and Emily," *Fight Like a Girl,* Quibi, April 16, 2020.

282 "List of WWE *Raw* Women's Champions," Wikipedia, last updated May 10, 2020.

made fun of Bayley's apparent inexperience with romantic relationships (Bayley is engaged IRL). Against Bliss, Bayley's goodness was a liability, causing her to hesitate in their kendo stick match and thus lose her championship rematch. This made both competitors appear weak and soured fans on Bayley, many of whom were already struggling to get behind a white-meat babyface who also happened to be a woman, while the rest lost faith in her for not being able to get the job done against the dastardly Bliss.

Though Bayley and Bliss aren't purported to be close friends (the tension between Bliss and Banks, however, is well-known), their storyline was one best forgotten and definitely not an example of shine theory.

This theme continued in Bayley and Banks's own narrative in WWE.

Their union as one-half of the Four Horsewomen was officially branded "The Boss 'n' Hug Connection," a poor play on The Rock and Mick Foley's "Rock 'n' Sock Connection" from the late 1990s, which itself was a "Rock 'n' Wrestling Connection" pun. Together they took on such other teams as Absolution (Mandy Rose and Sonya Deville, managed by Paige), but this was prematurely paused when Banks eliminated Bayley in the first women's Royal Rumble match in January 2018. Fans clamored for a match between the two at that year's *WrestleMania*, but they were disappointingly thrown in the obligatory preshow battle royal, a lower-stakes version of the Royal Rumble. Bayley got her revenge, however, and eliminated Banks from that match.

Tensions were rising between the former friends, who were sent to counseling to analyze their issues, which, if you'll remember Lynch's pronouncement, flies in the face of wrestling being a "conflict business" in which altercations are resolved in the ring.

Banks and Bayley hugged it out, their friendship back on track and viewers puzzled as to why they were even bickering to begin with. Contrary to their *NXT* feuds, this one seemed micromanaged and disingenuous, which is why it was received so poorly. When the Four Horsewomen are given minimal guidance and allowed to mine their personal connections for what feels honest to them, that is when their feuds connect the most.

There could only be one answer to Banks and Bayley's quick reformation: women's tag team championships.

With the creation of Absolution (renamed Fire and Desire when Paige took a step back from WWE to focus on other commitments), the Riott Squad, the IIconics, and Naomi and Asuka, the time for a championship for the women's tag team division seemed ripe. (There was gold for this division back when WWE was World Wrestling Federation and the titles were called the WWF Women's Tag Team Championships,[283] thus separating them from the new ones and allowing WWE to christen them the "first ever," which it loves to do.)

WWE's first all-women's pay-per-view, *Evolution*, was on the horizon, after all. But the majority of these teams were thrown into yet another battle royal, which usually serves as a way to get every woman on a traditional, dude-heavy show and has no business on an all-women show on which almost everyone should get a proper match. *Evolution* should have served as the perfect showcase for the crowning of the first women's tag team champions. What was the point of forcing the Boss 'n' Hug Connection back together if not for this?

The championships did finally come, in an Elimination Chamber match at the event of the same name in February 2019, almost a year after Banks and Bayley's initial main roster feud. By all accounts the Boss 'n' Hug Connection was largely responsible for getting WWE to put its support behind the women's tag team division, so it was only right that they be the inaugural champions.

"No one knows how hard we fought to get these," Banks said as she cried in the ring with Bayley upon their win. "If you guys legit only knew. We don't just do this for us. We do this for everyone in the back, this women's division. This is just the beginning of more change to come. Because we are here for a purpose, and we are going to continue to do what we love and do what we do best. That is why we are the Boss 'n' Hug Connection: your new WWE tag team women's champions."

The Boss 'n' Hug Connection took great pride in floating among WWE's three brands—*Raw, SmackDown,* and *NXT*—proclaiming to

---

283 "WWF Women's Tag Team Championship," Wikipedia, last updated March 30, 2020.

be fighting champions to all contenders. It was clear that there was a disconnect between what the champions wanted to do with their titles and WWE's own perception of them as low priority. This continued after their defeat at *WrestleMania 35* by the IIconics, who, as a comedy team, were perceived to diminish the titles' prestige and were pushed so far down the card that they seldom defended the belts in the time that they held them. It's not fair to blame the IIconics for the reemergence of a problem that the Boss 'n' Hug Connection had used their higher status to convince WWE to alleviate, if only briefly.

Banks retreated from wrestling in the months following her and Bayley's loss of the women's tag team titles at *WrestleMania*, allowing Bayley, perpetual horse girl and arguably the forgotten Horsewoman, to flourish on her own.

Bayley was no stranger to leading a locker room on her own, as she had done four years earlier when Banks, Lynch, and Flair were called up to the main roster as harbingers of the women's evolution.

"I try to be the best leader in the locker room that I can," Bayley said.[284] "I really enjoy helping and teaching. . . . It's a whole new level of learning when I'm able to help someone else out."

Sonya Deville has also affirmed Bayley's leadership skills. "She's someone you could go to for advice or if you have questions about how things work. . . . [S]he's definitely just a natural leader in the locker room," she said.[285]

From her own perspective, though, Bayley "felt very alone . . . I felt a little insecure," she said after Banks's departure.[286] "I had to snap out of it. I was like, 'What do you think you're going to do here if you sit here and feel sad or scared? You're just going to get walked all over.' So

---

284　Sam Roberts, *Sam Roberts Wrestling Podcast*, "Bayley," November 11, 2015.

285　LaToya Ferguson, "Fire and Desire's Sonya Deville 'Ain't Got Time for Hate,'" RondaRousey.com, February 14, 2020.

286　WWE, "Behind the Scenes of *WWE Stomping Grounds* with Bayley: *WWE Day Of*," YouTube, June 30, 2019.

I instantly had to change my mindset and the gears in my head, and I just had to freakin' go. I had to not stop, I had to not look back, and not think about the people [I was] leaving behind. 'Do not think about anything else. Just think about yourself for a change.'"

She moved from *Raw* to *SmackDown* during this time, quickly securing the Money in the Bank briefcase (containing a contract for a guaranteed championship match any time within the year of retrieving it from above the ring using a ladder) at the event of the same name in May 2019. Later in the night, Bayley cashed in her contract on Flair, who had only minutes before captured her record-setting ninth championship (until Flair herself broke that record when she won her tenth, also from Bayley) from Lynch. "I feel like I've started over. . . . I feel like I'm rewriting my own history," Bayley continued.

Despite the loss of Lynch's second title, demoting her from Becky Two Belts to Becky Red Belt (Bayley held the blue *SmackDown* women's championship), Lynch was still the most talked about person in wrestling. It seemed Banks's Four Horsewomen stablemates were doing fine without her.

The WWE women's division as a whole, though, was stagnating. Fans, myself included, had been agitating for Banks's return for months in lieu of Lynch's subpar challengers Natalya (who is an excellent wrestler and an icon and stalwart of women's wrestling, but who is lacking star power), Alexa Bliss, and the tiresome 1950s throwback housewife character Lacey Evans. So when Banks burst back into the wrestling stratosphere the night after *SummerSlam* in August 2019 to take out Nattie, it reignited the women's division and hailed the second wave of the women's evolution. Lynch, having developed respect for Nattie in their match the night prior, came to her rescue, meeting vicious chair shots from Banks for her efforts.

This same metal folding chair would be the weapon of choice for Bayley when she sided with her best friend and similarly attacked Lynch several weeks later. While Banks versus Lynch was set for the *Raw* women's championship at *Clash of Champions* in September 2019, Bayley versus Flair was taking place for the *SmackDown* women's championship at this event. What better way to raise the stakes of Flair and Bayley's match and indicate the first time the Four Horsewomen were enmeshed in parallel storylines than by turning Bayley heel?

As mentioned previously, in the age of the antihero, fans have a hard time supporting someone who is purely good. And as we saw with Lynch's character development from doormat to demigoddess of wrestling, it's far easier to connect with a multifaceted *human* than an outdated paragon of righteousness. Whereas Lynch wanted to break away from the attention-sucking Flair the year before, Bayley instead chose to stay by the side—and somewhat in the shadow of—Banks.

"Do you have a best friend?" Bayley asked a morning news host.[287] "Would you do anything for your best friend?"

"Of course," the newsreader replied.

In the romantic fables that litter the pop culture wasteland, women standing by their men are portrayed as the greatest expression of love, some more troublingly than others. By Boss 'n' Hug declaring their undying devotion to each other, they are declaring themselves the ultimate ride-or-dies and, thus, a glistening example of shine theory.

"I'm the hero, I'm the role model, and I'm trying to show your kids what it means to be loyal," Bayley said in explaining her actions,[288] perfectly encapsulating how the qualities that made her a fan favorite back in *NXT* have since turned sour.

Fellow wrestler and epochal good guy—until he wasn't—Sami Zayn likened his and, it could be inferred, Bayley's change of heart to a breakup.

"It's almost like when you're dating [someone], and [they] kind of have these quirks, but they're lovable," he said. "But once you break up, you're like [they were] so annoying! . . . The things you used to love about [them] now you hate about [them] because you don't love [them] anymore."

Bayley didn't abruptly do away with the inflatable men in her entrance or stop wearing her hair in a side ponytail (although she did eventually deflate the tube men and chop her hair off into a blunt, no-nonsense bob, leaving Flair the only Horsewoman who hasn't markedly evolved

---

287 @BayleyUpdates, Twitter, September 18, 2019.

288 WWE, "Bayley and Sasha Banks Make Charlotte Flair Their Latest Target" YouTube, September 3, 2019.

her look). But Bayley reserved her hugs for Banks.

As is evident throughout this chapter, Lynch has constantly encouraged her colleagues to meet her on her level, and that's what Banks, Flair, and Bayley have done.

Though not technically an illustration of shine theory, the Four Horsewomen's reformation as rivals for the first time on WWE's main roster in September 2019 exemplifies that although they might be fighting, they'll always do their best work together. Again, it's that passion and history, and the fact that they know each other so well. "Soul mates" is perhaps a better term for what these women are when they get in the ring, and for their connection outside of it. "We are connected, in the brain and the heart and the soul," Bayley said,[289] talking about Banks, but it could just as easily be applied to the rest of the Four Horsewomen of the women's wrestling evolution.

---

289 WWE, "Bayley & Sasha Banks Have Put Their Problems Behind Them" YouTube, July 30, 2018.

11. THE PROBLEM WITH RONDA ROUSEY

Content warning: *This chapter contains mentions of intimate partner violence (IPV), transphobia, and misogyny.*

As the timer counted down to reveal who would be the final entrant in the first-ever women's Royal Rumble match in January 2018 in Philadelphia, fans in attendance and internet pundits alike expected it to be the newly signed "Rowdy" Ronda Rousey.

The former Olympic judo competitor and MMA champion had transferred her athletic talents into a third career by joining WWE in late 2017. Rumors of Rousey's arrival in the company had swirled since the first women's version of the Royal Rumble match—a thirty-one-year tradition in which usually thirty participants, but sometimes forty or even fifty, attempt to throw one another over the top rope and out of the ring to earn a championship match at *WrestleMania*—was announced to much fanfare a month earlier. What would be more fitting than the woman who revolutionized combat sports making her debut during an event that signified one of the last remaining obstacles in the way of a full-blown women's wrestling evolution?

In fact, it wasn't Rousey who drew the thirtieth spot. When the timer reached zero, the giggle that begins the entrance music of legendary women's wrestler Trish Stratus crescendoed into Lil' Kim's vocal stylings as the seven-time women's champion made her way to the ring to a chorus of cheers. If Rousey wasn't taking the final slot, Stratus was perhaps the only woman who could have made the notoriously rabid Philly crowd forget its yearning for the former MMA champion.

But Rousey did make an appearance that night. After the undefeated Asuka eliminated Nikki Bella from the match in a frantic conclusion to earn a shot at the women's championship, her two possible opponents, *SmackDown* women's champion Charlotte Flair and *Raw* women's champion Alexa Bliss, who had been watching the match from ringside, approached the winner in the ring. In the closing moments of the show, as Asuka glanced from Flair to Bliss while considering which woman she would challenge at *WrestleMania*, she was interrupted by the opening chords of Joan Jett's "Bad Reputation" blasting over the Wells Fargo Center arena speakers. Wearing the late "Rowdy" Roddy Piper's oversized leather jacket, which was gifted to her by his son, Rousey strode to the ring to gate-crash Asuka's victory party and point at the *WrestleMania* sign—a tradition around that time of year—glowing above the ring. It would seem that Rousey, who had never had a wrestling match at that point, was indicating her intention to insert herself into the women's title picture on the grandest stage of them all, as wrestling fans fondly call the annual event.

Rousey ended up wrestling in a mixed tag team match at *WrestleMania* against Stephanie McMahon and Triple H, wrestlers and the real-life WWE executives responsible for luring Rousey to wrestling, with Olympic gold medallist Kurt Angle as her partner. However, the optics of her stealing the thunder of not just Asuka but also effectively the other women who had wrestled in the hour before she showed up and, indeed, throughout the history of women's wrestling, were skewed and ultimately reflected her rookie—and only, as of writing—year in WWE.

The common perception of Rousey's foray into women's wrestling is that she legitimized it. But perhaps a more apt statement is that Rousey got into sports entertainment *because* of the work done by countless women to legitimize it.

The mythology surrounding Rousey has always positioned her as the lone, superior woman athlete, rising above all others. *Rousey* was the first UFC women's champion and the first UFC women's bantamweight champion. *Rousey* was the first woman to headline a UFC pay-per-view. *Rousey* was the first woman to be inducted into the UFC Hall of Fame. It's an ideology she herself buys into: "I have this term for the kind of woman my mother raised me to not be, and I call it a Do Nothing Bitch," Rousey said in a 2015 UFC YouTube video.[290]

> "The kind of chick that just tries to be pretty and be taken care of by somebody else. . . . Just because my body was developed for a purpose other than fucking millionaires doesn't mean it's masculine. I think it's femininely badass as fuck, because there's not a single muscle in my body that isn't for a purpose, because I'm not a Do Nothing Bitch."

Rousey incorporated this sexist rhetoric into her storyline with Nikki Bella at WWE's all-women's pay-per-view *Evolution* in November 2018 for the *Raw* women's championship, which Rousey had held since August of that year, after wrestling for less than four months.

Even though *Evolution* was the first WWE-proper event to feature women-only matches (the *Mae Young Classic* preceded it, but took place in the same arena that WWE's minor-league program, *NXT*, emanates from, using many of the same wrestlers), it's plain to see that it was run by the same men who've been dictating the tastes of wrestling since time immemorial. The marketing for the milestone event took a back seat to WWE's Saudi Arabian show, which took place less than a week later and, notably, was men only, because women were not allowed to compete in the country at the time. What little buildup was done for *Evolution* bought into the age-old stereotypes about women in wrestling—and women more broadly—that many had fought to break

---

290 UFC—Ultimate Fighting Championship, "UFC 190 Embedded: Vlog Series–Episode 2," YouTube, July 29, 2015.

down in recent years.

In fact, the "breaking down" of barriers for women in sport is exactly what the narrative around Rousey and Bella's match encompassed. Bella "turned heel" (became a villain) on Rousey several weeks before *Evolution*, because Rousey "disregarded everything Nikki and I have done for this business," Nikki's twin, Brie, said in a promo.

The Bellas believed—and rightfully so—they didn't get enough credit for bringing about the women's wrestling revolution.

"It made me cringe to watch you at the forefront of this *evolution*," Nikki seethed. "I'm still trying to figure out why you're here. You're nothing but a loser who doesn't deserve it. You never deserved a title match, and you sure as hell don't deserve to be champion. I do. So let me give you a little history lesson. We made the word 'Diva' mean something. We and other women made Diva strong and powerful. Our hit reality show put more women and little girls in that crowd. . . . We made the world want to see women's wrestling even more. Ronda, you walked into an evolution that my sister and I started. I have done more in that ring than you will ever do. I am the longest-reigning Divas champion, and that means something."

Rousey retorted that Nikki was a "Do Nothing Bella": the kind of woman who used her looks and sexuality to get ahead instead of her talent, which was of "the absolute minimum amount."

This is the kind of slut-shaming that was prevalent in the Attitude era and has no place in wrestling now. With the increase in women and girls who are watching wrestling, as Bella noted, this is an unacceptable message to be sending to them and the men who internalize these messages about women and enact them in their own lives.

Bella didn't get much of a chance to get into the nitty-gritty of her so-called Bellalution and why she believed she and the women of her era were underestimated in the canon of women's wrestling on WWE programming. The following week's contract signing, the last segment to promote their feud before *Evolution*, consisted of Bella taunting Rousey about how ashamed her mother would be when "a Diva will beat you for your title," which didn't end up being the case. But Nikki was doing her darndest on social media and on TV, radio, and podcast interviews in the lead-up to *Evolution* to articulate the Bellalution.

"I'm here to remind people of [the history of the Divas championship, which preceded the current *Raw* and *SmackDown* women's championships]," she said on the *State of Combat with Brian Campbell* podcast.[291] "You want to discredit women who worked hard because of a butterfly on a championship that we didn't design? That's not OK with me. That's not empowering. I hope that after *Evolution* we can stop talking about 'Diva' being a bad word. My sister and I and the other *Total Divas* [cast members] are always like, 'Oh, we're sorry for giving you a hit reality show!'"

But while Bella was defending the women who had the misfortune of wrestling during a time when they were valued more for their looks than their athletic ability, Rousey was busy taking all the credit.

"Everything that the Divas era stood for made me sick to my stomach," Rousey said in the "Do Nothing Bellas" promo. "I tried to give you the benefit of the doubt: that you were just doing the best you could with what you had . . . [but] you are the embodiment of a stereotype. . . . You leeched off of the names of your men. You plagiarize and dilute their move sets. You're not pioneers, you're a callus. You're relics of the past waiting to be eviscerated like smallpox"—a misarticulation that Rousey herself was roundly eviscerated online for (smallpox is a disease to be *eradicated*, not *eviscerated*, and so concludes today's English lesson). "I will make the name Bella into a four-letter word that will be remembered as the societal sore it always has been."

When the Bellas defended themselves with the uninspired retort that Rousey was just jealous of their mainstream success and their pioneering role in breaking down barriers for women in wrestling, Rousey returned to the knocking-down-doors metaphor as she listed all of the career paths she chose to conquer: "I knocked down doors in judo. I knocked down doors in strikeforce. I knocked down doors in the UFC. And now I'm knocking down doors here at home in the WWE."

All of this may have been true in the *actual* competitive sports Rousey excelled in, where the aim of the game is to win, but wrestling

---

291 Brian Campbell, *State of Combat with Brian Campbell*, "WWE: Crown Jewel Criticism, *SmackDown* 1000…," Stitcher, October 17, 2018.

is about telling a story in the ring. And by definition this cannot be done alone. Wrestling can provide a place and a purpose for any and all women, from those who got into wrestling through modeling or other sports (the latter of which includes Rousey) to the "jobbers" (wrestlers destined to always lose to make their opponent look good) to those who have parlayed their wrestling careers into other industries.

But Rousey has never played well with other women. She is quick to slap a label on any woman she feels doesn't adhere to her stringent guidelines of what a woman should be (though she exempts the members of her Four Horsewomen of MMA group: two-time *NXT* women's champion Shayna Baszler, Jessamyn Duke, and Marina Shafir, who have all completed the transition to wrestling); they are the Do Nothing Bitches/Bellas, as established above.

They are the ring girls who use their bodies and sexuality to hype up the crowd between UFC fights. A handful of UFC ring girls have posed nude for *Playboy*, which Rousey doesn't like. "With all these ring girls and their vaginas—all of this goes back to advice my mom gave me," Rousey told *Tap Out Radio* in 2012.[292] "She gave me this one piece of advice, which I still hold dear. She said, 'Look, whatever pictures you put out there are gonna be out there forever, so just think that one day your twelve- or thirteen-year-old son or daughter is going to see those pictures. Whatever you want your son or daughter or even your thirteen-year-old little sister to see, keep that in mind.' So, whatever I'm not gonna show on a beach, I'm not gonna show in a magazine. These girls are going to have to explain to their kids one day why Mommy's ass and vagina are all over the place."

(I guess Rousey's 2016 *Sports Illustrated* swimsuit edition photoshoot, the infamously gratuitous cover of which her nude, body-paint-adorned form graces, is somehow different? She was on the beach in the shoot, so she was true to her word.)

---

292 Pedro Carrasco, "Ronda Rousey Reacts to Ring Girls in *Playboy* | They Will Have To Explain To Their Kids One Day (Explicit)," *BJPenn.com*, February 23, 2012.

It should be no surprise then that Rousey also abhors porn stars and celebrities with sex tapes, the most famous of whom is Kim Kardashian.

"I would beat the crap out of Kim Kardashian, actually," she said on the red carpet of the ESPY Awards in 2012.[293] "Any girl who is famous and idolized because she made a sex video with some guy and that's all that you're known for, 'Oh, I got my fame for sucking dick,' I think it's pretty stupid. Sorry, but it's true. . . . This girl should be selling lube or something like that instead."

Rousey is not shy about voicing her opinions on that topic, either, maligning women who use lubricant for sex as "gritty kitty bitches."[294] "You should never need lube in your life. If you need lube, then you're being lazy," she wrote ("wrote") in a 2015 *Maxim* advice column.

She's also a school-shooting skeptic, signal-boosting a since-deleted YouTube video questioning the veracity of the 2012 Sandy Hook massacre, which left twenty-six school children and teachers dead, in addition to the shooter, Adam Lanza, and his mother, Nancy Lanza.[295] She tweeted (also deleted) that the propaganda in the video was "extremely interesting" and "must watch." This, coupled with her penchant for doomsday-prepping and avoidance of "mainstream media,"[296] paints Rousey as a bit of a tinfoil-hat aficionada.

But whereas Rousey's preparation for the impending apocalypse doesn't really affect anyone other than herself and those sharing a bunker with her, her most egregious opinions—of which we've established there are many—are those about transgender athletes.

In 2013, Rousey endorsed comments by fellow mixed martial artist Matt Mitrione, who called transgender fighter Fallon Fox a "lying, sick, sociopathic, disgusting freak" who used her gender identity to

---

293   EsNews, "MMA Champ Ronda Rousey: I'd Beat the Crap Out of Kim Kardashian," YouTube, July 11, 2012.

294   UFC—Ultimate Fighting Championship, "UFC 193 Embedded: Vlog Series—Episode 1," YouTube, November 9, 2015.

295   McKinley Noble, "UFC Star Ronda Rousey Tweets 'Interesting' Sandy Hook Shooting Conspiracy Video," *Bleacher Report,* January 15, 2013.

296   @RondaRousey, Twitter, January 16, 2013.

beat up cisgender women.

"She can try hormones, chop her pecker off, but it's still the same bone structure a man has. It's an advantage. I don't think it's fair," Rousey told the *New York Post*.[297]

Fox took umbrage at Rousey's transphobia. "I mean her whole thing is like, 'Look at what I did. I was persistent. This is how I got women into the UFC. I didn't take no for an answer. I never stopped, and I rose to the top, and I convinced Dana [White, UFC president] because I was persistent,'" Fox said in a 2015 interview with *Jezebel*.[298] "But when I'm persistent? Yeah, when I'm persistent about transgender women they're like, 'You should just stop. Just go away don't even try to attempt it [sic].' Now Rousey is doing the gatekeeping."

Rousey prides herself on "doing the research":

"Asking questions . . . is more patriotic than blindly accepting what you're told," she tweeted in response to a fan who complimented her for promoting the Sandy Hook video.[299] In that case, she should know that bone density and muscle mass decrease in transgender women who undergo medical transition after a year of hormone therapy.[300]

Rousey should also know that being transgender is not a choice, but rather the way a person is born. But she insists on reinforcing that stereotype too.

"It's not something that happened to her," Rousey said about Fox. "It was a decision she made. What if she became UFC champion and we had a transgender women's champion? It's a very socially difficult situation."

Also socially difficult: Rousey's promotion of intimate partner violence

---

297   Marc Raimondi, "UFC Women's Champ Rousey Weighs In on Transgender Fighter Controversy," *New York Post*, August 10, 2013.

298   Katy Koonce and Susan Schorn, "'Fuck Moving On': Talking to Fallon Fox about Fair Fights, Ronda Rousey," *Jezebel*, July 29, 2015.

299   @RondaRousey, Twitter, January 16, 2013.

300   Steven Petrow, "Do Transgender Athletes Have an Unfair Advantage at the Olympics?" *Washington Post*, August 8, 2016.

(IPV). She bragged in her 2015 memoir, *My Fight/Your Fight*, about hitting her male partner when she was worried he would make public nude photos of her.

"I slapped him across the face so hard my hand hurt . . . " Rousey wrote, in partnership with coauthor Maria Burns-Ortiz. "I punched him in the face with a straight right, then a left hook. He staggered back and fell against the door. . . . I slapped him with my right hand. He still wouldn't move. Then I grabbed him by the neck of his hoodie, kneed him in the face and tossed him aside on the kitchen floor."

Rousey is, at the time of writing, married to Travis Browne, also an MMA fighter, who has had IPV allegations made against him by an ex-wife, though an independent investigation by the UFC found no evidence of this.

Given Rousey's outspokenness about about not wanting to fight transgender women, incorrectly likening their physiology to that of a cisgender man, it's confusing that Rousey has engaged in many intergender wrestling segments.

Intergender wrestling, which I wrote about at length in Chapter 9, is when competitors of different genders wrestle each other. In her first WWE match, the aforementioned mixed tag team bout at *WrestleMania 34*, Rousey backed Triple H into a corner with some punches, countered a kick with a judo maneuver, and hoisted him up onto her shoulders before Stephanie McMahon broke up the proceedings. This was after weeks of smaller-time intergender interactions with Triple H that included Rousey putting him through a table.

She's also attacked male security guards and fellow wrestler Baron Corbin and turned on her one-time tag team partner Kurt Angle.

Now, I can imagine you saying as you read this, "Doesn't this bitch know wrestling is fake?" Dudebros tweet similar rants at me whenever I write about Rousey or intergender wrestling on the internet. But, as evidenced by her reappropriation of her "Do Nothing Bitches" speech for a wrestling promo and her frequent boasting of her accomplishments in other sports, Rousey explicitly carries her real-life persona over into wrestling. Unlike pretty much every wrestler who has come before her, from Stone Cold Steve Austin to "The Boss" Sasha Banks, Rousey doesn't have a character that's distinct from her authentic personality. She deploys the same sobriquets—"Rowdy," "The Baddest Woman on the Planet"—that she did in UFC. Her opponents are seldom allowed to bring up her real-life MMA losses, which, given how she retreated from the sport and the public eye, as she would eventually do with wrestling as well, and went into another career following them, is a touchy subject and further evidence that her authentic personality is inextricably linked to her in-ring one.

This is why she couldn't resist bringing up gender in the lead-up to her match with Becky Lynch at *Survivor Series* in November 2018, which Lynch ultimately had to bow out of, after sustaining a broken nose and a concussion at the hands (or one hand, rather, formed into a stiff right hook, which is seldom used in professional wrestling) of Nia Jax.

Since putting to rest her feud with Charlotte Flair, Lynch had begun calling herself "The Man." This is because there is no female nomenclature for being at the pinnacle of the wrestling industry. But Rousey evidently saw this as an opening to shit on Lynch's masculinity and, thus, the masculinity of millennial men.

"Becky, you're so hypersensitive," Rousey said in a backstage promo. "You're not just 'The Man,' you're 'The Millennial Man.' You are the skinny jeans-wearing, V-neck sporting, avocado-toast-munching, wing-shoe-wearing Millennial Man, with a bubble wrapped ego and a porcelain self-perception. . . . Being offended doesn't make you right."

From there, Rousey continued to confuse gender with physical anatomy, accusing Lynch in multiple tweets of having "penis envy"[301,302] across the span of the buildup to their *WrestleMania* match. I might just be easily offended, but a noted transphobe accusing someone of having penis envy doesn't sit right with me.

As an aside, Rousey—who is two days younger than Lynch—is a

---

301 @RondaRousey, Twitter, November 20, 2018.

302 @RondaRousey, Twitter, March 1, 2019.

millennial. She crows about how she didn't wander aimlessly through jobs, unlike Lynch, who, after sustaining a head injury and leaving the industry, worked as a flight attendant, went to clown school, and turned to acting before refocusing on her true passion, wrestling, in 2012. But the flip side of the millennial coin is entitlement, which Rousey has benefited from in spades.

The bubble wrap began deflating when Rousey had her ass handed to her by Flair, who replaced Lynch in the *Survivor Series* match and beat Rousey black and blue with a kendo stick, because her fixation on what's in other people's skinny jeans was again showing. "You're not a man," she could be heard muttering to a heckling fan as she exited the arena.

As Fallon Fox inferred, Rousey doesn't play well with others.

This lone-wolf mentality was an asset in the individualistic sports of MMA and judo. I will concede that it is very unlikely that without Rousey women would have main-evented in the Octagon as early as she did, and certainly not with the same notoriety.

But she is not the only woman at the forefront of the women's revolution in sport. Serena Williams has been grand-slamming in tennis since the nineties. The US Women's National Soccer Team medaled in every Olympics between 1996 and 2012. In 2017 the women's national hockey team succeeded in receiving equal pay after winning the World Cup. And, as Nikki Bella said, there was a long line of women who paved the way for Rousey to make wrestling her third sport.

Though professional wrestling is not technically a sport, nor a team one at that, it is an industry that relies on everyone playing their part in the story to make whoever is on top of the mountain look good. For the better part of 2018, Rousey was the one erecting her flag at the summit, but the time to let someone else stake that claim came in the main event of *WrestleMania 35* in 2019, the first time women closed the biggest show in wrestling.

It also marked the end of Rousey's illustrious rookie year in WWE.

Rousey had long spoken of her desire to start a family, and come *WrestleMania*, she would pass the torch to Lynch as she retired to her farm.

Given what we know of Rousey, it's no surprise she didn't go down without a fight. In the months leading up to her *WrestleMania* match with Lynch for the *Raw* women's championship, Rousey fumbled her words as the crowd began to turn on her in favor of Lynch, who oozed charisma and self-assuredness both in in-ring promos and on social media. In further evidence that Rousey's wrestling "character" wasn't so much a character as it was a version of herself, it was plain to see she could not handle the souring of the fans. As a decorated professional sportsperson, Rousey was used to being adored by the masses except for when, you know, she wasn't, as in her previous sport. Hmm, what's the common denominator in these equations?

Lynch was "arrested" for showing up on *Raw* and attacking Rousey, violating her suspension from WWE in an effort to keep building up to the big match. (Funnily enough, I was supposed to interview Lynch for a profile the following day; however, it was canceled in order to keep kayfabe alive!). Rousey retaliated by accusing Lynch of "taking fake prison photos in the hallway"[303] and watering down the importance of their match.

"Fuck 'em. Fuck everybody. WWE Universe included," she said on her travel vlog *Ronda on the Road*.[304] "I'm going to disrespect the sport they all love so much.

"*Oh, don't break kayfabe Ronda*," she continued in a mocking tone. "Wrestling is scripted, it's made up, it's not real. None of those bitches can fucking touch me. The end."

Wrestling fans aren't always the smartest, but we are under no illusions that the fights taking place are legitimate. It was notable that Rousey got away with calling wrestling fake, because this has long been believed to be the biggest insult to the business one could possibly espouse. There was no need for Rousey to preface her inevitable loss

---

303 @RondaRousey, Twitter, February 28, 2019.

304 Ronda Rousey, "*Ronda on the Road* | WWE *RAW* Philadelphia," YouTube, March 7, 2019.

with this. If anything, it signified that the unsportswomanlike behavior that had followed her throughout her career had led her to an industry in which she could influence the outcome using her mainstream clout, because she clearly couldn't handle it being left up to chance and her once-enviable skills.

When the time came for Rousey to "do the job" (lose), she awkwardly kept one shoulder up from the crucifix pin that Lynch surprisingly won the match and both women's championships with (as mentioned in the previous chapter, Charlotte Flair and the *SmackDown* women's championship were needlessly added to the match in the months and weeks before in an attempt to keep the storyline going). Is it any wonder that someone who had never been booked to take a pinfall during her career would inevitably flub it?

Rousey, looking visibly pissed, nursing a broken pinky finger and her dignity, exited the arena. "A backstage interview?"[305] she questioned as someone approached her for comment after the match. "To promote what? It's already over."

This offhand dismissal reflects the attitude that Rousey developed over the course of her monopoly of the women's division during her time in WWE. The other women whom I've written about throughout this book laid the foundation for the women's wrestling evolution, which was then falsely attributed to Rousey. Therefore her unceremonious departure should have allowed other women to step into the spotlight, but what it ended up doing was taking with it WWE's faith and investment in a division that fell by the wayside.

---

305 Ronda Rousey, "*Ronda on the Road | WrestleMania 35*," YouTube, April 13, 2019.

Epilogue:

WE STILL NEED A REVOLUTION

On April 7, 2019, the stars aligned so that *WrestleMania* was in my favorite city—(technically New Jersey, but billed as being in the shadow of) New York—the year I was able to save up enough money to tick off every wrestling fan's ultimate bucket-list item, something that I had never thought would be remotely possible up until a few years prior.

I'd grown up watching the "Super Bowl of wrestling" crisscross North America, traveling to a different city every year. The first time I watched "the granddaddy of them all" (another telling nod to the patriarchal structure of wrestling) was in 2002, when it emanated from Toronto. I remember the tiny red maple leaf emblazoned on hometown heroine Trish Stratus's white booty shorts. I remember Stephanie McMahon's shimmery turquoise—the fabric du jour that adorned shopping-mall windows of the era—jumpsuit and her crimped hair as she tried to interfere in the main event, the closest a woman had ever gotten to the final match at that point, and for many years after. I remember Mighty Molly Holly (who, you'll recall, shaved her head in order to get on the card two years later) being one of the only women to win the Hardcore championship, if only for a portion of the night, and Stacy Keibler in her signature role of distracting eye candy, wiggling her butt at Jeff Hardy to divert his attention during a tag team match.

Though the evening featured just one women's match (albeit two women champions), it was surprisingly better than many of the *WrestleMania*s that followed. Over the following sixteen years, women wrestlers were thrown into a chaotic battle royal that was won by a man (Santino Marella as his problematic drag "sister," Santina Marella), engaged in *Playboy* pillow fights and evening gown matches, and were denied the opportunity to wrestle for the division's top prize, the Divas championship for seven orbits of the Earth around the sun.

But it just so happened that the year I got to attend my first *WrestleMania* was the same year that for the first time in three and a half decades, women wrestlers would close the show by fighting for a proper championship in a serious match for which they were able to wear their regular wrestling gear.

The last time *WrestleMania* was in MetLife stadium, six years prior, for the twenty-ninth installment, the only women's match scheduled— the Bella Twins and the Funkadactyls (Naomi and Cameron) were partnered with men in a mixed tag bout—was canceled lest the show run over schedule. Not coincidentally, that was the first *WrestleMania* I watched after a few years away from wrestling. Though I didn't realize it at the time, this was likely the catalyst for my dogged pursuit of equality for women in the industry. Everything was brought full circle for me as I watched a warm afternoon turn to an overcast and chilly night in East Rutherford.

It all started with the punch heard 'round the world when Nia Jax knocked Becky Lynch, who was scheduled to wrestle Ronda Rousey in the upcoming champion-versus-champion match at *Survivor Series* in November 2018, unconscious, breaking her nose and forcing her to miss the match. Rousey and Lynch continued to spite each other over the coming months, going at it on Twitter and Rousey costing Lynch her title at *TLC* in December 2018. Lynch won the Royal Rumble match the following month, putting her in contention for a women's championship match of her choosing, and she immediately called out Rousey for her *Raw* women's championship at *WrestleMania*.

Repeated references were made to this match being the main event of *WrestleMania* months even before it was made official, two weeks out from the actual event, the same day I arrived in New York in anticipation that it would be.

But what of the other women's championship, Asuka's *SmackDown* title, heading into *WrestleMania*? On March 26, Charlotte Flair had won her eighth women's championship, from Asuka, usurping a previously advertised match in which Naomi, Carmella, Mandy Rose, and Sonya Deville were to compete in a Fatal Fourway to become the number-one contender to the title at *WrestleMania*. Instead, all competitors were relegated to the now-annual preshow battle royal that was originally named after alleged sex trafficker The Fabulous Moolah, while both singles women's titles would be featured in the main event, with a winner-take-all stipulation.

Many defended the move by arguing that adding the *SmackDown* women's championship to the match raised the stakes. But the first women's main event of *WrestleMania* is high stakes by virtue of it being *the first women's main event of WrestleMania*! There was no need to add the only other singles women's championship to the match and snuff out the progress of the rest of the division.

It was also special because Becky Lynch was able to do what only a handful of people (read: men) had done before, which was to create such a buzz that she was the only choice to close *WrestleMania*, by finally besting Ronda Rousey, who, let's face it, was always going to be a part of that conversation regardless of whether she had paid her dues, as so many of the women wrestlers who came before her had.

By shoehorning Flair (which became her nickname for a time) into the match, along with a second title and the winner-takes-all clause, WWE clearly demonstrated that it was unable to see what the rest of us did: that the chemistry between Lynch and Rousey and the crowd reaction that had been bubbling up around them was all the match needed. Instead, what we got was this: too many cooks in the kitchen and a screwy finish in which Rousey had her shoulder off the mat when Lynch pinned her to win in an upset that we knew was coming but was absent of the pomp and circumstance usually reserved for main event wins.

The swindling of the *SmackDown* women's division in the lead-up to *WrestleMania* indicated that WWE saw the women's main event of *WrestleMania* as the end of the women's wrestling evolution. The absence of an *Evolution 2* and *Mae Young Classic 3* and the bone throw of allowing women to wrestle in Saudi Arabia are further evidence of that: *Women are equal now, what more do you want?* And if we've learned anything throughout the course of this book it's that if WWE says the evolution is over, then it's over.

But was there ever really an evolution if only a select few of the species—those deemed genetically superior, as Flair was initially marketed as, which is troubling considering they're all cisgender, able-bodied White women—were able to evolve to the status that has been afforded to men?

"Tonight an evolution will be complete," Michael Cole, lead WWE commentator, actually did say. But that's not how evolution works.

In order for there to be a women's wrestling evolution, we have to acknowledge women's wrestling history. As poet and essayist Mairead Small Staid wrote[306] in *The Ringer* ahead of *Evolution*, "There's a blank space where the past should be." I hope I've shed light on some of the dark past of women's wrestling in this book.

We also have to confront that past. Lest we think women's wrestling has come so far from the days of little-to-no women's matches at *WrestleMania*, we should be mindful of the fact that in 2019 we may have gotten the first women's main event, but there was only one other women's bout on the main card, for the women's tag team championships. Granted, it included eight women, increasing the number of women competitors from six the year prior, which actually featured three women's matches on the main card (one of which was a mixed-gender tag match).

Though the women's wrestling evolution of WWE began in response

---

306 Mairead Small Staid, "Does WWE Really Want a Revolution?" *The Ringer*, October 5, 2018.

to the short match discussed in the prologue, the measure of its success should not just be quantity, but quality.[307] High-quality matches and storylines that showcase the plentiful skills of WWE's women wrestlers and get fans invested. More opportunities inside and outside the ring for women wrestlers who aren't White, blonde, straight, cisgender, slim, conventionally attractive, and able-bodied. Quotas in place to insure equal representation and remuneration. And, finally, recognition that the women's wrestling evolution is far from complete, and a commitment to seeing it reach the next stage.

"What do you do when all your dreams come true?" Lynch asked[308] in the *WWE 24* documentary episode about her journey to the main event of *WrestleMania 35*. Though on a smaller scale, my dreams also came true on the night of *WrestleMania 35*. I was able to witness history being made, as WWE so often likes to tout.

But for some reason I felt empty after getting the *WrestleMania* women's main event I had yearned for for so long, and disillusioned for months after by the state of WWE's women's division.

As it turns out, so did Banks, my OTWP (one true wrestling pairing), who left WWE for several months after *WrestleMania 35*. "Wrestling saved my life, and it felt like [wrestling] was destroying it, so I wanted to take a step back and figure out what the problem was," she said[309] of her return, which, not coincidentally, brought me back to the sport.

"I've only known this . . . . I've only watched this . . . . So all I know is this," she continued. "And I had to rediscover new things. . . . I love wrestling, but this is not always going to be here."

Though I have many varied interests (I've been told that I have too many), I empathized with Banks. When it appeared that the second

---

307   Charlotte Flair said in 2020 that "fighting for airtime is a weekly thing." Girl Up, "#SportsForAPurpose: Media Coverage in Sports Virtual Panel," YouTube, April 14, 2020.

308   "Becky Lynch: The Man," *WWE 24*, WWE Network, May 19, 2019.

309   "Sasha Banks," *WWE Chronicle*, WWE Network, September 14, 2019.

wave of the women's wrestling evolution that I'd invested so much in was not imminent after *WrestleMania 35*, I took a little break from wrestling. I was tired. Not only physically, from six uninterrupted days of watching wrestling, including the eight-hour outdoors spectacle that is *WrestleMania*—by far the most wrestling consumed in succession in this introverted homebody's life—but also emotionally. I was still following developments on social media, but I was tired of fighting so passionately for something for the better part of five years to so little avail.

So, like Banks, I laid low and took stock.

Lynch and Banks are two sides of the same coin and, it just so happens, two sides of the inspiration wall I have in my bathroom: Bloody Becky and a rendering of Banks's aforementioned return, a smug smile on her face as she looks back on the fire she lit under the women's division, not unlike the meme of a smirking girl standing in front of a burning house. These portraits, made by cover artist Lauren Moran, may be an odd choice for a vanity decoration, but like some people might hang affirmations or beauty inspiration, I display these women's visages to remind me to never give up.

Banks's vision of her future may have been blurry after she achieved all of her goals, but Lynch was able to look toward her next target from the vantage point of the top of the industry.

"That happiness, that contentment really is the worst thing in the world for somebody like me. I can't be happy. I always have to be fighting. I always have to be fighting against something," she continued.

"A lot of people's goal is 'I just want to be happy.' Well, that's just an emotion, that's fleeting. You've gotta chase the things that mean something to you," Lynch said.[310] "And for me, it's defending this title, making this business the coolest thing on TV, it's making my matches must-see. And that to me feels purposeful, and that is more important than happiness. Having a purpose and going after it. Because you're not always going to be happy. You're gonna be miserable a lot of the time in that [pursuit], but it's gonna have meaning and it's gonna have a greater purpose than just being happy. It might inspire somebody. It might change the course of history, which is what's happened."

I strongly identify with Lynch's trajectory from someone with potential who was ultimately overlooked to a fed-up trailblazer, so hearing Lynch say something similar solidified just how much of a woman after my own heart she is.

And so the fight begins again.

I signed the contract for this book a week before the final pay-per-view of 2019, *TLC*, which women, specifically Flair, Lynch, Asuka, and Kairi Sane, main-evented for the second year in a row.[311] It was serendipitous to close out the most revolutionary decade in women's wrestling history—one that began with an untelevised women's battle royal (and the televised match between Mickie James and Michelle McCool lasted twenty seconds[312])—with the women's tag team titles, an emblem for forward movement in the division.

There were four women's matches in the two-day, empty-arena version of *WrestleMania* the following year, just a few weeks after the COVID-19 pandemic changed life as we knew it. Several weeks after that, Lynch forfeited her *Raw* women's championship due to pregnancy rather than losing it in a match, going out on top as the longest-reigning women's champion of the modern era.

---

310   WWE, "Live Becky Lynch Interview About Her Impressive 2019 & More: WWE Now," YouTube, n.d.

311   Three of whom—Lynch, Flair, and Asuka—were in both matches.

312   James was being referred to with the unfortunate nickname of "Piggy James" at that point.

The women's wrestling evolution is not over because WWE says it is. As long as wrestling is a male-dominated industry in a patriarchal society, there will always be room for evolution. From bra and panties to the pinnacle of the industry; the green room to the main event; a Diva to a wrestler. And that will be truly revolutionary.

A SYLLABUS OF WOMEN'S WRESTLING

Unladylike: A Grrrl's Guide to Wrestling by Heather Bandenburg, Unbound Digital, 2019.

Banner Days by Penny Banner with Gerry Hostetler Banner, Flying Mare Publications, 2004.

Incomparable by Brie and Nikki Bella with Elise Loehnen, Gallery Books, 2020.

Lita: A Less Traveled R.O.A.D.—The Reality of Amy Dumas by Amy "Lita" Dumas with Michael Krugman, World Wrestling Entertainment and Pocket Books, 2003.

The Fabulous Moolah: First Goddess of the Squared Circle by Lillian Ellison with Larry Platt, Regan Books, 2002.

An Encyclopedia of Women's Wrestling: 100 Profiles of the Strongest in the Sport by LaToya Ferguson, Sterling New York, 2019.

Second Nature: The Legacy of Ric Flair and the Rise of Charlotte by Ric Flair and Charlotte Flair with Brian Shields, St. Martin's Press, 2017.

If They Only Knew by Joanie "Chyna" Laurer with Michael Angeli, Regan Books, 2001.

Sisterhood of the Squared Circle: The History and Rise of Women's Wrestling by Pat Laprade and Dan Murphy, ECW Press, 2017.

The Queen of the Ring: Sex, Muscles, Diamonds and the Making of an American Legend by Jeff Leen, Atlantic Monthly Press, 2009.

Crazy is My Superpower: How I Triumphed by Breaking Bones, Breaking Hearts and Breaking the Rules by AJ Mendez Brooks, Crown Archetype, 2017.

Women Love Wrestling: An Anthology on Women and Professional Wrestling by Jason Norris (editor), independently published, 2020.

A Star Shattered: The Rise & Fall & Rise of Wrestling Diva by Tammy "Sunny" Sytch, Riverdale Avenue Press, 2016.

ACKNOWLEDGEMENTS

Thank you to my cheer squad and my biggest supporters: *my mom, April, Lana,* and *Linzie.*

Thank you to *Lauren Moran* for designing the cover of my wildest dreams. And to *Jay Zeller,* who provided last-minute edits to the back cover over the Christmas break.

Thank you to *Scott* and *David* of *Fayetteville Mafia Press* for taking a chance on me and this book. David's edits preserved my voice while making this a better book.

Thank you to *LaToya Ferguson, Heather Bandenburg,* and *Bill Hanstock* for blurbing this book.

Thank you to the early readers of some of these chapters— *Chelsea Spollen, Nicole Brinkley, Jetta Rae Robertson, Kristin Lagerquist, Mira Adama, Marilyn,* and *Stephen*—for making sure what I was writing wasn't actually trash.

Thank you again to *April,* and *Julian* who, perhaps unbeknownst to them, planted the seeds of this book in my brain.

Thank you to *Matt Phaedonos*, who helped with the legalities.

Thank you to *Kristine Archer*, who bid on this mention as part of the #AuthorsforFireys fundraiser for Country Fire Authority Victoria during the 2019/2020 Australian bushfire disaster that was unfolding around me as I wrote some of this book. Climate change is real and we need to take action, like, yesterday.

Thank you to the women's wrestling community who inspire and support me; from the wrestlers themselves to my peers, especially *Kristen Ashly, Harmony Cox, Patricia Rogers, Ashly Nagrant, Kate Foray, Shane Thomas, Warren Hayes, David Bixenspan, Michael Greene, Dakari Barnes* and many others.

Thank you to everyone who bought and read this book. Thank you for supporting women's wrestling.

ABOUT THE AUTHOR

Scarlett Harris is a culture critic from Melbourne, Australia. She has been published in such outlets as *The New York Times*, *The Guardian*, *Harper's Bazaar*, *Playboy*, *Vox*, *Vice*, and many more. You can read the rest of her work at her website, scarlettwoman.com.au/about, and follow her on Twitter @ScarlettEHarris. *A Diva Was a Female Version of a Wrestler* is her first book. She is the editor of the collection *The Women of Jenji Kohan: Orange Is the New Black, GLOW, and Weeds*, forthcoming from Fayetteville Mafia Press in 2022.

SCARLETT HARRIS RETURNS

WITH NER NEXT BOOK IN 2022:

The Women of Jenji Kohan:
Orange Is The New Black, GLOW,
and Weeds

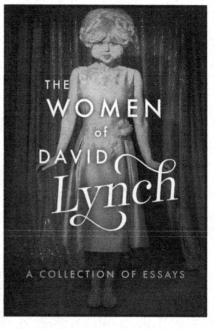
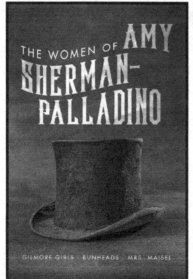

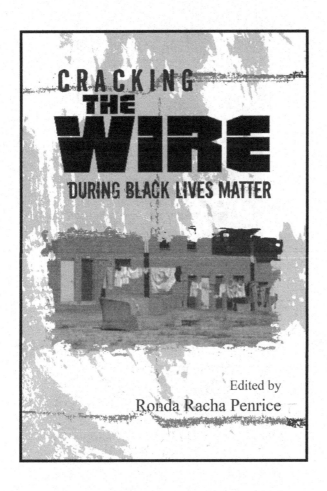

A book of essays by all African-American writers about HBO's *The Wire*.

9781949024289 Paperback
9781949024296 Ebook

The Common Angler
by Jack Wollitz

Essays about the sport and lifestyle of the fisherman from a nothern Ohio reporter.

ISBN: 9781949024227

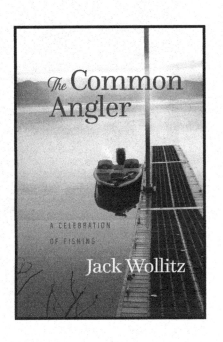

The Massillon Tigers: 15 for 15 by David Lee Morgan, Jr., with a foreword by Jim Tressel. Follow along with the Ohio high school football powerhouse team the Massillon Tigers as they hunt for a state championship in 2019.

ISBN: 9781949024166

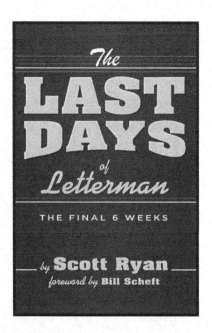

Read an inside look at the final six weeks of *Late Show with David Letterman,* all told through the words of the staff that wrote, directed, and produced those iconic last twenty-eight episodes in 2015. *The Last Days of Letterman* by Scott Ryan

ISBN: 9781949024005

Mark Frost cocreated *Twin Peaks*, wrote for *Hill Street Blues,* and has written over ten books. Learn about his life, his craft, and his career in this new book by David Bushman.

ISBN: 9781949024104

Ken Fortenberry solves one of the greatest real-life mysteries in aviation history as he searches for the killer of his father and the cause of the crash of Flight 7.

ISBN: 9781949024067

Laura's Ghost: Women Speak about Twin Peaks
by Courtenay Stallings with a foreword by Sheryl Lee.
Women discuss how Laura Palmer influenced their lives.

ISBN: 9781949024081